LEARNING AND TEACHING WITH COMPUTERS

LEARNING AND TEACHING WITH COMPUTERS

Artificial Intelligence in Education

Tim O'Shea
Lecturer in Educational Technology,
The Open University

John Self
Lecturer in Computer Studies,
University of Lancaster

A SPECTRUM BOOK

PRENTICE-HALL INC., ENGLEWOOD CLIFFS, N.J. 07632

Library of Congress Cataloging in Publication Data

O'Shea, Tim, (1983)
   Learning and teaching with computers.

   "A Spectrum book."
   Bibliography: p.
   Includes index.
      1. Education — Data processing.   2. Computer-
assisted instruction. I. Self, John.
   II. Title.
   LB1028.43.083   1983   370'.28'5   83-4546
   ISBN 0-13-527770-1
   ISBN 0-13-527762-0 (pbk.)

10   9   8   7   6   5   4   3   2   1

Prentice-Hall International, Inc., *London*
Prentice-Hall of Australia Pty. Limited, *Sydney*
Prentice-Hall Canada Inc., *Toronto*
Prentice-Hall of India Private Limited, *New Delhi*
Prentice-Hall of Japan, Inc., *Tokyo*
Prentice-Hall of Southeast Asia Pte. Ltd., *Singapore*
Whitehall Books Limited, *Wellington, New Zealand*
Editora Prentice-Hall do Brazil Ltda., *Rio de Janeiro*

CONTENTS

PREFACE

The microcomputer revolution has greatly exercised the minds of some educators. The focus, however, has been almost exclusively on the equipment and the software available today. Microcomputers have, it seems, made twenty years' experience of computer-assisted learning irrelevant and long-term research programmes unnecessary. Microelectronics have undeniably changed the reality of computers in education but have solved few of the fundamental problems. In this book, these problems are considered from the new perspective offered by the subject of artificial intelligence which is the science of developing computers to carry out functions normally associated with human intelligence, for example, to teach.

The book is intended to be of interest to anyone concerned with the future of education, including teachers of all kinds, educational administrators, and practitioners and researchers in computer-assisted learning. No previous computing experience is required.

Chapter 1 introduces the main themes of the book as well as the nature of computers and programming. Some understanding of programming, the central new skill of computing, is necessary for a proper appreciation of the role of computers in education. Chapter 2 explains the relevance of artificial intelligence to computer-assisted learning and serves to motivate our history of computer-assisted learning in Chapter 3. The next two chapters consider in detail the two most promising modes of computer-assisted learning – computer as teacher and computer as tool. Our arguments are supported by descriptions of research programmes and projects which are already sufficiently developed to have been used to aid teaching and learning. Chapter 6 is concerned with the practical problems that arise when computer-based innovations are introduced into the educational system. The final chapter is the obligatory session with a crystal ball.

Concerning our use of pronouns, we ask the reader to accept that the male embraces the female, and vice versa.

We are grateful to the following people who read parts of the manuscript or contributed in other ways: Bruce Anderson, Alan Borning, Ben du Boulay, Marc Eisenstadt, Ann Floyd, Lindsay Ford, Laura Gould, Roger Hartley, David Hawkridge, Euan Henderson, Jim Howe, Bob Hudson, Ann Jones, Paul Lefrere, John Maddison, John Mason, Tony Priest, Peter Ross, Eileen Scanlon, Ruth Self and Mike Sharples. We thank Claire Jones, Di Mason and Liz Rowley for help in preparing the manuscript. Our greatest debt is to Margaret Boden who first persuaded us to start this book, and then patiently encouraged us to complete it.

Tim O'Shea
John Self
Stony Stratford
July 1982

1. INTRODUCTION

Computers will cause great changes in education. Already there are examination halls in American universities where rows of nervous students type answers to multiple-choice questions at computer consoles and anxiously await their grade. There are also experimental classrooms where young children happily and confidently command a computer to draw pictures or play music, and articulately explain their latest computer program. Motivated by cost-effectiveness and efficiency, educators may try to use computers to turn classrooms into human battery farms. But there is a possibility that computers will be used to enhance the educational process and equip each learner with an exciting medium for problem-solving and individual tuition. In this book we discuss some current educational applications of computers, and draw attention to those which offer the potential for improving the quality of education.

Even in a recession, governments have felt it wise to encourage the use of computers in education. There are three reasons:

1. Children need to be aware of the nature and uses of computers in order to be able to cope with the present and future technological society.
2. Computers can help with certain administrative chores, such as the maintenance of student records and the scheduling of classes.
3. Computers can help to improve the learning process.

The first two reasons are clearly sound, and we shall have no more to say about them. The third, however, is more controversial and is the subject of this book.

Why should anyone believe that computers could help learning?

Like the blind men groping round the elephant, advocates of computer-assisted learning have different visions. Here are a sample of some of the reasons that have been given:

By eliminating the drudgery of numerical calculations and the bother of erasing and retyping, the computer increases the net joy of learning and frees time for the more significant aspects of scholarship. (Licklider, 1979)

The uniqueness of a computer-assisted instruction system resides in the computer which provides two significant capabilities: a large memory and flexible logic. While memory in a directly displayable form also is provided by a variety of other teaching aids, only the computer provides the detailed collated random-access memory of each student's responses to individual displays of instructional materials in a form that is directly useful for automatic processing. No other aid provides the computer's logical capability for organizing information to make it dependent upon the characteristics of the individual student. (Stolurow, 1969)

The interactive capacity afforded by a computer with suitable input-output equipment is really a new tool not heretofore available to the researcher studying learning nor, of course, to the educator. (Rigney, 1962)

Potentially a very important educational use of the computer's capacity to handle data and to store and retrieve information is the presentation of complex simulations which it would be difficult, impossible, too time-consuming or too costly to set up otherwise. (NCET, 1969)

A computer allows us not only to simulate all other classes of teaching machines but also to approach full simulation of the human tutorial process. In this sense a computer represents the only research tool that does not limit our imagination and creativity. (Uttal, 1962)

The computer can act as a mentor or coach, and 'observe' the use of the medium by the student. It can interrupt students at appropriate times to get them out of ruts or to point out how some aspect of their current activity illustrates an important principle. (Brown, 1979)

Children can learn to use computers in a masterful way, and . . . learning to use computers can change the way they learn everything else. (Papert, 1980)

The basic components of pocket teaching computers are no different from those of calculators – a larger keyboard and a more elaborate display are the only minor changes – and once a commercial impetus is given to their development, the production lines will roll them off, by the million and then by the billion, and each unit will shortly be as cheap as today's calculators . . . Teaching computers are basically all-electronic, with no moving parts – other than electrons – and are easy to mass produce. They cost little more than the raw materials of which they are made, and they have the great advantage of being extremely reliable. (Evans, 1979)

2

It is all very bewildering: how can one machine support such a variety of opinions? Well, the fact is that a computer is an exceptionally flexible device and, while it is premature for us to try to justify or disagree with the above opinions, it is sufficient for now to accept that there might be something in any of them. Developments in microelectronics have now made computers so cheap and reliable that there will be no shortage of people attempting to realise their own vision of computer-assisted learning. The challenge, then, is clear: to make the educational use of computers maximally beneficial to all concerned.

You may have noticed that some of the quotations are rather dated. Some even pre-date the microcomputer, the harbinger of a new dawn of civilisation. The microcomputer is first and foremost a computer, and it is one of the aims of this book to show that there are many lessons to be learned from computer-assisted learning projects dating back to 1960. There is every sign that the headlong rush into micros is causing a reversal to techniques and philosophies which had been discredited in computer-assisted learning many years ago. It is not that such techniques and philosophies are wrong – nothing in education is that simple – but that they present an impoverished view of what computer-assisted learning could be about. We believe that computers can radically enhance the quality of education. To support this belief we shall describe computer-assisted learning research programmes and projects which are already sufficiently developed to have been used for teaching. This work gives us a much better picture of what computer-assisted learning should and could be like within ten years (or sooner) than we would get by looking at the 'educational software' that is available today from microcomputer manufacturers.

The large majority of the thousands of computer-assisted learning programs in existence 'do not know what they are doing' when they teach. The idea of computers 'knowing' anything is a difficult one, but for the moment let us simply say that most programs do not know the subject under discussion in the sense of being able to answer unanticipated questions, and do not know enough about an individual student to be able to adapt the teaching session to his needs. If we want to build computer-assisted learning programs to answer unanticipated questions and to individualise

3

teaching – and we assume we do – then we must try to make the necessary knowledge available to the computer. This means that the knowledge must be represented symbolically and stored in the computer's memory (as we shall describe).

Now, the question of how to represent knowledge has been recognised as the central one in a branch of computer science called artificial intelligence. This subject, then, is the main source of the ideas and examples described in this book. Artificial intelligence is the science of making machines do things that would require intelligence if done by humans, for example, play chess, make hypotheses about a patient's illness, prove mathematical theorems, translate from one language to another, or teach geography. But to list activities is to miss one of the main points made by such work, namely, that there are general processes common to these activities. For example, artificial intelligence programs are often involved with processes such as:

remembering and accessing relevant knowledge;
using this knowledge appropriately, for example to reason and to form plans of action;
revising and extending their knowledge;
searching in some more or less systematic way for a solution to a problem;
recognising similarities and drawing analogies between things;
and attempting to understand some aspect of their surroundings, for example, something communicated to them in English.

In principle, therefore, artificial intelligence should be relevant to the design of teaching and learning systems since these processes are generalisations of particular teaching and learning activities.

So far we have tended to assume that computers will be used to teach students. It is natural to look at the present educational process and to imagine how computers could patch it up, but this is too blinkered. Computers can add new dimensions to education. To take one example, before the advent of computers it was obviously not possible for computer programming to be a classroom activity. Even today, only a tiny proportion of primary schoolchildren have written computer programs, although it is known that many of them are well able to do so, and that there are

4

good reasons for believing that programming is a worthwhile activity in itself. Of course, we need to think carefully about the nature of computer programming to be able to devise successful computer-based learning environments for children, and in a later chapter we shall discuss in detail the requirements for such environments.

The interesting fact is that one of the sources of inspiration for the designers of computer-based learning environments is, as for the designers of intelligent teaching systems, the subject of artificial intelligence. On reflection, however, it is not so surprising. Research workers in artificial intelligence study how knowledge has to be organised in a computer to enable it to carry out intelligent activities. We are bound to speculate on the similarities of such organisations with those that presumably develop to enable us to carry out intelligent activities. The ways by which good organisations of knowledge in a computer are developed suggest guidelines and insights into how learning environments might lead to the development of good organisations of knowledge in a child's brain.

Comparisons between computers and humans, which is one of the main themes in artificial intelligence, may seem repellent at first, reflecting a dehumanising, mechanistic view of human nature. At this stage, we can only say that by the end of the book we hope to have shown that programs based on ideas from artificial intelligence are considerably less dehumanising than those that are not.

Artificial intelligence also allows us to put the more grandiose claims for computer-assisted learning into perspective. The most fundamental problems in the design of good educational programs are essentially ones which have been studied in artificial intelligence for many years and, while some progress has been made, it is clear that there are unlikely to be simple solutions. In fact, artificial intelligence research itself demonstrates that there are limits to what can be achieved in computer-assisted learning in the foreseeable future.

Let us pause now to summarise our thesis in the form of a logical argument with several premises and one main conclusion:

Premises
1. Computers will be widely used in education.
2. Most present programs are unsatisfactory.
3. The main reason for 2 is that the programs lack knowledge of various kinds.
4. Artificial intelligence is concerned with making explicit the kinds of knowledge mentioned in 3.

Conclusion
The designers of computer systems to be used in education should take account of the subject of artificial intelligence, and the users of such systems may expect them soon to provide facilities considerably more sophisticated than those available today.

We shall justify this argument not merely by rhetoric, but by a detailed examination of computer-assisted learning systems that *already exist*.

The organisation of the book is as follows. Chapter 2 considers in more detail arguments concerning the relevance of artificial intelligence to computer-assisted learning. The chapter first describes a program which illustrates many of the techniques used in artificial intelligence. We then imagine how this program, and ones like it, could be used in education. Artificial intelligence is then related to contemporary ideas in developmental psychology, with which it is in considerable sympathy.

Chapter 3 surveys the multitude of methods used in computer-assisted learning. The background provided by the previous chapter enables us to appreciate the merits and limitations of each method and the educational philosophy on which each is based. The intention is not to give an exhaustive, and exhausting, survey (although we have given liberal references in footnotes for those who wish to read further), but the historical treatment enables us to conclude that there has been a trend from rigid, mechanistic, statistically-based teaching systems to ones which treat the student as a thinking, understanding and contributing individual – a trend which microcomputers have to some extent put in abeyance.

In the next two chapters we consider the two approaches which seem to hold the most promise for improving education. Chapter 4 is concerned with the issues that arise during the construction of computer tutors, namely, program competence in the subject being taught, student modelling, representing tutorial strategies, and communication. Chapter 5 considers the computer as an educational resource and emphasises the use of programming languages as tools for problem-solving, modelling and self-expression.

In Chapter 6 we are concerned with the problems that may arise when computer-based innovations are introduced into the educational system. We try to identify some groups who seem to have the most to gain from the developments described and summarise evidence for changes in communication skills, motivation and self-confidence.

The final chapter looks ahead to the likely developments in educational computing in the next ten years or so.

The remainder of this introductory chapter is intended for those readers who know little of computers and how they may be used. It attempts to remove some of the mystique attached to computers. Readers with previous experience of computers may of course skim through to Chapter 2.

Using computers

It isn't necessary to know how a computer works before we can use one, just as we can drive a car without knowing what is under the bonnet. So imagine that we are given a box with buttons on it as shown in Figure 1.1 and that this box is connected to a computer which can cause a mechanical device called a turtle (shown in Figure 1.2) to move over a sheet of paper drawing a line as it moves. Pressing the button labelled 'FORWARD 50' makes the turtle move forward 50 units, let's say millimetres. Pressing the button labelled 'RIGHT 90' makes the turtle turn 90 degrees to the right from whatever direction it is facing at the time. We can therefore draw on the paper by pressing buttons. So let us try to draw a queue of people, something like Figure 1.3 (we're not seeking realism!).

We shall start with the first man, naturally. There are many ways

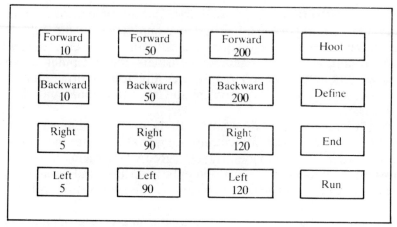

Forward 10	Forward 50	Forward 200	Hoot
Backward 10	Backward 50	Backward 200	Define
Right 5	Right 90	Right 120	End
Left 5	Left 90	Left 120	Run

Figure 1.1 *A button box*

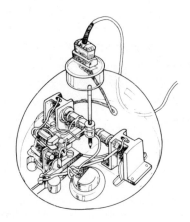

Figure 1.2 *A turtle.*

this man may be drawn, corresponding to drawing lines in different orders. We shall adopt a top-down strategy. We can draw his triangular head by pressing these buttons, in order:

FORWARD 50, RIGHT 120, FORWARD 50,
RIGHT 120, FORWARD 50, RIGHT 120

Sure enough, our turtle draws

We could now go on to draw the neck, arms, body and legs of the first man and then do something similar for all the other men in the queue. This would be extremely tedious and error-prone. Devices like button-boxes are intended only to help beginners to get started: to do anything worthwhile with a computer we need a more sophisticated set of commands than that shown in Figure 1.1.

The commands that we have used so far are in fact statements in a particular programming language, called Logo.[1] We shall now introduce some more Logo for, as programming languages go, it is relatively easy to understand and since it can be used to draw pictures we can actually see what the commands do.

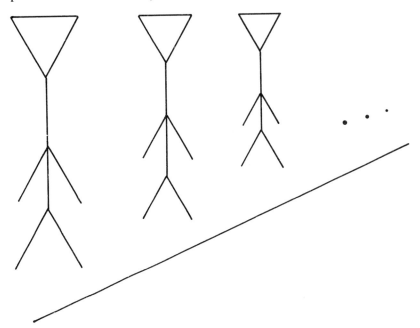

Figure 1.3. *A queue.*

The version of Logo which we shall use is that implemented on the Terak computer (and similar to ones available on the Apple II and the Research Machines' 380Z). In Terak Logo we communicate our commands to the computer using a keyboard and these commands are displayed on a television screen.[2] Messages from Terak Logo to us also appear on the screen. For example,

    W:

means that the computer is in the 'waiting state' and is waiting for us to type in a command.

    W: FORWARD 50

makes the turtle move forward 50, as before, or if we are using the television screen to draw on an imaginary turtle will draw a line of length 50 on the screen.

In Logo we can associate a name with a series of commands, as follows:

    W: BUILD 'TRIANGLE

Logo now responds with

    TRIANGLE

and we then type in the series of commands to be associated with this name:

    1 FORWARD 50
    2 RIGHT 120
    3 FORWARD 50
    4 RIGHT 120
    5 FORWARD 50
    6 RIGHT 120

(terminated by pressing the ESCAPE key).

The BUILD command puts the computer in the 'defining state', which it stays in until we press the ESCAPE key. In the defining state we can, as you can see, type in the series of commands which we wish to define, preceding each command by a number, the 'line number', which orders the commands. The name which we want to associate with the series of commands is specified in the BUILD command – in this case, TRIANGLE. A named series of commands is a *procedure*. Defining a procedure doesn't draw anything – to actually draw a triangle we must, as we say, *call* the procedure, as follows

W: TRIANGLE

The ' that appeared in the definition needs some explanation. There is an analogous use of quotes in English. Consider

Honesty is a virtue.

'Honesty' has three syllables.

The latter sentence refers to the word enclosed in quotes (literally); the former refers to the meaning of the word 'honesty'. Similarly, in Logo, we might say that TRIANGLE refers to the meaning of the word 'TRIANGLE (we are excused the closing quote!). Thus, 'TRIANGLE (with a quote) denotes the name of the procedure and TRIANGLE (without a quote) denotes a call of the procedure.

Now let's build a procedure to draw our man. This might be:

W: BUILD 'MAN

MAN

   1 HEAD

   2 NECK

   3 ARMS

   4 BODY

   5 LEGS

The HEAD, NECK, etc. that appear in this definition are not part of the Logo language and we must also define these. (Remember that we have not called MAN yet, only defined it.) Our HEAD procedure might be:

W: BUILD 'HEAD

HEAD

   1 TRIANGLE

The TRIANGLE procedure, which we have already defined, can now be used as though it is a command in the Logo language itself. So we can define procedures in terms of other procedures, creating ever more complicated commands. Similarly, we can define the other procedures we need:

W:BUILD 'NECK
NECK
  1 FORWARD 50
W: BUILD 'ARMS
ARMS
  1 RIGHT 30
  2 FORWARD 50
  3 BACKWARD 50
  4 LEFT 60
  5 FORWARD 50
W: BUILD 'BODY
BODY
  1 FORWARD 50
W: BUILD 'LEGS
LEGS
  1 ARMS

Having now defined all the procedures that MAN needs, we can call it to see if it works. If you have been concentrating, you will know that it won't. In fact, it draws the figure shown:
  W: MAN

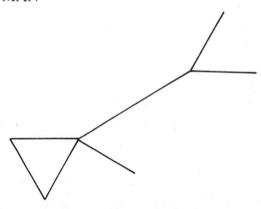

Do not despair! Few people would get this man drawn correctly first time. It is not necessary to start again from scratch for we can see that our attempt is along the right lines: some of the lines are in the wrong direction, that's all. If we were to watch carefully while the drawing was being made we would see that the lines were drawn in the order indicated

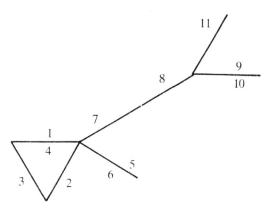

(assuming our turtle to be facing east at the start). If we look closely at the individual commands in HEAD, NECK, etc. we will see that this is exactly what we have defined. Our mistake (or *bug*, as we say in the trade) lies in not making sure that the turtle was in the right place and facing the right direction before drawing the next part of the figure. For example, the HEAD procedure leaves the turtle here

but the NECK procedure assumes it to be here

There are several ways in which we can improve matters. We could redefine NECK:

```
W: SCRAP 'NECK
W: BUILD 'NECK
NECK
    1 RIGHT 60
    2 FORWARD 50
    3 RIGHT 30
    4 FORWARD 50
```

13

Similarly, ARMS should be changed to leave the turtle where it was before the arms are drawn:

    W: CHANGE 'ARMS
       6 BACKWARD 50
       7 RIGHT 30

(In Terak Logo the old definition appears on the screen and we can add, delete or alter commands in it.)

    Now we can call MAN again

      W: MAN

to give us

We can now draw a man – indeed, **any number of men**. All that remains is to get them the right size and in the **right place**, to look like Figure 1.3. Our procedures all draw lines of length 50. We do not want to have to define different procedures for every different sized man, and in Logo we do not have to. We just make the size a *variable*, that is a number which may differ on different calls of the procedures. Then when we call the procedure we say what size we actually want. So let us type in a new definition of TRIANGLE:

14

W: SCRAP 'TRIANGLE
W: BUILD 'TRIANGLE
TRIANGLE 'SIZE
   1 FORWARD VALUE 'SIZE
   2 RIGHT 120
   3 FORWARD VALUE 'SIZE
   4 RIGHT 120
   5 FORWARD VALUE 'SIZE
   6 RIGHT 120

The name of the variable is 'SIZE (as specified after Logo's echo of the procedure name) and its value is given by VALUE 'SIZE. We say what the value is to be by giving it in the call.

   W: TRIANGLE 50

This draws us the same sized triangle as before. The call

   W: TRIANGLE 100

draws a triangle with sides twice as long.

We say that TRIANGLE needs one *input*. In Terak Logo, a procedure is called by giving the procedure name (without the ') followed by any inputs it requires. We can now redefine all our other procedures to need one input as well:

W: SCRAP 'MAN
W: BUILD 'MAN
MAN 'SIZE
   1 HEAD VALUE 'SIZE
   2 NECK VALUE 'SIZE
   3 ARMS VALUE 'SIZE
   4 BODY VALUE 'SIZE
   5 LEGS VALUE 'SIZE
W: SCRAP 'HEAD
W: BUILD 'HEAD
HEAD 'SIZE
   1 TRIANGLE VALUE 'SIZE
W: SCRAP 'NECK
W: BUILD 'NECK
NECK 'SIZE
   1 RIGHT 60
   2 FORWARD VALUE 'SIZE
   3 RIGHT 30
   4 FORWARD VALUE 'SIZE

15

(and so on). All these VALUE 'SIZEs take a lot of typing, and so Logo kindly allows an abbreviation, namely :SIZE (and similarly, of course, for variables with other names), and we will adopt this from now on.

We can now define a procedure for drawing a queue of men as follows:

>W: BUILD 'QUEUE
>QUEUE 'SIZE
>   1 MAN :SIZE
>   2 REPOSITION :SIZE
>   3 QUEUE :SIZE

where REPOSITION repositions the turtle for the next man. (Let us not linger over details, but, for completeness, here is the definition of REPOSITION:

>W: BUILD 'REPOSITION
>REPOSITION 'SIZE
>   1 RIGHT 180
>   2 FORWARD :SIZE
>   3 FORWARD :SIZE
>   4 RIGHT 30
>   5 FORWARD :SIZE
>   6 RIGHT 60
>   7 LIFT
>   8 FORWARD :SIZE
>   9 PENCIL

Here, the LIFT is to lift the imaginary pen up so that the turtle can move without drawing a line, until the command PENCIL is carried out to drop the pen down on the paper again. With QUEUE, this enables us to leave a man-sized gap between men.)

The call

>W: QUEUE 50

gives us the drawing shown opposite all the way across the paper (or screen). The call of QUEUE from within QUEUE may look a little odd but it is quite sensible – the definition says 'to draw a queue of men, draw one man and then draw a queue of men'.

We must now make each man a constant fraction (say ¾) of the man to his west. First, we need to say something more about procedures in Logo. So far all our procedures except one have

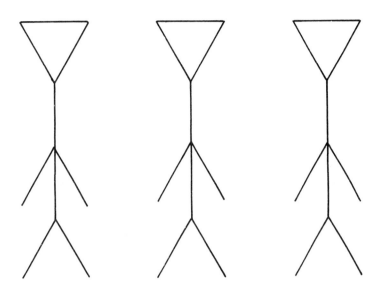

done things, or as we say had an *effect*, such as draw something. The exception was VALUE which did not draw anything but enabled the value of a variable to be used as input to some other procedure. In general, then, some Logo procedures calculate a *result*. So, for example, in

    W: FORWARD ADD 10 20

ADD is a procedure which takes two inputs and produces a result which in this case is used as input for the FORWARD procedure. The net effect, of course, is that the turtle moves forward 30. Notice that in Terak Logo all procedures precede their inputs (and therefore we do not write '10+20' as in conventional arithmetic notation). Now, to return to our QUEUE, we want to make all men after the first ¾ of the size of the one to their west. This we may do as follows

    W: CHANGE 'QUEUE

       3 QUEUE DIVIDE (MULTIPLY 3 :SIZE) 4

(We can use round brackets to make Logo a little more readable.) Now the call

    W: QUEUE 50

17

produces our queue as in Figure 1.3.

We have now completed our little project, but we must not simply be pleased with the product (or not, as the case may be). Our aim was not to produce a masterpiece but to introduce some important ideas about using computers. Let us therefore summarise some of these.

First, there is the idea of problem decomposition, that is, of setting about solving a problem by breaking it down into simpler subproblems (and so on if necessary) until we get to problems which we can actually solve. With programming languages, this leads to the use of procedures, small programs to solve specific problems. In Logo there are two kinds of procedure, those which have an effect and those which calculate a result. Then we have the concept of a variable in a procedure, which enables a small piece of program to produce a large range of behaviour.

We were also made aware that computer programs can, and usually do, have bugs. The activity of finding and removing bugs from programs ('debugging') is far from a trivial operation. The relationship between a programmer and his program is much like that between a scientist and his theory, and this comparison has encouraged the opinion that children might benefit from learning to program. The whole sequence of 'teaching the computer' to drive the turtle can serve as a precise, easily grasped metaphor for the child to use in understanding his own thinking and learning.

Once we have written a few procedures we are, of course, free to use them as we fancy, just for fun or in the spirit of scientific exploration. Here, for example, is a procedure using our TRIANGLE

```
W: BUILD 'SHELL
SHELL 'SIZE 'ROTATION
    1 TRIANGLE :SIZE
    2 LEFT :ROTATION
    3 SHELL (ADD :SIZE 5) :ROTATION
```
The call
```
W: SHELL 25 20
```
draws us the shell shown in Figure 1.4.

We would like to leave you with the impression that computer

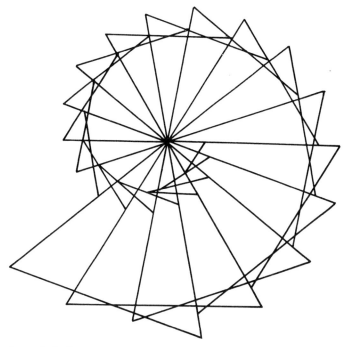

Figure 1.4   *A shell*

programming is child's play; but some programs are rather serious
matters. So, in order to introduce a few more programming concepts which we shall need, let us develop a program which, as we
shall see, is not very different from many which have actually been
written to teach.

First we shall write a procedure to bombard a student with a
series of questions, and to respond 'GOOD' if the student answers
correctly and 'WRONG' otherwise. The Logo language can be
used not only to draw pictures, but also to print messages on the
screen. So, we imagine our student sitting reading questions on the
screen, and typing in answers on a keyboard.

Our BOMBARD procedure will consist of a series of calls of
another procedure, TEST, which will do three things: present a
question, accept the student's answer, and respond 'GOOD' or

'WRONG' as appropriate.

The first two may be done in Terak Logo by using the ASK command. ASK takes one input and causes it to appear on the screen, followed by a question mark. ASK then waits for a response to be typed on the keyboard and returns this response as its result. So, if we type in the command

W: PRINT ASK [WHAT IS THE CAPITAL OF ARGENTINA]

first of all the question will appear on the screen, to which we provide an answer

WHAT IS THE CAPITAL OF ARGENTINA? BUENOS AIRES

The answer is returned by ASK as its result, which our command then PRINTs:

[BUENOS AIRES]

In Logo, square brackets are used to enclose a series of items to form what is called a *list*. A list can serve as the one input required by ASK, as shown above. The PRINT command is used to cause a number, word or list, provided as its input, to appear on the screen. In our TEST procedure, of course, we do not, in fact, want to echo the answer but to remember it (so that we can compare it with the correct answer). We do this by 'assigning' the list to a variable, that is, by making the variable have the list as its value:

W: MAKE 'SA ASK [WHAT IS THE CAPITAL OF ENGLAND]

WHAT IS THE CAPITAL OF ENGLAND? LONDON

Now the variable SA has the value [LONDON]. (Note that ASK always returns a list even if only one word is typed in as answer.)

Finally in TEST we need to compare the student's answer SA with the correct answer, and respond appropriately. EQUALQ is a procedure for comparing two inputs − if they are the same its result is 'TRUE, otherwise it is 'FALSE. Procedures which return 'TRUE or 'FALSE (called 'question procedures' in Logo and given names ending with Q, by convention) can be used in *conditional commands*, as in, for example

W: IF EQUALQ :SA [LONDON] THEN PRINT 'GOOD ELSE PRINT 'WRONG

If EQUALQ returns 'TRUE then the command between the THEN and the ELSE is carried out, otherwise the command after

ELSE is carried out. (The ELSE part can be omitted if nothing is to be done in the 'FALSE case.) The conditional command is an important programming idea for it is the basic mechanism by which the execution of a program may be made to depend on information read in or computed.

We are now in a position to define TEST. We want it to work for any question, so we shall require the actual question and its correct answer to be provided as inputs. Here it is:

    W: BUILD 'TEST
    TEST 'Q 'CA
        1 MAKE 'SA ASK :Q
        2 IF EQUALQ :SA :CA THEN PRINT 'GOOD ELSE
            PRINT 'WRONG
Now we can define BOMBARD:
    W: BUILD 'BOMBARD
    BOMBARD
        1   TEST [WHAT IS THE CAPITAL OF BRAZIL]
            [BRASILIA]
        2   TEST [WHO KILLED COCK ROBIN] [THE
            SPARROW]
        .
        .
        .
        99 TEST [WHY DID THE CHICKEN CROSS THE
            ROAD]
            [TO GET TO THE OTHER SIDE]
and call it
    W: BOMBARD
to give a computer-student dialogue, perhaps this one
    WHAT IS THE CAPITAL OF BRAZIL? *RIO DE
        JANEIRO*
    WRONG
    WHO KILLED COCK ROBIN? *THE SPARROW*
    GOOD
        .
        .
    WHY DID THE CHICKEN CROSS THE ROAD? *I
        DON'T KNOW*
    WRONG

21

(We have italicised the student's answers in this dialogue to clarify what the student has typed, and we shall adopt this convention throughout the book.)

We might perceive some educational merit in this, so let's improve it a little. Some wrong answers are less wrong than others, and we could try to be a little more sympathetic with these. To ask the first question above, we might try:

```
W: BUILD 'Q1
Q1
    1 MAKE 'SA ASK [WHAT IS THE CAPITAL OF
      BRAZIL]
    2 IF EQUALQ :SA [BRASILIA] THEN PRINT
      'GOOD
      ELSE IF EQUALQ :SA [RIO DE JANEIRO] THEN
      SAY [IT USED TO BE] AND Q1
      ELSE IF EQUALQ :SA [BUENOS AIRES] THEN
      SAY [THAT'S THE CAPITAL OF ARGENTINA]
      AND Q1
      ELSE IF EQUALQ :SA [GIVE UP] THEN PRINT
      'BRASILIA
      ELSE PRINT 'WRONG AND Q1
```

The only new piece of Logo here is the AND which allows us to have two commands for the price of one: wherever we are normally allowed one command we can put two provided we put an AND between them. SAY is the same as PRINT except that the square brackets are omitted from the output.

Now the call

```
W: Q1
```

might give us this dialogue:

```
WHAT IS THE CAPITAL OF BRAZIL? RIO DE
            JANEIRO
IT USED TO BE
WHAT IS THE CAPITAL OF BRAZIL? CARACAS
WRONG
WHAT IS THE CAPITAL OF BRAZIL? GIVE UP
BRASILIA
```

What we have gained using Q1 is the ability to handle a large number of different dialogues, corresponding to different paths through Q1. (A simple refinement to count the number of wrong answers and to abort after so many would make the number of possible paths finite.) What we have lost is our 'general-purpose' TEST procedure, for now we are thinking of writing a different version of Q1 for every single question, since we shall need to program different comments for every anticipated wrong answer.

As a final programming example, let us consider asking questions for which there is no one correct answer, such as 'Name a country which borders Paraguay'. A simple procedure to do this is:

```
W: BUILD 'Q2
Q2
    1 MAKE 'SA ASK [NAME A COUNTRY WHICH
        BORDERS PARAGUAY]
    2 IF MEMBERQ :SA [ARGENTINA BRAZIL
        BOLIVIA]
    THEN PRINT 'GOOD ELSE PRINT 'WRONG
```

MEMBERQ is a procedure which, when called, determines whether the item specified (as first input) occurs somewhere in the list specified (as second input). (MEMBERQ is a predefined procedure in some Logo implementations but not in Terak Logo. It is, however, easily defined in terms of simpler procedures for handling lists.[3]) So MEMBERQ :SA [ARGENTINA BRAZIL BOLIVIA] returns 'TRUE if :SA is one of the countries named in the list, 'FALSE otherwise.

The items in a list may themselves be lists. So this

```
[PARAGUAY [ARGENTINA BRAZIL BOLIVIA]
ECUADOR [COLUMBIA PERU]
CHILE [BOLIVIA PERU ARGENTINA]]
```

is a perfectly acceptable list. Here is another:

```
[APOLLO [11 1969 [SEA OF TRANQUILITY] [1 N 3 S]]
       [12 1969 [OCEAN OF STORMS] [3 S 24 W]]
       [17 1972 [SEA OF SERENITY] [20 N 31 E]]]
```

The list notation, therefore, can be used to represent complicated pieces of information, and we can write procedures to look for items in such lists, and indeed to add items or to change the lists around (e.g. to sort the items into some order). Logo provides procedures to enable us to do this, as do most of the languages which have been used to write the programs described in this book.

This emphasises the fact that, contrary to popular belief, computers are not merely (or even mainly) devices for performing numerical computations. Computers are general-purpose, symbol-manipulating machines, as our examples already show.

So we have seen that programming languages enable us to use computers without knowing anything about the way computers actually work. None the less, you might feel uneasy about this and so, for those who feel they need reassurance, in the rest of this chapter we shall introduce some of the technical terms used in computing, and try to give some idea of how computers work.

The cheapest calculator you can buy in the local general shop is a computer in all but one respect. Let us look at the similarities first. Visualise using such a calculator by, say, pressing the buttons labelled 2, +, 3, = in turn and you will see that the calculator consists essentially of five units:

1. *An input unit*, i.e. something which enables the user to communicate with the calculator – the keyboard.
2. *An output unit*, i.e. something which enables the calculator to communicate with the user – the display.
3. *A memory*, i.e. somewhere where the number or numbers to be operated on are stored, e.g. the number 2 in the above sequence needs to be remembered while the second number is being typed.
4. *An arithmetic unit*, i.e. a device which performs the actual operations themselves, e.g. by taking two numbers stored in specific places in memory, adding them together, and putting the result in a specific place in memory.
5. *A control unit*, i.e. a device which coordinates the activities of the other units, e.g. by sending appropriate signals to the output unit to ensure that the result of a calculation is displayed.

Now, even the largest computer has only these five units, although of course they differ in appearance, size, how fast they work, etc. The input unit may consist of a variety of input devices: perhaps, paper tape-readers and card-readers, although these are fast becoming obsolete; teletypes and terminals, in which a keyboard is combined with a printer or television screen so that the user can see what he has typed; more specialised devices such as sketchpads, light pens and touch-sensitive screens, and speech input devices. Some of these devices, in particular terminals, double as output devices, enabling the computer to be used *interactively*, that is, in a mode in which the computer and the user take turns in sending messages to each other. Special output devices include visual displays and speech generators. The input and output devices may also be other pieces of equipment, e.g. a model train or a nuclear reactor, which can thereby be controlled by the computer.

The memory of a large computer is of two kinds: main memory and secondary memory (or *backing store*). Numbers, or more generally data, which are in the main memory can be transferred to the arithmetic unit to be operated on. Since the time it takes to find and move data in the main memory largely determines the overall speed of the computer in performing its calculations this is designed to be as short as economically feasible. Main memory is therefore expensive relative to backing store, which is used for data which are not actually required in main memory and when the volume of data would overflow the main memory. Magnetic tape (as in cassettes) and floppy discs (thin, flexible, plastic discs held in a protective cardboard envelope) are examples of media used for backing store. Consider, for example, a computer-assisted learning program which deals with a class of 100 students, only one of whom may use the program at any one time. Information about each student would normally be kept in backing store; when a student used the program, his own 'student record' would be transferred to main memory, where it may be used as specified by the program. At the end of the session, an updated student record may be transferred back to backing store.

The large computer's arithmetic unit and control unit differ only in degree from those of the calculator. The arithmetic unit will be capable of more operations than the $+, -, *, /$ of our calculator and the control unit will have considerably more complex units to supervise. Incidentally, the adjective 'arithmetic' is now misleading since most of the built-in operations are not arithmetical at all but are concerned, for example, with comparing or moving data. The arithmetic unit, control unit and main memory may not be three physically distinct devices – since they are usually hidden from the user (as in the calculator) he cannot tell, and does not care. Together these three units constitute the central processing unit or *processor*. The other units are called *peripherals*.

As this description implies, computers all have the same functional organisation – that shown in Figure 1.5. In a theoretical sense all computers are the same in that anything that can be done with one can alsr be done with any other, assuming that there is sufficient memory, and we don't mind how long it takes. Consequently, technical details of the various devices are largely irrelevant to us, for developments here do not change the computer's fundamental capabilities.

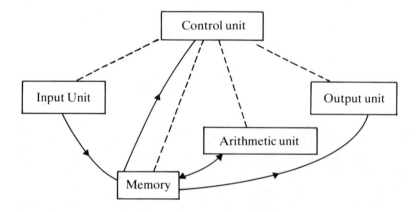

Figure 1.5 *Components of a computer* (broken lines indicate the paths of control signals; solid lines indicate the paths of data)

But there are horses for courses, and different kinds of computers are useful in different ways. The large, expensive, 'traditional' computer – now called a *mainframe* – is usually organised as a *time-sharing system*, i.e. a system which can be used simultaneously by several users at different terminals. Because the speed at which input and output units can communicate information is much slower than the processing speed, it is possible for the computer, by means of a special program called the operating system, to share its time among the users, each of whom (ideally) appears to be receiving the computer's undivided attention. The system's *response time*, i.e. the time it takes the system to reply to the user, is an important measure for such systems. It is not a constant, for it will depend on how many other users there are, and what they are up to, but delays of more than a second or two would certainly detract from the effectiveness of a teaching program meant to engage a student in some discussion. The terminal may be far from the computer itself, in which case one talks of the user having *remote access* to a computer system. The constellation of terminals and other peripherals, which may indeed be further computers, is called a *computer network*. It is also possible to use mainframes in a *batch-processing* mode, in which the user submits a job to the computer and must then wait for it to be dealt with, and for the results to be returned at some unpredictable time, typically an hour or so later.

At the other extreme we have microcomputers, including *personal computers*, which are computers affordable by a person of average means. These microcomputers are based on microprocessors, which are processors manufactured as integrated circuits. An integrated circuit is a small (25 mm $\times$ 12mm $\times$ 2mm) piece of plastic which contains a wafer of silicon (the silicon chip) onto which have been etched many circuit elements and which has metal leads extending from it for connections to other components. A personal computer is usually supplied with a keyboard, television screen (or monitor), and perhaps one or two floppy disc drives. As the name suggests, a personal computer has only one user at a time, and the system is invariably an interactive one.

We said earlier that a cheap calculator differed from a computer in one respect. We could remove this difference by spending a little more money on a 'programmable' calculator. To explain this concept we need to say more about the way memory works.

The size of a computer's memory is said to be so many bytes or so many words. A *byte* is the size of memory needed to hold a single character (i.e. letter, digit or other symbol). More technically, a byte is eight bits, where a *bit* is the smallest possible amount of information, i.e. it specifies one of two alternatives, which we can denote by 0 and 1. So a byte can contain one of the 256 (i.e. 2^8) possible permutations of eight 0s or 1s. A *word* is a certain number of bytes – the actual number may differ from computer to computer. A word is usually the smallest number of bits which the electronic circuitry has been built to be able to transfer from memory in one go. In main memory, the time taken to access a word is the same for all words: such a memory is called a *random-access memory* (or *RAM*). In microcomputers, a distinction is drawn between RAM, the contents of which can be changed by the user's program, and *read-only memory* (or *ROM*), the contents of which are fixed once and for all by the manufacturer.

A few figures might help. To take a typical, large computer, Newcastle University's IBM 370/168, its main memory is 6,291,456 bytes. Since an average-sized book has about half a million characters, we could say this is equivalent to about twelve books. For backing store, there is a disc of $2*10^9$ bytes (or 4000 books), capable of transferring about 10^6 bytes (or two books) per second to main memory, and magnetic tapes, each of which holds $4*10^7$ bytes (or 80 books) which can be transferred at $2*10^5$ bytes per second. Over 200 terminals are connected to the system. The IBM personal computer, on the other hand, has a main memory of 64,000 bytes (or 1/8 book) of RAM and 40,000 bytes of ROM. Its floppy discs hold a mere 160,000 bytes.

At any time a byte is in one of 256 possible states, given by the particular pattern of 0s and 1s contained therein. The state of a byte does not, by itself, mean anything: it does only when it is interpreted according to some convention. So we may say that the state 00000000 represents the concept symbolised by the number 0, the state 00000001 represents the number 1, and so on. This would be sensible, corresponding as it does to the system of binary arithmetic. But we may equally well say that the state 00000001 represents the letter 'A', or the date '1 January 1984', or indeed anything we like. It is necessary, then, to arrange that the computer interprets the states in the desired way, as numbers, letters, dates or whatever. For the common kinds of information, such as numbers, we would expect common operations, such as addition, to be handled by 'hardware', that is, by specially designed electronic circuitry in the arithmetic unit; for operations on the kinds of information which only crop up occasionally, such as dates, we would expect to have to write a *program*, that is, a sequence of instructions which can be broken down into operations for which circuitry has been provided. For the ordinary user of computers, the distinction between operations performed by hardware and those performed by program or 'software' is of no real concern (but hardware operations are faster than programmed ones). Most computers are *general-purpose* in that the hardware operations provided ('the machine instructions') are broad enough to be usable to solve many different problems. It is precisely this generality which makes the program necessary – to say how a specific problem is to be solved.

General-purpose computers have only a small number (around 100) of machine instructions and it is possible to associate each instruction with a distinct state of a byte. It is the computer manufacturer's responsibility to ensure that these states are interpreted correctly by the circuitry. Now we can see that the main memory can contain not only the data we wish to work on, but also the instructions constituting the program to process the data. Without this facility, a specification of each operation would have to be input immediately before being obeyed. This is what we have to do with our cheap calculator. To repeat the calculation with different data we have to type the operations in again. With a programmable calculator or any other computer, we can put the program in memory, from where it can be run more quickly and repeatedly if we wish.

Sometimes we have a piece of data which is too large to fit in one byte. With our convention for numbers we could store only the numbers from 0 to 255. For larger numbers we could arrange to use more bytes: four, for example, would give us numbers up to 2^{32} (about $4*10^9$). This works as long as we know, when we write our program, how large the piece of data is. But consider a program which stores the names of each student in a class, putting the characters of the names neatly into consecutive bytes of main memory. Now, owing to unforeseen circumstances, Miss May becomes Mrs February: there is no space for the extra characters, and she is probably in the wrong place anyway. Instead of shifting innocent characters about to make space, a better solution is obtained by realising that we can associate with each byte (or word) of memory a unique number (called its *address*) and can therefore interpret the state of a byte (or word) as the address of another byte (or word). A large piece of information does not have to be stored in adjacent bytes, i.e. bytes whose addresses differ by one, but can be distributed in smaller pieces around main memory and backing store, if necessary, provided we have a record of the addresses of these smaller pieces. We can now build up arbitrarily complicated *data structures*, as they are called, with the particular advantage that this enables us to retrieve and to change parts of a body of information independently of other parts.[4] The organisation of these data structures, and how they may be used in computer-assisted learning programs, will be considered in the next chapter.

Notes

1. Abelson (1982) describes a version of Logo for the Apple II and includes appendices listing differences for TI 99/4 Logo and a second Apple Logo. Terak Logo and 380Z Logo are defined in manuals obtainable from the micro manufacturers.
2. The computer has a certain number of primitive operations built into it. The operations of a programming language like Logo have to be converted into these primitive operations. Special programs, called compilers or interpreters, are provided to make this conversion automatic.
3. The procedure MEMBERQ can be defined in terms of three more basic procedures for dealing with lists, FIRST, REST and EMPTYQ. FIRST returns the first item in a specified list as its result:
    W: PRINT FIRST [ARGENTINA BRAZIL BOLIVIA]
gives
    ARGENTINA
on the screen. The result of REST is the list that remains after removing the first item:
    W: PRINT REST [ARGENTINA BRAZIL BOLIVIA]
gives
    [BRAZIL BOLIVIA]
on the screen. EMPTYQ returns 'TRUE if the list given as input has no items in it at all, otherwise 'FALSE. The definition of MEMBERQ is:
    W: BUILD 'MEMBERQ
    MEMBERQ 'ITEM 'LIST
        1 IF EMPTYQ :LIST THEN RESULT 'FALSE
        2 IF EQUALQ :ITEM (FIRST :LIST) THEN RESULT 'TRUE
        3 RESULT MEMBERQ :ITEM (REST :LIST)
In a procedure which is to calculate a result we must, naturally, say what the

result is to be – we use the command RESULT for this. Since a procedure can have only one result it stops as soon as it carries out its first RESULT.

4. To see in more detail how data structures may be stored, let us take the list [ARGENTINA BRAZIL BOLIVIA] again. Since a list may contain any number of items we cannot sensibly allocate a fixed number of words in memory to store it in. Instead, we may take each item of the list, store it in a fixed number of words, and then associate with it the address of the next item in the list, that is, diagrammatically,

where ARGENTINA denotes the state which represents the sequence of characters 'ARGENTINA', the arrow from a box means that the state of that box is the one which represents the address of the word containing the item pointed to, and END represents a state indicating the end of a list. If we now put some addresses on these boxes

25		64		18	
ARGENTINA	64	BRAZIL	18	BOLIVIA	END

we can follow what happens with the call

    W: MEMBERQ 'BRAZIL [ARGENTINA BRAZIL BOLIVIA]

The value of a variable which is a list is effectively given by the address of the beginning of the list (25, in this case) and so this call may be thought of as equivalent to

    W: MEMBERQ 'BRAZIL 25

Now, EMPTYQ 25 is 'FALSE, and :ITEM (i.e. 'BRAZIL) is not equal to FIRST 25 (i.e. 'ARGENTINA). Therefore, the result is given by MEMBERQ 'BRAZIL 64, where the 64 is the result of REST 25, i.e. the address of the rest of the list. So MEMBERQ is entered a second time and in this case :ITEM is found equal to FIRST 64 (i.e. 'BRAZIL), giving a result of 'TRUE for this and the previous call of MEMBERQ.

It should be clear that the actual addresses do not matter. Pieces of information can, therefore, be put wherever in memory is convenient (and languages like Logo take on the responsibility for this), as long as the addresses are recorded. Also, we can operate on the list by changing the addresses rather than by moving around the (possibly very large amounts of) information itself. For example, the above list may be sorted into alphabetical order just by rearranging the addresses stored in the boxes:

25		64		18	
ARGENTINA	18	BRAZIL	END	BOLIVIA	64

2. ARTIFICIAL INTELLIGENCE, TEACHING AND LEARNING

Like many Latin abstract terms, the origin of the noble concept of 'education' is to be tracked down to the agricultural vocabulary of the farmyard (*v*: L.R. Palmer's *The Latin Language, passim*). It is indeed related to *edere* − to eat, but is derived from its variant *educare* − to cram, to stuff full, applied to geese and the like. (From a letter to the *Guardian*, 1980)

In the first chapter we argued that if we wished to use computers in an intelligent way in education, then we should look to the science of artificial intelligence for ideas and examples. In this chapter we shall first describe in some detail one artificial intelligence program, a program called MYCIN which performs medical diagnosis (Shortliffe, 1976).[1] This program will be discussed from two perspectives. First, we shall use it as an example of some contemporary techniques used in the construction of artificially intelligent programs. Then we shall explore the various educational uses to which this and similar programs might be put. The description of the MYCIN program should provide a general appreciation of the achievements and goals of artificial intelligence research. We then relate this new field's ideas about thinking and learning to more general questions of educational philosophy and, in subsequent chapters, to the design of computer-assisted learning systems.

MYCIN – An artificial intelligence program

MYCIN attempts to diagnose bacterial infections in the blood, and to suggest appropriate treatment. It is used by a doctor who interacts with the program via a computer terminal. An example of a dialogue is given in Figure 2.1.

Figure 2.1   *Part of a dialogue with MYCIN* (from Shortliffe, 1976)*

.

.

.

I will refer to the most recent positive culture for which you desire therapeutic advice as – culture1 – .
4) From what site was the specimen for culture1 taken?
[MYCIN numbers questions so that they can be referred to.]
blodd
=blood
5) How many days ago was this blood culture (culture1) obtained?
2
I will refer to the first offending organism from this blood culture (culture1) as – organism1 – .
6) Enter the identity (genus) of organism1:
unk
[i.e. unknown]
7) Staining characteristics of organism1 (gram):
?
[consultant asks to see some recognised responses]
What is the stain of organism1?
Expected responses are: acidfast grampos gramneg
Enter 'help' for list of user options.
gramneg

.

.

.

19) What is the suspected non-sterile portal of entry of organism1 into this sterile site?
rule
[to see the rule which has caused this question to be asked]
rule 121

---

*In this book, all dialogues are from published descriptions and have been modified only to convert them into a standard form, in which all computer output is in small type, and student input is in italics, and a sequence of vertical dots denotes an omitted extract. [Explanatory comments are enclosed in brackets as this sentence is.]

if: 1) the site of the culture is one of: those sites that are normally
      sterile, and
   2) the portal of entry of the organism is the same as the site of a
      prior organism with the same identity as this current
      organism
then: there is further suggestive evidence (.3) that each of them is
      a prior organism with the same identity as this current
      organism

gu
20) Did organism1 grow aerobically?
yes
21) Did organism1 grow anaerobically?
no
22) Was any chemotherapy recently begun specifically to combat
organism1?
qa
[consultant wants to enter the explanation system for a question-
answering session]
type help for the list of question options.
iq what do you think the identity of organism1 is at this point?
The identity of organism1 is pseudomonas (.333) klebsiella (.333)
enterobacter (.333)
return
[to return to the consultation system]
.
.
.
26) Has Jeremiah Sample [patient1] had any gu surgery or manipulation of the urinary tract? (e.g. indwelling catheter, cystoscopy,
etc.)
why
[to see a more detailed explanation of why the question was asked]
I am trying to find out about the identity of the organism.
I already know that:
The portal of entry of the organism is upper-gu
The morphology of the organism is rod
The stain of the organism is gramneg
The site of the culture is blood.

Therefore, if:
1)the patient has not had a genito-urinary manipulative procedure, and
2)urinary-tract-infection is not a problem for which the patient has been treated
then:
there is suggestive evidence (.6) that the identity of the organism is e.coli.
(Rule 156)
.
.
.

47) Were any additional positive specimens recently drawn from Jeremiah Sample [patient1] which revealed one or more organisms for which you wish therapeutic advice?
no
My therapy recommendation will be based on the following possible identities of the organism(s) that seem to be significant:
<Item 1> The identity of organism1 may be pseudomonas
<Item 2> The identity of organism1 may be klebsiella
<Item 3> The identity of organism1 may be enterobacter
<Item 4> The identity of organism1 may be e.coli
<Item 5> The identity of organism1 may be proteus (subtype unknown)
48) On a scale of 0 to 4, where higher numbers indicate increasing severity, how would you rate Jeremiah Sample [patient1]'s degree of sickness?
4
49) Does Jeremiah Sample [patient1] have a clinically significant allergic reaction to any antimicrobial agent?
no
[Considering gentamicin for use against organism1 . . .]
[Rec 1] My preferred therapy recommendation is as follows:
In order to cover for Items <1> <2> <3> <4> <5>:
   Give the following combination:
   1 Gentamicin
      Dose: 1.7 mg/kg q8h-iv or im
      Comments: Modify dose in renal failure

2 Carbenicillin
    Dose: 25 mg/kg q2h-iv
    Comments: Modify dose in renal failure
Do you wish to see the next choice?

.

.

.

[consultant may now ask MYCIN questions, e.g.]
What made you think organism1 might be a proteus?
I used Rule 163 to conclude that the identity of organism1 is proteus. This gave a cumulative c.f. of .277. The last question asked before the conclusion was made was 26.
I used Rule 084 to conclude that the identity of organism1 is proteus. This gave a cumulative c.f. of .119. The last question asked before the conclusion was made was 24.

.

.

.

The program's knowledge about bacterial infections is expressed as a few hundred 'production rules'. A production rule is a way of representing knowledge of the form: 'If some condition is true then do some action', for example: 'If you have a headache take an aspirin'. A production rule is therefore rather like a Logo conditional command:

    IF EQUALQ :SYMPTOM 'HEADACHE THEN
    PRESCRIBE 'ASPIRIN.

Obviously, with MYCIN, the suggested treatment will depend on the diagnosis of the infection and causative organism. One of the production rules actually used in MYCIN looks like the following:

    Rule 129:

    IF EQUALQ :INFECTION 'PRIMARY-BACTEREMIA
    THEN
        IF EQUALQ :ENTRYPOINT
        'GASTRO-INTESTINAL-TRACT THEN
            IF EQUALQ : CULTURESITE 'STERILE-SITE
            THEN
                MAKE 'ORGANISM 'BACTEROIDES

We say 'looks like', because MYCIN's production rules are not the same as Logo's conditional commands for the following reason. In Logo all variables have values, which can of course be used as inputs to EQUALQ. With MYCIN, however, variables may not have values – for example, the program may get to Rule 129 without having found out what the infection is. In such a circumstance, MYCIN ought perhaps to ask the doctor: 'Do you know what the infection is?' Consequently, the designers of MYCIN wrote a special program (called an interpreter) to interpret the production rules as required. The interpreter operating on Rule 129 might initiate the following dialogue:

MYCIN: What is the infection?
Doctor: Primary-bacteremia.
MYCIN: What is the entry point?
Doctor: Gastro-intestinal tract.
MYCIN: What is the culture site?
Doctor: Csf.

With these answers the interpreter would not then go on to make the value of ORGANISM 'BACTEROIDES (because the answer to the last question was not 'a sterile site'). Once these questions have been asked, the interpreter will not need to ask them again when operating on other rules which deal with INFECTION, ENTRYPOINT or CULTURESITE.[2]

A set of production rules (which is called a *production system*) can be interpreted in two distinct ways. Consider this very simple production system ('mini-MYCIN'):

1. rash, swollen gland → german measles
2. rash, fever, cough → measles
3. quick pulse, high temperature → fever
4. measles → keep in bed for two days
5. german measles → isolate until rash gone

which we shall use to diagnose a case with the symptoms: rash, high temperature. One way to interpret a production system is to work through the rules one by one until a rule is found for which the condition (the 'left-hand side') is true. When such a rule is found the corresponding action (the 'right-hand side') is carried out. So our diagnosis might proceed like this:

'Do you have a swollen gland?'   'No'
'Do you have a fever?'   'I don't know'
'Do you have a quick pulse?'   'Yes'

Now Rule 3 succeeds, and we deduce that the patient does in fact have a fever. The diagnosis is not yet complete and so we go back to the beginning and work through the rules again:

'Do you have a cough?'   'Yes'

Rule 2 now tells us that the patient has measles, and Rule 4 gives the treatment. In general, then, with a more realistic production system such as MYCIN's, we might scan through the rules several times to complete a chain of reasoning steps from the symptoms to the treatment (including, perhaps, several steps which turn out to be irrelevant to the final diagnosis). Under this interpretation the rules are run from 'left to right'.

Alternatively, the production system could be 'run backwards', with the rules being run from 'right to left'. Imagine that the case is presented with the symptoms above and an initial hypothesis: 'I think it's measles.' Now the interpreter could go through the rules looking at the *right-hand sides* until it finds one which matches the hypothesis (with mini-MYCIN, Rule 2). The corresponding left-hand side gives conditions which, if true, support the hypothesis. If the truth of a condition on the left-hand side is not known it could form a sub-hypothesis to be checked out using the production system in exactly the same way. With our measles case above, this interpretation would lead to the same sequence of questions above, except that we would not ask about swollen glands. With MYCIN, this kind of interpretation would correspond to the situation where we suspect the patient has some particular disease or infection and we want to know what symptoms or clinical facts would support this diagnosis.[3]

As it happens, MYCIN does run backwards. The main reason for this is that the generation of sequences of questions associated with some particular hypothesis makes sense to a doctor, whereas if MYCIN were to run forwards it would appear to jump from topic to topic, asking questions in a seemingly haphazard order. (If this is not clear, imagine our mini-MYCIN with 100 or more rules, in no particular order, and having nothing to do with measles.)

Many of MYCIN's diagnosis rules express knowledge that is not absolutely certain. For example, in Rule 129, if the condition holds then this might be considered only 'suggestive evidence' that the organism is bacteroides. So each rule in MYCIN has a 'certainty factor' associated with it to indicate its reliability – say 0.7 (on a scale from 0 to 1) for Rule 129. Some of the facts that the doctor types in will also have a certainty factor. These are combined as the interpreter runs so that some measure of the reliability of a deduction based on the use of a series of rules can be calculated by the program. Obviously, deductions with high reliability are taken more seriously by MYCIN than those with low reliability.

The use of production rules to express pieces of medical knowledge enables MYCIN to be made easy to use in a number of important ways. First, it is easy to add new rules to the system, in order to include special cases or new medical knowledge or to correct omissions. This is so because each rule expresses (in principle, anyway) an independent 'chunk' of knowledge, and therefore when adding rules one does not have to worry about complicated interactions with existing ones.

Secondly, it is possible to write a program to enable the doctor to communicate with the system in English. This is because the rigid format of the production rules makes it not too difficult to translate them into readable English, e.g. to pull Rule 129 apart and to produce, for example, 'What is the infection?'

Another important facility which MYCIN offers is that of being able to explain its diagnosis by reference to its rules. So that if we ask the system:

'Why did you decide the organism was not bacteroides?'
it might reply, by virtue of Rule 129,

'The culture site was not a sterile site.'
As Figure 2.1 shows, the doctor can ask for an explanation of a particular rule, of why a particular question is being asked, and of why a particular conclusion is reached. A medical expert can therefore monitor the conclusions that are generated. A doctor unsure of the validity of a conclusion could get MYCIN to go through the rules that were used to reach this conclusion, and, if necessary, could then change a faulty rule or replace an over-

40

general one with a number of special case rules.

It should be emphasised that MYCIN's diagnoses do not come with a money-back guarantee. Computers are machines which slavishly follow their instructions, without error, but it is a mistake to believe that their pronouncements are therefore without error. Within its speciality MYCIN performs as well as an expert, and of course better than the run-of-the-mill doctor, but this is not perfection. It is important therefore that the doctor using MYCIN should know that the responsibility remains his and that he should be given ways of understanding (and overruling) MYCIN's decisions.

To summarise, then, the important features of MYCIN are that it has

1. an appropriate way of representing medical knowledge, i.e. as production rules;
2. a reasonable initial set of facts and relations which can easily be extended;
3. a natural and comprehensible mode of reasoning, i.e. running the production system backwards;
4. an ability to carry out plausible reasoning;
5. a dialogue capability using an adequate subset of English;
6. an ability to explain its decision-making processes.

Intelligent computer-assisted learning systems

A program with the features just described for MYCIN could be a valuable part of a computer-assisted learning system. We shall now imagine the roles that MYCIN could play in a computer-based learning environment, either as it stands or with suitable extensions, and consider further the question of knowledge representations, which seems to be the key to developing intelligent programs.

Most obviously, MYCIN can be used in 'apprentice-master' mode. MYCIN's therapy recommendations compare well with those of human experts in infectious diseases, and trainee doctors could simply be asked to look over MYCIN's shoulder as it sets about solving its problems. One may have doubts about the efficacy of this procedure – it's like hoping to learn how to play golf by watching Jack Nicklaus on television – but, if the experience of the designers of MYCIN is at all typical, human experts at such specialised skills have some difficulty in explaining why they do what they do, especially when the reasoning is judgemental. Masters know more than is in the textbooks and it is this 'lore of the subject' which an apprentice is asked to absorb.

We ought now to think briefly about what other areas of human expertise could be covered by 'master programs' like MYCIN and indeed to speculate on whether there are any limitations in this direction. First, the MYCIN approach has already been adapted to several other specialist problems[4] – the production system interpreter, and the programs for giving explanations and for changing the production system, can be carried over virtually unchanged. And, as we shall see, other domains have been tackled with success by different means. Programs which try to solve problems which would otherwise require specialist human skill are called *expert systems*. But the art of 'knowledge engineering' is still a new one, and in most areas requiring great expertise the human remains unchallenged. However, most workers in artificial intelligence believe that there is no reason in principle why a computer program could not be written to perform satisfactorily at a given problem-solving task. (There may be reasons why such programs *should* not be written, but that's another story, told by Weizenbaum (1976). He believes that certain activities, such as psychotherapy, making judicial decisions and perhaps teaching, are essentially human ones and that it is a gross offence to moral feelings to entrust them to a computer.)

The student-apprentice does not have to play silent partner to the MYCIN master. Since MYCIN can explain in English what it is doing, the student could be provided with a way of interrupting MYCIN to ask why a particular question has been asked or conclusion has been reached. Or perhaps MYCIN could be modified to print out step-by-step explanations while working through a diagnosis.

42

This idea of a computer program giving a 'trace' of its own performance is not quite as straightforward as it may seem. On most computer systems there is a way of running any program under a 'trace option', which typically gives a list of the procedures entered, in order, and of the values of variables. This trace is supposed to help the programmer understand why his program has run amok, assuming it has. To achieve this the trace has to be comprehensible – a list of computer addresses and contents, for example, probably would not be. Similarly, with MYCIN, an explanation such as 'Because Rule 129 failed' would not help the student much. In general, the program has to express its explanations in terms of what the student knows, and this implies that the program should know what the student knows, an issue to which we shall return shortly. Moreover, traces can make very tedious reading unless the program is clever enough to be able to select only that which is really worth saying.

Now, a very important point: MYCIN's explanations of its decision-making processes will not help the student unless these processes are similar to those which the student is supposed to be developing. It is possible that medical diagnosis could be done on a purely statistical basis by taking all the clinical data, and perhaps working through a medical database to come up with a verdict: '95.3 per cent of similar cases had primary-bacteremia.' A program written along these lines would be able to say little about its intermediate stages and would capture little of the reasoning of expert diagnosticians. MYCIN's production rules have been developed in consultation with human experts, suggesting that the rules should be at a level appropriate for human comprehension.

Put another way, MYCIN, like all artificial intelligence programs which attempt to model human reasoning processes, embodies a commitment to the view that these processes are best understood in terms of symbolic processing and rely little on numerical computation. In artificial intelligence, a *symbol* is a representation of a 'chunk' of knowledge which a program can execute, or look at, or describe, or compare with other symbols, or use in whatever other way is necessary.

The expertise of MYCIN depends crucially on the way in which knowledge is represented within it. Production rules are particu-

43

larly appropriate as they can be used to relate premises about facts determined by questioning to conclusions about possible diagnoses. These rules can then be used in reasoning. For other domains or types of expertise it may be better to use some other form of representation.

With most programs we can see that some knowledge is contained in the programs themselves and some in the data they work on. Suppose, for example, that a telephone directory were stored in a computer database and that we had a program which could look up a particular person's number in the directory. The representation of the directory would be an example of a *declarative* representation, i.e. one in which there is a set of independent facts. The program itself, however, contains knowledge about how a directory is searched. The specification of methods is called a *procedural* representation.

Are MYCIN's production rules declarative or procedural? If we emphasise the way one rule encapsulates a piece of medical knowledge which can be understood and explained in isolation and the fact that a new rule can easily be added to the system, then we are emphasising the declarative aspect. If, on the other hand, we stress that the rules are similar to Logo's conditional commands and that the whole production system is really only a program which requires a rather specialised interpreter, then we are emphasising the procedural aspect. So our question presents a false dichotomy. There is no fundamental difference between the declarative and procedural representations, for any program is merely data for some other program. And yet, while it is conceded that 'the proceduralists and the declarativists secretly agree' (Winston, 1977), the procedural versus declarative issue has been the subject of much discussion in artificial intelligence.[5] This discussion is of relevance to computer-assisted learning because the view we adopt of a knowledge representation helps to determine what we do with it.

In general, for programs that must answer questions about 'how', a procedural view is useful; for programs that must know facts, a declarative view may be more appropriate. So a program to work out a complex series of events to answer 'How will precipitation be affected by increased temperature and reduced wind-

44

speed?' might be implemented using procedures for determining meteorological changes. On the other hand, a program to answer 'What is the population of San Francisco?' might better make use of a database of geographical facts. In the MYCIN system, when the consultant asks 'How did you reach the conclusion that organism1 was proteus?' the production system needs to be looked upon in procedural terms, to explain the conclusions reached from the rules which were carried out. If the question were 'Which rules are useful in deciding that organism1 is proteus?' then the declarative view is needed – the rules are to be looked up.

Thinking a little more carefully about the MYCIN system, we can see that it contains more knowledge than is in the rules alone: it 'knows' how to interpret the rules. This knowledge is represented procedurally, within the production system interpreter. In theory, MYCIN could introspect about this knowledge and explain it to us, but in practice it would be very difficult for it to do so because the knowledge is not organised into tidy, explicit forms, like production rules. The practical consequence is that MYCIN cannot explain how the production rules are used, in a global sense. MYCIN can answer 'how' and 'why' questions about a specific diagnosis but it cannot stand back and say 'In general, the way to carry out a diagnosis is . . . ' It may seem unreasonably optimistic to expect such explanations from a program, but we should bear in mind that it is after all what a MYCIN tutor would be trying to teach – not so much what the rules are, but how in general they are to be used. We shall see much more mundane examples of teaching programs which are limited by being unable to explain what they can do. The general point is that the designer of an intelligent computer tutor needs to consider carefully which levels of knowledge need to be made explicit (i.e. examinable and explainable by the tutor) if it is possible to do so.

In other domains it may not be sensible to try to divide the relevant knowledge up into independent chunks. Even with MYCIN it may well be that certain diseases are associated with the same symptoms and, therefore, rather than repeat conditions in several rules, we may want to say something like 'If these conditions hold try Rule 283 next (which will assume these conditions)'. This however would be against the spirit of production systems since it would now be impossible to understand, explain or change one rule in ignorance of the rest. But, of course, pieces of information are interrelated, and it may be crucial that these links be represented. For example, suppose you were in the habit of maintaining a notebook in which you jotted down facts and gossip about your acquaintances:

Elsie's phone number is 234.

Ken is a school teacher.

Sue is pregnant.

Len is living with Elsie.

etc.

As the number of facts grows, so it becomes more difficult to find what you want: 'What's Len's phone number?' So you organise your notebook – you gather together facts about the same person, you arrange things in alphabetical order. In computing terms, you no longer have a set of independent facts but a data structure.[6] It is relatively straightforward to write a computer program to find its way about such a structure, to add new facts in the right place, and to apply rules of inference to deduce facts not stored (and 'certainty factors' would be a good idea here as well!).

The extreme view is that all knowledge is an organised, coherent structure and should be represented as such in a program which needs to make use of this knowledge. Then no concept would be meaningful in isolation but would acquire meaning only from its relationships to other concepts in the entire structure.

The advantages and disadvantages of the various knowledge representations are still under active consideration in artificial intelligence research.[7] Let us just summarise the properties on which these comparisons are made:

1. Modularity – the degree to which part of the representation can be understood independently of the rest;
2. Changeability – how easy it is to change (add, delete) parts of the representation;
3. Power – the extent to which what ought to follow from the knowledge represented does in fact follow from the representation and how it is understood;
4. Explicitness – how much of the knowledge represented is

explicit, i.e. interpretable (and hence in principle explainable) and not merely executable.
5. Conciseness – how little of the knowledge represented is redundant.

So far we have just thought about letting a student watch MYCIN in action. Suppose a student were simply given the MYCIN program and left to do what he liked with it. What would *you* do? Here are some possibilities: try to 'break the system' by finding some input data for which the program fails disastrously; print out the program and try to make some sense of it; delete a few rules to see what happens; extend the program to deal with different illnesses; sell it to a gullible friend. A prospective doctor might learn more from some of these activities than others. But some educationalists would argue that computer tutors should not be over-dogmatic and should give the student some freedom over his activities. Of course, the MYCIN system, because of its narrow specialist skill, does not leave much scope even for the inventive student. Imagine, instead, that the student is given access to a computer to use and develop programs as he wishes. Is programming an educationally worthwhile activity? The designers of programs like MYCIN learn a great deal about the specialist knowledge involved and how it should be organised: likewise, we may expect a child asked to write a program to, say, make our turtle (Chapter 1) draw pretty patterns, to absorb certain mathematical ideas and to develop ways of organising his own knowledge. This argument will be pursued in Chapter 5.

Now imagine that the tables are turned: the student is to attempt the diagnosis while MYCIN looks over his shoulder. The simplest way to do this would be to change MYCIN so that it selected a case (from a database of cases or, perhaps, by making one up) and then asked the student to diagnose it. MYCIN could surreptitiously complete a diagnosis itself (or look up the diagnosis if this is also in the database) and at the end of the session indicate whether it agrees with the student's verdict. This is a drill-and-practice. One complication needs mentioning: MYCIN's language understanding capability would need improving since the student is now expected to ask arbitrarily complicated questions and not, like the consultant, type in short responses to questions.

We can think about improving on a straightforward drill-and-practice in various ways. MYCIN could work through the diagnosis at the same time as the student and try to monitor what he does. Unusual steps, i.e. steps which do not correspond with those that MYCIN would take in the same circumstances, could be commented on, and the student perhaps could be given advice or hints to keep him on MYCIN's path. This would not be easy to do satisfactorily, however: since MYCIN does not always come up with 'correct' solutions it cannot be sure that the student's unusual step is not, in fact, an improvement on its own.

When the student comes up with a hypothesis with which MYCIN does not agree, MYCIN could present him with a counter-example. This might lead the student to think about the reasoning processes involved more than would a blunt 'I do not agree'.

Also the cases presented to the student could be selected specifically to give the student practice in some area. This presumes that our extended MYCIN has a reason for believing that the student needs practice in this area. How could MYCIN develop such a belief? Well, apart from the obvious answer of looking the student up in some giant file, MYCIN could keep track of the rules which the student has successfully used and therefore probably understands. MYCIN could then select cases which required other rules. This again confirms that it is desirable that each rule should be an independent chunk, so that it could be said to be understood as a whole, or not.

What MYCIN knows about the student must be in terms of what it itself knows about the problem domain, for of course MYCIN knows nothing else. This is why expert systems, to be useful teaching vehicles, should be realistic models of human intellectual structures, and especially of their dynamic nature, i.e. of how they develop and change.

We have stressed the following points about MYCIN: the way its expert knowledge is represented; that it is not perfect yet is useful; that its rules can be easily added to; and that a student might learn from studying its problem-solving processes. It would be inconsistent not to recognise that exactly the same points should be made about our extended MYCIN, an 'expert teacher'. Its teaching rules should be explicit, and indeed the attempt to make them so may be particularly fruitful: the rules would then be studiable by student-teachers just as MYCIN's are by student-doctors. And again, since the rules would not be perfect, the system should have some means of improving them, either from a medical expert (or a competent student) or a teaching expert, i.e. either at the level of medical expertise or teaching expertise.

Let us now summarise the ways in which MYCIN could be used as a computer tutor:

1. by stepping through a diagnosis, explaining each step;
2. by following a student engaged in a diagnosis and commenting on unusual steps;
3. by generating cases for a student to practise on;
4. by keeping track of a student's capability, to be used for example to give appropriate practice;
5. by explaining and improving its own teaching ability.

In Chapter 4 we shall see the extent to which such intelligent computer tutors have been implemented.[8]

Artificial intelligence and educational philosophy

Artificial intelligence attempts to study intelligence and the knowledge that makes it possible by developing computer programs and representations of the knowledge they need. To the extent that this enterprise is successful, we are justified in saying to a student 'Organise your own knowledge as this program does', and in believing that writing programs helps to develop intelligent thought-processes.

Structure
It has been found that the computational analogue of thinking depends partly on general-purpose procedures, like the laws of logic, but rather more on the skilful use of specific knowledge retrieved from memory. For this retrieval to be passably efficient, the knowledge has to be well-organised or highly structured. The

knowledge so retrieved is not necessarily mere information, but may be procedures for processing other data structures, by, for example, creating, changing or comparing them. Artificial intelligence sees learning to depend upon the possession of these active structures and tries to study it by studying their content, organisation and development.

One of the aims of artificial intelligence is to implement and investigate possible mechanisms to demonstrate and explain learning behaviour. It does not aim to develop the mathematically-formulated laws of learning more familiar to psychologists.

Artificial intelligence is a young science and does not speak with one voice: no one program, like MYCIN, can be considered typical. Perhaps more of the consensus view of learning is captured by Winston's program to learn structural descriptions from examples (Winston, 1975). This program is presented with a series of descriptions of line drawings and told in each case whether or not the drawing is an instance of some concept, such as 'a house'. The program's task is to develop a way of being able to distinguish between, for example, houses and non-houses (including, of course, previously unseen examples) – in other words, to learn, to some extent anyway, what is meant by 'a house'.

The program works by building up a data structure to represent the concept, and then comparing this with a representation of the example given. The differences found determine the changes to be made to the structure.[9] Thus, the program learns from well-chosen examples and not by some drawn-out statistical process (as implied by many learning theories). Winston stressed the idea of 'near-miss' examples, i.e. ones which did not differ too much from the structured representation at that time – otherwise the program would be overwhelmed by all the mismatches, and be unable to work out how to modify its understanding of the concept.

As we explained when describing MYCIN, the way knowledge is represented within a system is often crucial in determining that system's performance. The representation adopted by Winston can be thought of as a network of linked nodes, the nodes denoting objects and the links denoting relationships between objects. It would be nice to have a good general representation which could be used to solve a range of problems and, with this aim in mind, workers in artificial intelligence have recently been grappling with ideas of considerably more detailed networks than Winston used. In artificial intelligence such a network is generally called a *frame* but we shall use the term 'schema' instead, as psychologists have long used this word to denote much the same idea (and we shall meet a different sort of frame in the next chapter). As described by Minsky (1975), a schema is a data structure for representing a stereotyped situation, such as a children's birthday party. Within a schema are various kinds of information: some facts that are always true about the situation (e.g. there will be party games); some questions to resolve (e.g. what present to take); some default assumptions (e.g. the children will be smartly dressed); the expected order of events (e.g. candle-blowing and 'happy birthday to you'); and so on. The proposal is that a situation is understood (by human or program) by retrieving an appropriate schema from memory and adapting it as necessary. Related schemata are linked together to form 'schema-systems' by, for example, sharing parts of their structure and by specifying transformations from one schema to another, e.g. to represent actions or cause-effect relations. Learning is then to be interpreted in terms of the storing and modifying of schemata as a result of experience.

Artificial intelligence endeavours to make concrete various rather abstract ideas about thinking. These artificial intelligence ideas mesh intriguingly with those of modern developmental psychology, which studies the mental development of children. In particular, we must look at the work of Piaget, a genetic epistemologist, who has been increasingly influential on educational practice. His ideas are the inspiration for the educational computing systems described in Chapter 5. For fifty years or more, Piaget argued against the behaviourist tradition in psychology and it is only recently (particularly in America, where the behaviourist tradition was stronger) that he has been recognised as *the* psychologist of cognitive development.[10]

Epistemology is the theory of knowledge, and hence a genetic epistemologist is concerned with the origin and development of knowledge. Piaget tried to change our understanding of children and what they know. There is no Piagetian dogma about education, and in fact Piaget himself wrote comparatively little that is directly addressed to education, but what he did write is of profound significance for teachers.

He emphasised structure: 'the essential functions of intelligence consist in understanding and inventing, in other words in building up structures by structuring reality' (Piaget, 1970). At any point in the development of the intellect it can be described as a set of organised structures or schemata. These structures are built by the child in interaction with the environment: objects and events are 'assimilated' to these structures, which thus function and grow without structural change. When this is not possible because the existing structures are inadequate, they may modify themselves or 'accommodate' and thus undergo structural change. The structures are equilibrated systems – meaning that they can cope with input requiring only minor changes to the structure – which can undergo more radical reorganisation to take the child to a higher level of intellectual development.

Schemata can assimilate one another to form further schemata and thus structures can be common to many 'higher-level' structures. The combination of mental structures may produce new ways of thinking and behaving and this theory enables explanations of insight and invention to be suggested. For example, 'invention . . . is nothing other than a spontaneous reorganisation of earlier schemata which are accommodated by themselves to the new situations, through reciprocal assimilation' (Piaget, 1966).

So, knowledge is always structured in some way at all age levels. A baby's knowledge is organised in terms of his motor actions and sensations; by two years, the organisation of knowledge begins to exist in thought, and so on through increasingly rich structures. Since understanding comes only from assimilation into existing structures, children at different developmental stages see different worlds. But while a child's progression through the stages of intellectual development is considered to be immutable, Piaget is not saying that the child's cognitive structures change only in some pre-established or entirely predictable way: the child is always considered to be the centre of activity, being constantly involved in self-regulating processes.

This necessarily brief description of Piaget's ideas may suggest that they are somewhat vague, an impression not entirely dispelled by an assiduous reading of his sixty-odd books.[11] Piaget did try to add precision by adopting classical mathematical terminology, groups, lattices and the like, but the tools were not adequate to the job. To describe a theory of change, you need to be able to describe the process of change – as artificial intelligence's computational metaphor for thinking tries to do.

Teaching style

As we saw, the MYCIN program could be used to support a variety of teaching styles, each of which has its merits. We have expository styles, in which the student looks and listens; we have more open styles, in which the student is largely responsible for his own activities.

The expository style is closer to the conventional classroom lesson or lecture and is relatively easy to implement, even when enlivened by the occasional question or joke. So easy, in fact, that simple machines can do it, as discussed in the next chapter. Piaget was surprisingly complimentary about such machines, but perhaps only because they 'demonstrate beyond all possible doubt the mechanical character of the schoolmaster's function as it is conceived by traditional teaching methods . . . the ideal of [which] is merely to elicit correct repetition of what has been correctly transmitted' (Piaget, 1970).

Piaget believed that the role of language in learning is a minor one. He suggested that the sources of thought are to be found not in language, but in the pre-verbal actions performed during the first two years of life. A young child demonstrates operational thinking before developing the ability to explain or describe it. It is, however, probably an unwarranted extension to hold that language has no role in thought for older children or adults.

The concept that language reflects thought, rather than that thought depends on language, carries with it the view that a teacher is not a mere explainer or imparter of information, and that a student's verbal responses may tell us little about his understanding. Instead, Piaget stressed the spontaneous interaction with the environment by which mental growth occurs, and concluded that the teacher's main task is to foster conditions under which each child can think freely. Duckworth (1964) quotes Piaget as follows:

The chief outcome of this theory of intellectual development is a plea that children be allowed to do their own learning . . . you cannot further understanding in a child simply by talking to him. Good pedagogy must involve presenting the child with situations in which he himself experiments, in the broadest sense of the term.

Piaget's use of the word 'active' to describe his approved teaching methods has led to some confusion. The fundamental belief that learning is an active process, since knowledge is a construction from within, leads naturally to the idea that young children should manipulate objects: it does not mean that all learning environments should ensure that the learner is perpetually 'doing something'. 'Authentic activity may take place in the spheres of reflection, of the most advanced abstraction, and of verbal manipulation' (Piaget, 1970). So, for example, Piaget felt able to approve of the Socratic method – a verbal, essentially expository one – since it engages the learner in actively constructing his own knowledge. The confusion arises perhaps because of Piaget's idiosyncratic view that thought is implicit action: '[mental] operations are nothing but interiorized actions whose efferent impulses do not develop into external movements' (Piaget, 1954). Most researchers, especially those in artificial intelligence, where theories perforce are more concretely expressed, would hold that thinking involves the processing and changing of symbolic structures in memory.

Regardless of merits, teaching styles can be characterised in various ways: the emphasis on efficiency; the use of behavioural objectives and prescribed strategies; the degree of response to changing interests and abilities of the learner; the view of learning as cumulative or insightful. As later chapters and our discussion of MYCIN show, a computer is not constrained to any specific teaching style. But, as Piaget (1970) writes, 'the better our teaching methods, the more difficult they are to apply', and this holds for computer and human teachers alike.

Learning style

To say that learning involves changing cognitive structures still leaves many difficult questions: Just when do these changes occur? What if anything can teachers do to promote these changes? How do these changes differ between individual students?

Piaget has given deceptively straightforward answers to some of

54

these questions. Central to his theory is the idea that there are definite stages of development (the major of which involve sensorimotor, concrete operational and formal operational thought), and that these stages occur universally in a fixed order. This being one of the few hypotheses of Piaget's theory to lend itself to experimental test, it is inevitable that a mini-industry has developed to determine whether the order is, in fact, immutable and the extent to which the development can be accelerated. To a large extent, these experiments are beside our point: they accept Piaget's fundamental ideas, and aim to refine rather than overthrow them.

Piaget has, however, drawn a distinction between development and learning, a distinction which does not find much sympathy within the artificial intelligence community, at least. He writes:

The development of knowledge is a spontaneous process, tied to the whole process of embryogenesis. . . . Learning presents the opposite case. In general learning is provoked by situations – provoked by a psychological experimenter; or by a teacher, with respect to some didactic point; or by an internal situation. . . . In addition, it is a limited process – limited to a single problem or to a single structure. (Piaget, 1964)

Now, one difficulty here concerns what happens after the formal operational stage is reached in adolescence: is there no further cognitive development, or does each student thereafter develop an individual learning style? In either case, Piaget's theory would appear to offer little of direct help in the design of computer-assisted learning systems which deal with post-adolescent students.

In addition, if we look at computer programs to investigate learning, we do not find that 'development' gets treated very differently (perhaps because it is difficult to conceive of what would constitute embryogenesis with a computer!). 'Development' may involve more drastic changes to symbolic structures than 'learning', but in artificial intelligence it seems to be assumed that they are basically of the same sort. For example, Young (1976) used production systems to investigate children's ability to solve the Piagetian problem of length seriation, and found that adding one or two production rules at a time yielded a sequence of production systems which displayed many of the developmental phenomena which had led Piaget to divide the children's ability into three stages, and to claim that there is a 'restructuring' between stages.

Young was thus able to account for the development of the child's skill as a gradual acquisition of production rules.[12]

Within the framework of stages, Piaget does of course allow that children learn in their own ways, and yet he does not say much about how different styles are recognised and taken into account by the teacher. 'Individualised instruction' is now in fashion: 'The practical consequence of the fact of individual differences is that every general law of teaching has to be applied with consideration of the particular person in question.' This appeared in Thorndike (1906)!, but there are still few convincing demonstrations of teaching programs which systematically capitalise upon individual differences. One such is described by Pask and Scott (1972).[13] They distinguish between serialists, who habitually learn a body of information in terms of a series of items related by simple links, and holists, who learn as a whole forming more complex structures. To illustrate the difference, Pask and Scott set up an experiment in which students had to learn a taxonomy of unfamiliar objects ('Martian fauna') under 'free learning' conditions. Information about the taxonomy was written on cards which were divided into various classes, e.g. one class showed pictures of typical members of subspecies, another stated the structure of the taxonomy, and so on. A student 'asked a question' by turning over a card, but first had to give a reason for asking the question concerned. The degree to which a student tested for hypotheses based on complex predicates rather than simple ones enabled a discrimination to be made between serialist and holist competence. It was found that the different competence types had different behaviour patterns, i.e. they had different card-turning strategies.

Pask and Scott then devised two kinds of training programme, one intended to be suited to serialists and the other to holists. The serialist programme referred to a kernel of strictly relevant concepts presented in orderly fashion; the holist programme was based on 'overall' concepts. Both programmes conveyed exactly the same strictly relevant information. It was found that a student learned effectively if given a programme which matched his sort of competence, serialist or holist, but did not do so if there was a mismatch. To sum up, Pask and Scott showed that it is possible to detect differences in cognitive style and to devise teaching strategies slanted to suit an individual with a given sort of competence. Much of this could be done automatically. Computer-assisted learning is well-suited to the experimental investigation, and subsequent implementation, of programs based on individual differences.

Motivation

There is no doubt that using computers can be an intrinsically motivating activity. All computer-assisted learning projects report cases of students doing voluntary overtime at the computer. The average teacher's response to this strange phenomenon may range from tolerance to alarm. Concern is voiced on various grounds: that many computer-based activities are frivolous and a waste of a student's time; that long hours at a terminal will harm the student's social integration; that the development of a 'computer élite' may be socially harmful. These concerns cannot be dismissed, but since we do not contemplate deliberately making computers less motivating we are bound to adopt a positive attitude to them.

First, many superficially frivolous activities have considerably more educational meat in them than may be apparent, as we shall describe. And, regardless of any contribution to cognitive development, computer games may resonant with the student's affective component of behaviour leading to improved attitudes to the educational process. Secondly, the computer addict is indeed a sad and familiar sight, but one which we hope is the product of an outmoded view that computer programming is best done in isolation, both from other programmers and the 'outside world'. Professional programming is now largely a team activity, and it is accepted that most of the work is not done at the computer but in discussion of the problem and program design. Similarly, well-designed, computer-based learning environments increase rather than decrease social interaction. Thirdly, as regards the computer élite, this élite is not the same set of students as the 'mathematics élite', or any other élite. Thus, computing provides another field in which a student may enhance his self-respect. Unfortunately, at the moment many computer systems are so badly designed as to encourage too many students to believe they belong to the 'no good at computing' class.

57

Now, why are computers so motivating? Ultimately, explanations of motivation rest on philosophical assumptions, concerning, for example, the nature of free will. We assume that behaviour is determined by cognitive and affective processes. Humans act as determined by their thoughts and feelings. An 'intrinsically motivating' activity is one for which there is no apparent reward except the activity itself. Since there is no external reward, intrinsic motivation can only be explained in terms of 'internal consequences' which are experienced as rewarding. According to Deci (1975), 'intrinsic motivation is based on the human need to be competent and self-determining'.

Let us consider 'self-determining' first, since it is the more difficult of the two. Intrinsically-motivated behaviours result from a desire to feel personal causation (even though behaviour is predictable – in principle – if we had a full knowledge of the cognitive and affective processes involved). When the locus of causality becomes external, then motivation disappears or becomes extrinsic. Computers encourage self-determination in two main ways. First, they facilitate autonomous learning: students can, ideally, learn whatever, whenever (and soon wherever) they wish. Secondly, computers provide an environment in which mistakes are expected, and consequently in which students feel more free to experiment.

The 'need to be competent' suggests that behaviour seeks some optimum challenge to be overcome. When a problem is too hard, or completely solved, interest wanes. Computer programming is an activity which presents a student with optimum challenges: all computing teachers are familiar with students whose programs 'are nearly working' or 'need just one more improvement'.

Implicit in Piaget's work is the idea that children are intrinsically motivated to develop schemata through the processes of assimilation and accommodation. If there is a discrepancy between an informational input and a cognitive structure, then the assimilation schema tries to return the structure to equilibrium. The child is, according to Piaget, by nature motivated toward the development of increasingly complex cognitive structures. Thus, children are seen as builders of their own intellectual structures. Computers provide a new building material, one which helps the child to develop self-respect through a better appreciation of the power and limitations of his own theory building.

Educational technology and the computer

An old joke has it that the only successful piece of educational technology is the school bus. We recognise this as an old joke because educational technologists have now redefined their subject – no longer is it in terms of devices or equipment, but it is seen as a branch of behavioural science. Educational technology is concerned with the design and evaluation of curricula and learning experiences, and with the problems of implementing and renovating them (Rowntree, 1979). It does not imply an engineering view in which students are manipulated, and it carries no commitment to any particular theory of learning (although its very existence does not entirely accord with the Piagetian view that learning occurs by the natural process of assimilation).

Educational technologists would not, therefore, consider the computer as just another piece of equipment. If educational technology is concerned with thinking carefully about teaching and learning, then the computer has a contribution to make irrespective of its use as a means of implementation, for the design of computer-based learning environments gives us a new perspective on the nature of teaching and learning and indeed on general educational objectives. Papert (1980) presents a vision of how the computer presence could revolutionise learning procedures, and we shall return to this in Chapter 5.

But learning systems do have to be implemented, and we should therefore consider how the computer, as equipment, differs from other media. Despite prodigious efforts, researchers have provided very little evidence to contradict the conclusion of Oettinger (1971) that 'learning as now measured is largely independent of the details of means'. On the whole, the 'new' media have been used to re-implement existing curricula and teaching methods, and it is therefore not surprising that changes in learning have been marginal. It is difficult to believe, however, that learning cannot be improved by capitalising upon the computer's distinctive properties, which, to recapitulate, are:

1. It can make decisions. The computer is the only medium, other than the human teacher, able to take significant decisions whilst teaching. Moreover this decision could be based on more information than is usable by any other medium.
2. It is reactive, i.e. it can be programmed to respond to a student's actions with apparent interest and initiative (rather than with 'knee-jerk' reflexes), increasing the likelihood that the student will continue to engage in meaningful interaction with it.
3. It understands, i.e. it can in principle be programmed to understand a student, just as a good teacher does, and to use this understanding to determine its teaching actions.
4. It can control other devices, and can therefore capitalise on whatever advantages are offered by other media, such as graphical displays, speech input and output, and so on.
5. It is itself worthy of study. Its mere use can give insights into other subjects, such as mathematics, physics, psychology, etc.
6. It is not designed to accord with any specific educational theory (as teaching machines were to behaviourism). A computer can be programmed to reflect any view of a student, not necessarily a solely mechanistic or otherwise demeaning one.

These points need elaboration and that is the purpose of the rest of the book. It might appear that as an educational medium a computer has its limitations. For example, computers tend to be unsympathetic to first-time users, they do not understand conversational English, they do not get any better at teaching, and so on. But these are limitations of current practice, not of principle: a few systems already exist which, to some degree, do not have these limitations. The limitations are imposed by our own incompetence and lack of imagination.

Notes

1. The name MYCIN is taken from the common suffix of several of the antimicrobial agents, e.g. clindamycin.
2. If we were to write such an interpreter in Logo, then the production rules would

have to be stored as lists, for example Rule 129 as something like:
```
[[AND [SAME INFECTION PRIMARY-BACTEREMIA]
     [SAME ENTRYPOINT GASTRO-INTESTINAL-TRACT]
     [SAME CULTURESITE STERILE-SITE]
  [CONCLUDE ORGANISM BACTEROIDES]]]
```
where the interpreter would be written to 'know what to do with' AND, SAME and CONCLUDE. The original MYCIN system occupied 130,000 bytes on a DEC KI-10 and was written in INTERLISP, a version of LISP, the language most commonly used for writing artificial intelligence programs, and one designed specifically for processing lists. As Davis and Lenat (1982) remark, 'the reasoning performed by these programs requires removing the distinction between programs and data, which LISP does, in order to treat the rules and heuristics in the knowledge base sometimes as data to be reasoned about and sometimes as code to be executed.'

3. The two processes described are not in fact strict alternatives. A production system can be interpreted in many ways: for example, we could subtly mingle the running forwards and backwards modes. This is possible because the rules exist in memory as list structures to be interpreted as we wish by the program which looks at these structures. The two 'alternatives' just correspond to two straightforward ways of writing this program.
To see in more detail how this can be done, let us represent our mini-MYCIN production system as a list:
```
[[[RASH SWOLLEN-GLAND] [GERMAN-MEASLES]]
 [[RASH FEVER COUGH] [MEASLES]]
 [[QUICK-PULSE HIGH-TEMPERATURE] [FEVER]]
 [[MEASLES] [KEEP IN BED FOR A FEW DAYS]]
 [[GERMAN-MEASLES] [ISOLATE UNTIL RASH GONE]]].
```
Any particular part of this list can be picked out by a suitable combination of calls of the FIRST and REST procedures (see Chapter 1, n.3). For example, to get the first 'left-hand side' of a production system PS we could define:
```
W: BUILD 'FIRSTLHS
FIRSTLHS 'PS
  1 RESULT FIRST FIRST :PS
```
and to get the first 'right-hand side' :
```
W: BUILD 'FIRSTRHS
FIRSTRHS 'PS
  1 RESULT FIRST REST FIRST :PS
```
Now to see whether a left-hand side holds, we could take each item in turn and see whether it exists in SYMPTOMS, a list of symptoms e.g. [RASH HIGH-TEMPERATURE], and if not ask 'Do you have a whatever-it-is?' A simple version of such a procedure is:
```
W: BUILD 'HOLDSQ
HOLDSQ 'LHS 'SYMPTOMS
  1 IF EMPTYQ :LHS THEN RESULT 'TRUE
  2 IF MEMBERQ (FIRST :LHS) :SYMPTOMS THEN
```

61

RESULT HOLDSQ (REST :LHS) :SYMPTOMS
3 MAKE 'REPLY ASK PUTLAST[DO YOU HAVE A] (FIRST :LHS)
4 IF EQUALQ :REPLY [YES] THEN RESULT HOLDSQ (REST :LHS) :SYMPTOMS
5 RESULT 'FALSE

(On line 3 we have used the Logo procedure PUTLAST which joins its second input onto the list given at its first input.)

To run a production system PS forward, with given symptoms SYMPTOMS, we could now define:

W: BUILD 'RUNFORWARD
RUNFORWARD 'PS 'SYMPTOMS
1 MAKE 'P :PS
2 WHILE NOT HOLDSQ (FIRSTLHS :P) :SYMPTOMS
MAKE 'P (REST :P)
3 MAKE 'SYMPTOMS JOIN (FIRSTRHS :P) :SYMPTOMS
4 RUNFORWARD :PS :SYMPTOMS

We have a new Logo command here, the WHILE, which needs explaining first. The general form is

WHILE E S

where E is something which evaluates to 'TRUE or 'FALSE and S is a command. The idea is that if E is 'TRUE then S will be carried out, and then if E is still 'TRUE then S will be carried out again, and so on until eventually E becomes 'FALSE. So line 2 of RUNFORWARD assigns (REST :P) to P (which effectively skips past the first item, i.e. the first production rule, in P) as long as HOLDSQ (FIRSTLHS :P) :SYMPTOMS is 'FALSE. When line 3 is reached therefore, (FIRSTRHS :P) is the right-hand side to be carried out. On line 3, we assume that we just need to add the right-hand side to SYMPTOMS – for a general production system, we would need a procedure CARRYOUT to carry out the right-hand side. And then line 4 just repeats the whole process.

If we let the value of the variable DOCTORSPOCK be the list representing our mini-MYCIN production system then a call of RUNFORWARD could be

W: RUNFORWARD :DOCTORSPOCK [RASH HIGH-TEMPERATURE].

One or two minor problems remain, for example, knowing when to stop and avoiding carrying out the same rule repeatedly, but these are 'mere' programming details. We hope to have convinced you that it is possible to write a program like MYCIN – not that it is easy.

Now to run the system backwards is a little more tricky. Let the variable HYPOTHESIS be a suspected illness. Then an outline of RUNBACKWARD is

W: BUILD 'RUNBACKWARD
RUNBACKWARD 'PS 'SYMPTOMS 'HYPOTHESIS
1 MAKE 'P :PS
2 WHILE NOT MEMBERQ :HYPOTHESIS (FIRSTRHS :P)
MAKE 'P (REST :P)

    3 RESULT CHECKQ :PS :SYMPTOMS (FIRSTLHS :P)
Here, CHECKQ is a procedure which determines whether the left-hand side of a rule holds by looking each symptom up in SYMPTOMS, by running the system backwards with it as hypothesis, or by asking the user (it needs therefore to know which of these is appropriate). Assuming we have written CHECKQ, the call
    W: RUNBACKWARD :DOCTORSPOCK [RASH HIGH-TEMPERA TURE] 'MEASLES
will result in a series of questions about a fever, quick pulse and cough.

4. Feigenbaum (1980) summarises 'expert systems' similar to MYCIN for mass spectra interpretation, pulmonary function diagnosis, signal understanding, crystallographic data interpretation, and planning experiments in molecular genetics. See also other papers in Michie (1980) and Davis and Lenat (1982).
5. See, for example, the discussion by Winograd (1975).
6. This data structure may be represented by a list something like that shown in Figure 2.2(a). This may look fearsome, but it is not difficult to write programs to deal with such structures. Incidentally, when we want to depict a complicated data structure we avoid the box notation of Figure 2.2(a), to help preserve the forests of the world. Instead we may use the square bracket notation, e.g.
    [ELSIE [PHONE-NO 234]. . .]. . .
or the network shown in Figure 2.2(b). Such a schematic drawing does not give all the details about how a list is stored in memory but shows how the items in a list are related to one another.
7. For a survey of this research see the ACM SIGART Newsletter 70, February 1980.
8. In particular, we shall describe a program which accomplishes much of what has been suggested for our imaginary extended MYCIN (Clancey, 1979a, b).
9. Figure 2.3 illustrates the concept learning process. The program has previously been shown an example of a house (a), a 'wedge supported by a brick'. The program's understanding is represented by the 'old model' network. A near-miss-house (b), a 'wedge alongside a brick', is then presented to the program, which by comparing the two networks concludes that the wedge must be supported by the brick. The 'supported-by' link in the 'old model' is then replaced by a 'must-be-supported-by' link in the 'new model' network. Illustrations like Figure 2.3 are seductively convincing: they may however bear little relation to the actual program written. The details of Winston's program are still a matter of controversy and it is a symptom of epistemological malaise that much artificial intelligence research is difficult to evaluate.
10. The authoritative *Theories of Learning* of Hilgard and Bower contained only a single mention of Piaget (and that in a footnote!) in its third edition (1966), but the 1975 edition gave him a chapter.
11. Perhaps the easiest entry into Piaget's writings is Gruber and Voneche (1977). For summaries of Piaget's work, see Flavell (1963), McNally (1977) and Boden (1979).

63

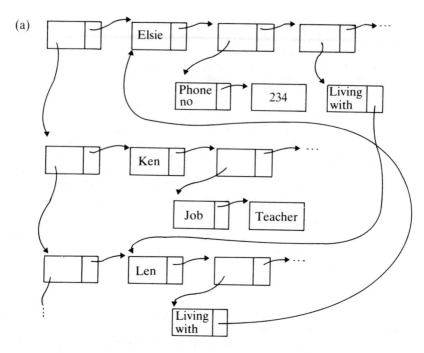

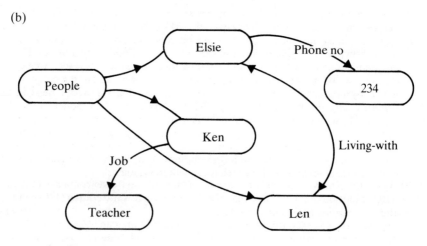

Figure 2.2 *Representing facts by networks*

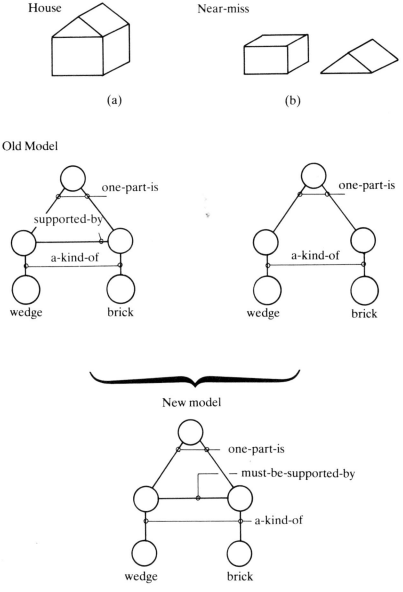

Figure 2.3   *Learning concepts by Winston's program* (from Winston, 1975)

12. Young did not write an automatic learning program – he added the new production rules himself, by hand. There has, however, been some research into the automatic addition of rules to production systems (e.g. Waterman, 1975).

13. Pask is a cyberneticist who has long advocated adaptive teaching systems (see Lewis and Pask, 1964) – and indeed been building them, the first apparently in 1953. His best-known machine, SAKI – self-organising automatic keyboard instruction – was devised for the training of card punch operators and used a computer which 'senses the characteristics of the trainee and adjusts the training routine to suit his requirements'. His more recent 'conversational theory' (Pask, 1975) is perhaps equally foresightful, but largely impenetrable. He appears, however, to see the computer as a regulator or controller of the educational process, without the constructive role with which we are mainly concerned.

3. A HISTORY OF COMPUTERS IN EDUCATION

There is an educational theory prevalent that might be called the Hydraulic Theory. It is a practical rather than a formal theory in that its disciples do not advocate the theory in any formal way: they merely act as though they believe it. Nevertheless, the Hydraulic Theory is respectable, its practitioners many, its tradition long, and its influence dominant. According to the Hydraulic Theory, knowledge is a kind of liquid which resides copiously in teachers and books, as in great vessels, and hardly at all anywhere else. Particularly is it scarce in the small vessels known as students. The purpose of education, then, is to transfer this liquid from the larger to the smaller vessels. Fortunately, this liquid has certain peculiar and mysterious properties that facilitate the process of transfer. For one thing, effluence from the larger container in no way diminishes the supply. (In some cases, it actually appears to have the opposite effect, as witness the increasing authority with which lecturers repeat the same material in consecutive terms.) Another remarkable property is that the effluence can be shared among a number of recipient vessels with no apparent reduction in the amount received by each. There are cases on record in which as many as 600 containers have been simultaneously filled from one great vessel in this way. The most recent advance in Hydraulic Theory, and certainly the most exciting, is the use of the computer and the multimedia console as a means of mediating Programmed Instruction. The console, with its graphic display and audio channel, is able to inundate the student with a flood of visual and auditory stimuli, literally filling every channel, inlet, passage, and canal leading to the student's brain. (Paul M. Davies, *The Hydraulic Theory of Education,* 1969)

The aim of this chapter is to survey past work in computer-assisted learning. The various approaches that have been developed will be described and their advantages and limitations discussed. We hope thereby to put current trends in computer-assisted learning in context and, particularly in the later sections of this chapter, to provide a background for Chapters 4 and 5, which discuss the use of the computer as a teacher and a tool respectively.

Our history will begin in the late 1950s. Any reader dissatisfied by our skimpy treatment of work carried out in educational psychology and educational technology before this time is referred to Saettler (1968).

The chapter is not organised on a strictly chronological basis since the development of ideas, which is what we are trying to convey, rarely follows an orderly path in time. The main underlying theme is the trend from rigid computer-oriented approaches towards more sensitive learner-oriented ones. Each approach will be described in general terms, and illustrated by a specific example. The selection of appropriate examples presents problems. Few successful programs demonstrate a single approach to computer-assisted learning: their success is often related to their marriage of two or more different approaches. We shall therefore concentrate on those aspects of the examples which are relevant to the point at issue. More serious are our difficulties in actually describing the examples adequately. Since our account is based on the premise that computers are different from more conventional media, such as books, we must say that there are features of these examples which we cannot convey, in particular, the interactiveness, the visual displays and the sense of seeing things happen and making them happen. We can only appeal to the reader's imagination.

The following table gives a guide to the chapter.

Approach	Distinguishing characteristics	Illustration
Linear programs	Derivation from behaviourism; systematic presentation; reinforcement and self-pacing.	Last (1979)
Branching programs	Corrective feedback; adaptive to student response; tutorial dialogues; use of author languages.	Ayscough (1977)
Generative computer-assisted learning	Drill-and-practice; use of task difficulty measures; answering student questions.	Palmer and Oldehoeft (1975)

Mathematical models of learning	Use of statistical learning theories of limited applicability; response-sensitivity.	Laubsch and Chiang (1974)
TICCIT	Team production of courseware: 'mainline' lessons; use of television and minicomputers; learner control.	Mitre Corporation (1976)
PLATO	Multi-terminal interactive system; visual displays; 'open shop' approach; concern over cost.	Bitzer (1976)
Simulation	Computer as laboratory; interactive graphics; typically small programs.	McKenzie (1977)
Games	Intrinsically motivating; audio-visual effects; often lacking educational aims.	Malone (1980)
Problem-solving	Computer as milieu; programming by children; derivation from Piaget's theory and artificial intelligence.	Papert (1973)
Emancipatory modes	Computer as labour-saving device; task-oriented; use of microcomputers and public information systems.	Lewis and Tagg (1981)
Dialogue systems	Tutorial strategies; use of natural language; mixed initiative; use of complex knowledge representations.	Carbonell (1970)

Linear programs

The methodology of linear programming is derived from the principles of operant conditioning, the basic law of which states 'if the occurrence of an operant is followed by the presentation of a reinforcing stimulus, the strength is increased' (Skinner, 1938).

This statement is a rephrasal of the Law of Effect (Thorndike, 1898). An 'operant' is a unit of behaviour which is not consistently elicited by any particular stimulus, as opposed to a 'respondent', which is. Teaching then becomes 'simply the arrangement of contingencies of reinforcement' (Skinner, 1968). Since the important event is considered to be the reinforcement and this should only follow the occurrence of desired behaviour, it follows that the teaching material should be organised so as to maximise the probability of correct responses. Moreover, since the desired behaviour is often complex and therefore unlikely to occur spontaneously, teaching should proceed by reinforcing successive approximations to the desired behaviour.

So much for the pedagogy: let's now summarise the distinctive features of Skinnerian programs in practice. We have only three procedures to describe.

1) *Program output*: Some material (a 'frame') is presented to the student. This material has been arranged to take the student one small step towards the desired behaviour.
2) *Student input*: The student makes some kind of response, for example, by filling in a missing space or two. He is immediately informed whether he is right or wrong (and if the program has been designed according to the principles he will be right).
3) *Program reaction*: The program moves on to the next frame. This next frame has been predetermined by the author of the teaching material and is independent of the correctness of the student's response.

As far as we are concerned, the main contribution of linear programming is its emphasis on the importance of *feedback* and *individualisation*, twin gods much worshipped in the computer-assisted learning literature. Of course it is important that the student be informed of the correctness of his response, and that the student be taught in a manner reflecting his ability and performance. But in linear programming the gods are but pale images. Feedback is considered to be important only after correct responses – indeed there shouldn't be any incorrect responses – whereas there is a much more constructive role for feedback to play, as discussed further in the next section. And in linear programming, the only individualisation that the student receives is

70

that he may work through the material at the pace which suits him best. There is no way that he may receive material different from that received by any other student.

From the beginning, Skinner contended that effective linear programming required mechanisation: only later was it emphasised that the principles of linear programming were independent of any particular teaching medium. 'As a mere reinforcing mechanism, the teacher is out of date,' declared Skinner. An industry duly developed to market programmed teaching machines. Only one of the problems associated with them needs to be mentioned now. The devices were supposed to be able to compare the student's response with the required answer but, given their reliance on push-buttons, cranks and similar contraptions, this often restricted the kinds of answer that could be required, or demanded that the student should evaluate his response by himself.

By an unfortunate accident of history, computers were becoming widely used at just the time when the 'teaching machine' bandwagon began rolling. Inevitably, people began to use computers to do their linear programming. This was very easy to do – for example, in Logo, the teaching material could simply be a series of calls of the procedure TEST we defined in Chapter 1:

W: TEST [IN A LINEAR PROGRAM LIKE THIS, ALL QUESTIONS ARE SUPPOSED TO BE ANSWERED —][CORRECTLY]
W: TEST [IF MORE THAN SAY 5% OF STUDENTS GIVE AN — ANSWER TO ANY QUESTION IT SHOULD BE MODIFIED] [INCORRECT]
W: TEST [THIS IS USUALLY DONE BY INCREASING THE NUMBER OF FRAMES SO THAT EACH STEP IN THE LEARNING PROCESS IS —] [SMALLER]

etc.

The poverty of linear programming is so manifest that the technique has long been extinct in computer-assisted learning. However, its ghost is still with us. For example, Last (1979) describes a program to teach German which is strictly Skinnerian (apart from a generous concession to allow two tries at each question). Here is a short, but adequate, section of a dialogue given:

To sleep
schlawfb
Sorry, no: have another try
schlafen
Correct

.
.
.

The evaluation of student responses by computer presents no problem (as long as they are expected to match the given answer exactly), the teaching material is relatively easy to change, and one can accumulate statistics on students' performances. Such advantages cannot, however, justify the extra cost.[1]

Branching programs

One change that could be made to a linear program is to use the student response to control the material that the student sees next. For example, in Logo, we might write

W: BUILD 'LESSON

.
.
.

120 MAKE 'ANSWER ASK [WHAT IS THE REAGENT
    REQUIRED FOR THIS REACTION:
        $C6H6 \rightarrow C6H5BR$]
121 IF EQUALQ :ANSWER [FE AND BR2] THEN
    PRINT 'YES AND GO 130
122 IF EQUALQ :ANSWER [BR2] THEN
    SAY [YOU ALSO NEED SOME FE] AND GO 120
123 SAY [THIS IS AN ELECTROPHILIC
    BROMINATION]
124 GO 120
130

.
.
.

The 120 simply labels the frame. If the student responds correctly (line 121), the program GOes to the next frame (labelled 130), as with linear programs. If he gives a wrong answer (e.g. BR2), he receives an appropriate explanation or suggestion and is retested on the current frame. For each anticipated wrong answer some comment could be provided.

To a computer programmer this might seem an obvious and unobjectionable development, but to a linear programmer it was heresy: as a teaching process, it does not accord with the principles of operant conditioning. It was Crowder (1959) who, proposing essentially the above, really set the cat among Skinner's pigeons. He wrote that 'the essential problem is that of controlling a communication process by the use of feedback. The student's response serves primarily as a means of determining whether the communication process has been effective and at the same time allows appropriate corrective action to be taken.' While the basic belief that students 'learn by being told' remains, the emphasis now is on the exposition itself being sensitive to the requirements of the student at all times, with the implication that this sensitivity demands an analysis of the student's actual responses.

We can summarise the main differences between linear programming and Crowder's approach, which he called 'intrinsic programming', with respect to the three procedures we discussed in the section on linear programs:

1. *Program output*: Frames tend to be larger units, since the author does not have to try to ensure that the student responds correctly.
2. *Student input*: The student responds to a question (a multiple-choice one in intrinsic programming). Alternative answers may be more or less acceptable, rather than totally correct or incorrect.
3. *Program reaction*:The student receives some comment upon his response and either repeats the frame or moves on to the next in a predetermined sequence of frames.

With intrinsic programming, we seem to be getting a firmer grip on the elusive 'feedback' and 'individualisation'. Feedback serves mainly to correct misunderstandings on the student's part, and this accords with current ideas about the role of feedback. For example, Kulhavy (1977) considers that 'supplying feedback after an error is probably far more important than providing confirmation'.[2] Of course, feedback now can range from a simple yes/no to the provision of substantial corrective information, which can itself take on the form of new instruction.

Since teaching actions are determined by student responses, two students will not in general receive the same material. The less able student will receive more explanatory corrections. We now have an *adaptive teaching program*, i.e. one in which the sequence of instructional actions taken by the program varies as a function of a given student's performance history (Atkinson, 1976).

The implementation of intrinsic programming does not demand a machine but there are disadvantages with the familiar programmed texts:

their size, and hence the course taught, is limited;

the constant page-turning is inconvenient;

the student can look up the required answer;

they are not enjoyable to read.

Crowder himself was enthusiastic about a particular device mainly because it could be fitted with a recording mechanism to recover a complete record of the student's progress – the microfilm projector! But with most machines except computers there are problems in accessing required frames, for example, with Crowder's projector the student himself had to enter the frame number on a keyboard.[3]

As suggested by the little piece of Logo above, intrinsic programming can be implemented by a computer program without much difficulty. Even this, however, was thought to be beyond the competence, or at least the interests, of most authors of computer-based teaching material. A special breed of programming languages, called *author languages*, developed to create the illusion that authors could write teaching programs without actually doing any computer programming. At their worst, such languages were extremely primitive, providing only routines to input, output and compare text, and to move between frames by means of a GO. Only dogma, however, stood in the way of extensions which soon became standard features of author languages:

Questions do not all have to be multiple-choice ones (as advocated by Crowder), since the program can compare the student's responses with a set of pre-specified alternative responses not accessible to the student.

Exact matches of student and stored responses do not have to be demanded, for one could try to allow for spelling mistakes, approximately correct numerical responses, and different word orders (although, of course, there are problems with allowing sentences which do not conform to some fairly rigid framework, as discussed in Chapter 4).

Other devices, such as audio-visual ones, could be controlled by the program.

The program could transfer to any specified frame (rather than just to the same or next frame), thereby allowing students to follow arbitrarily complicated paths through the material.

The program could accumulate statistics of the student's per-

unit	reagent	
at	710	[Specifies where text is to be written, namely on line 7 spaced over 10 spaces.]
write	Indicate the reagent required for this reaction.	
at	1318	
write	$C_6H_6 \leftarrow C_6H_5Br$	
arrow	1225	[Where the student's answer is to appear.]
answer	(Fe, FeBr$_3$, ferric*bromide) $<$and$>$ (Br$_2$, bromine)	[Words in brackets are regarded as synonyms; words in $<>$ are optional.]
wrong	(Br$_2$, bromine)	[Anticipated wrong answer.]
write	You also need some Fe.	[Response for this wrong answer.]
no		
write	entries $-$ 2, This is an electrophilic bromination, Try Br$_2$ and Fe.	[Response depends on the number of wrong answers – here, first a clue then a suggested correct answer.]

Figure 3.1 *An extract from a program in the TUTOR author language* (from Smith and Sherwood, 1976)

formance, either for the author's information, or to enable the program more appropriately to select the next frame (e.g. a simple count could be used to ensure that a particular frame is not presented too often).

Figure 3.1 gives an extract from a program in TUTOR (Sherwood, 1976),[4] one of the most widely used author languages. As the comments alongside indicate, it is a polished up version of our frame 120 above.

Figure 3.2 *Extract from a CALCHEM dialogue* (from Hooper, 1977)

In this section, you will be asked to decide which quantities you are going to measure in order to find E^*.
First read page 1 of B901L in the visicard, then type Z.
Z
Can you measure E^* directly? (Answer yes or no)
No
Correct.
To find E^*, you look at relationships involving E^* with
   a) other quantities which can be measured, or
   b) other quantities which themselves can be related to measurable quantities.
Do you know of any relationship involving E^*. If so name them.
The Arhenius equation
Yes.
We have seen that E^* can be found using the Arrhenius equation. What do you actually measure?
Rate constant and temperture
Yes, well done. You need to measure the rates of the reaction at different temperatures, but what do you actually measure to find the rate?
Concentration
Yes, measure the change in concentration with . . . (complete)
Time
Good.
  .
  .
  .

If the author is sufficiently industrious and ingenious, a student interacting with a program written in such an author language may well form the impression that he is communicating with an understanding teacher. See, for example, the fragment of dialogue with the CALCHEM program (Ayscough, 1977) given in Figure 3.2.

Since most tutorial programs are written in this style, it is worth considering further some of the problems that arise with them. Although intrinsic programming was supposed to be atheoretical, it does in fact share many similarities with Skinner's linear programming, to which it was in opposition. Both emphasise the importance of systematic presentation, and assume that this takes precedence over a learner's own activity. Both tend to treat the learner as a *tabula rasa*. Both are concerned with the efficiency of instruction rather than the quality of learning, seeing learning as the acquisition of 'knowledge' rather than 'experience' and ignoring the emotional and spiritual dimensions. Both tend to encourage the student to do what he is expected to do and not to offer his own interpretations. The outcome has been that the combined approach, *programmed learning*, has been taken by many to be that of all computer-assisted learning. For example, Laver (1976), in an introduction to the uses of computers, writes that computer-assisted learning 'stands or falls on the merits of programmed learning, for the computer is simply the means of increasing its convenience to the pupil'. This is complete nonsense, otherwise this chapter would end now.

Let us also consider some of the technical difficulties in writing good author language programs. The 'adaptivity' of our programs is still weak. With intrinsic programming, the program's next action is determined only by the student's last response. If the author language enables statistics to be kept, then this decision could be made (in principle) on the basis of the student's performance history. In practice, however, one can rarely do this effectively with author languages (as discussed in Chapter 4).

Moreover, with intrinsic programming, all the material and branching decisions are specified by the author. There is little scope for the program to determine, while it is running and on the basis of information gathered about the student, what to do next. The content of each frame is fixed, giving no real control of the level of difficulty. To make an author language program more adaptive in these respects is a time-consuming and wearisome exercise for the author, since the only method is to add more frames and more subtle branching tests. And it is no trivial programming task to ensure that all possible paths through the material are complete and make sense. The GO construction, upon which author languages rely, has long been criticised by programming experts as tending to lead to incomprehensible programs.[5]

Generative computer-assisted learning

Generative computer-assisted learning stemmed both from the practical desire to ease the author's task in preparing teaching material and, more importantly, from a different educational philosophy, one which held that in some situations students learn better from attempting problems of an appropriate difficulty than from attending to some systematic exposition. The method involves writing a computer program to generate material (i.e. problems, solutions and associated diagnostics) as and when it is needed during a teaching session. Consider an arithmetic drill. It would be absurd to write an author language program containing several frames, each with an explicit sum, solution and possible wrong answers. Far better, it would seem, to write a program which, in Logo, might be:

```
W: BUILD 'TESTADDITION
TESTADDITION
  1 MAKE 'X (PICK 100)
  2 MAKE 'Y (PICK 100)
  3 MAKE 'REPLY FIRST ASK PUTLAST
    PUTLAST PUTLAST[WHAT IS] :X '+ :Y
  4 IF EQUALQ :REPLY (ADD :X :Y) THEN
    PRINT 'RIGHT ELSE SAY PUTLAST [NO. THE
    ANSWER IS] (ADD :X :Y)
  5 TESTADDITION
```

where PICK is a Logo procedure which returns a randomly chosen number between zero and its input. (Line 3 is Logo's inelegant way

of putting together the question and then making the variable
REPLY take the number typed in as its value.) Then
        W: TESTADDITION
might proceed as follows
        WHAT IS 16+72?   88
        RIGHT
        WHAT IS 33+18?   41
        NO. THE ANSWER IS 51

        .
        .
        .

Figure 3.3   *A dialogue with a generative system* (from Palmer and Oldehoeft,
1975)

Find the equation of a line with slope 10 and y-intercept (0,2).
y = *10*x+2*
Good. Let's try another problem.
Find the equation of a line with slope 5 and passing through (10,
−5).
y = *5*x−45*
That's incorrect. Let's trace through the solution of the problem
together.
Step 1: Find the y-intercept by
        5 = (−5 − y-intercept)/10 => −(5*10)+(−5) = y-intercept
        => y-intercept = −55
Step 2: *Stop*
Okay. Let's try another problem.
Find the equation of a line with slope 3 and passing through (40,
10).
y = *3*x−110*
Good.
Find the equation of a line that passes through (10, −5) and (−1,
−2).
y = *−3/11*x−25/11*
That's very good

        .
        .
        .

The potential advantages of generative systems are:

(a) they provide an unlimited resource of teaching material;

(b) the store occupied by teaching material is reduced;

(c) they can provide as many problems as the student needs to achieve some level of competence;

(d) they may be able to control the level of difficulty of problems so that the student is presented with problems appropriate to his needs at any time.

Figure 3.3 shows an extract from a dialogue with a typical generative system (Palmer and Oldehoeft, 1975).

The implementation of such a system involves the following three steps:

1. Parameterise the components of a problem statement.
   For example, the first three questions in the dialogue shown may be derived from the general problem
   FIND THE EQUATION OF A LINE WITH SLOPE x AND PASSING THROUGH (y, z).
   Here, x, y and z are parameters to be replaced by randomly generated integers. Sometimes the parameters are interdependent, i.e. some condition between them needs to be satisfied.

2. Relate the problem types to expected solution processes.
   For example, the solution to the above problem type involves
   a. finding the y-intercept ($= z - x^*y$)
   b. substituting in $Y = x * X +$ y-intercept.

3. Decide on a teaching strategy, i.e. on an ordering of difficulty of problems and a way of moving from one to another (or to a different kind of problem for which steps 1 and 2 have also been completed).
   For example, one could generate progressively larger random numbers and decide that three successive correct answers are sufficient to move on to a different kind of problem. As these suggest, this step relies largely on intuition and commonsense.

In summary, then, the flow of a generative system is

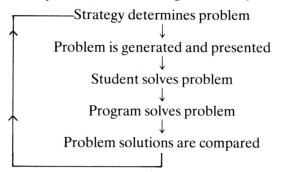

We can now put some flesh on this skeleton. The fact that the system can itself solve the problems it generates gives us several potential advantages. First, the program can do more than simply respond 'yes' or 'no'. It can, for example, present a step-by-step solution to the problem (as in the dialogue of Figure 3.3). It could also try to get the student more involved with (and thereby perhaps more receptive to) this feedback by, for example, asking relevant questions, such as 'What do you think the y-intercept is?' The system could also be programmed to answer questions like the ones generated but presented by the student. For example, the student may be unsure of a particular case (e.g. when the slope is zero), and ought to be able to ask about it. For this to be possible the system must of course be able to understand the student's questions, and this is usually achieved by insisting on a rigid format.

The Palmer and Oldehoeft system used as an illustration here shows the generative approach, as originally conceived, taken to its limits.[6] No further significant development seems possible other than the use of new modes of presentation, such as graphics. Our illustration should therefore show the advantages and, more importantly, the limitations of the approach. Generative systems are oriented towards providing a drill rather than a tutorial, and therefore do not compete with, let alone improve upon, the bulk of branching programs.

Very few subjects are sufficiently well-structured that they can be cast into the generative mould. To explain this, let us consider improving our TESTADDITION procedure. In order to be able to generate appropriate numbers to add we need a *task difficulty model*, that is, a way of predicting the difficulty of a particular addition task for a particular student. Let us hypothesise (simplifying from Woods and Hartley, 1971) that the pupil undertakes a mental ordering corresponding to the natural number sequence, and that the addition of a number involves 'moving a pointer' the appropriate distance along this sequence. If m is the probability of successfully moving the pointer along one place and the average size of digit is s, then the probability of adding two one-digit numbers successfully is m^{2s}. (We might suspect that the first number is treated differently, but let us proceed.) Assuming that the hypothesis receives some experimental verification, the model can be used to generate examples at specified difficulty levels. We first estimate m, and continually re-estimate it for a particular child, and for a given desired probability of success p, calculate s $= (1/2) \log_m p$, within some tolerance, to give variety. Notice that even this elementary model involves a bit of computation which the ordinary teacher cannot indulge in.

But if the successful use of the generative approach presumes the availability of a task difficulty model, with parameters which can be altered systematically, how could we use it to teach, for example, politics or poetry? What determines the difficulty of questions such as 'What was the cause of the Korean war?' and 'What is the rhyming scheme in the sestet of a Miltonic sonnet?' It is not easy to say exactly when the generative approach may be appropriate. If you have a topic in mind and can answer 'yes' to each of these questions:

Do you have 'standard format' questions?

Is there only one method of solution for each problem?
Can you identify intermediate steps (assuming you want to comment on these)?

Is it easy to estimate the difficulty of a problem?

Is it easy to find out what you need to know about a student to be able to give him appropriate problems?

Can you put the different sorts of problems in an order of difficulty (if you have more than one sort)?

then you might be able to write a generative program, otherwise probably not.

Mathematical models of learning

Skinner, in his theory of operant conditioning, deliberately avoided two things: a consideration of internal 'cognitive' processes (preferring to deal with measurable behaviour), and the use of formal notations (preferring to express rules in English). With their emphasis on the constructive role of feedback, branching programs and generative systems are a reaction to the first of these but, like linear programs, they are still derived from informal theories of learning. Dissatisfied with this lack of academic rigour in computer-assisted learning, some researchers tried, towards the end of the 1960s, to define precise theories of learning which predicted the effects of alternative teaching actions, and then to develop programs which used such theories to choose between these alternatives.

These theories of learning were expressed in mathematical notation, the use of which is not of course reserved to those of any particular theoretical orientation. But these so-called mathematical models of learning have developed a distinctive style in which learning is represented probabilistically or statistically, and which deal mainly with stereotyped learning situations.

Our illustrative example deals with the learning of a vocabulary or, more generally, a set of stimulus-response pairs (Laubsch and Chiang, 1974). As in the previous section, we have taken what we suspect to be the last of a line of development in order to see the limitations more clearly.[7] As before, we shall describe the steps that need to be followed to produce such a program:

1. Define the set of teaching actions.
   For example, with vocabulary learning, let us assume that in each session with a student one can present to him only m of the M words to be learned.
2. Define the objectives.

For example, the objective could be to maximise the number of words learned by the student after S sessions. The problem, then, is to determine which m words to present at each session. In general, there may be several objectives, perhaps conflicting with one another, and some weighting would have to be attached to them.

3. Define the costs of each action.

Some actions may 'cost' more than others, e.g. by taking longer or by being more expensive or otherwise undesirable, and it will be necessary to decide whether any increased benefit from them is 'worth it'. For the vocabulary learning problem, this step does not arise since we may assume that the cost of presenting m words is independent of which particular m it is.

4. Define the learning model.

For example, for vocabulary learning the model might assume that each word is in one of small number of states and then specify the probabilities of words transferring from one state to another between teaching sessions and if presented to a student during a teaching session. The Laubsch and Chiang model, for example, had three states, corresponding to words which were 'permanently learned', 'learned but forgettable' and 'un-learned'.[8] If the probabilities of a word being in the various states at one particular time are known (or estimated), the model enables these probabilities to be calculated at subsequent times.

For the kinds of learning situations for which this approach is useful, the first three steps above are usually straightforward. The definition of the learning model, however, is not. But whether or not (or rather to what extent) a particular model is valid is not the issue here: we are concerned only with how, having defined it, it may be used to derive teaching strategies.

If the four elements (briefly, actions, objectives, costs and effects) are precisely defined, then the derivation of an optimal teaching strategy may proceed as follows. First, one has to estimate the learner's initial state (e.g., for Laubsch and Chiang's model, one might assume all words were initially 'unlearned'). Then, for the first session, one can use the learning model to predict the effect of presenting any particular m words. In principle, one now repeats this process for each combination of words for all sessions. The definition of objectives and costs would then enable the best such series of presentations to be determined. In practice, since the computational effort of finding optimal solutions is often exorbitant, one settles for near-optimal ones. For example, with vocabulary learning one could proceed session by session, i.e. use the objectives and costs to determine the first session, present the m words, then determine the second session, and so on.

The strategy thus derived for teaching a vocabulary is not adaptive at all. So far we have been concerned only with presenting words, with the student being a passive spectator, and there is therefore nothing to adapt to. If, however, we require the student to respond to a word before the correct response is given, then we ought to be able to use the information provided by his response to refine the predictions of the learning model. This is not very difficult,[9] and ought to lead to an improved teaching strategy. This is an additional reason for determining the strategy session by session and not completely in advance.

There are two other ways in which the strategy may be individualised. First, we may know something about the student's prior knowledge of the vocabulary. Secondly, we may know (or find out during the teaching) something about his particular learning processes, i.e. we can make the learning model parameters a function of the student. Otherwise all students would receive identical teaching sessions, as in linear programming (although the emphasis on hypothesised states and transitions is a marked change from the behaviourist philosophy underlying linear programming).

Mathematical learning models usually generate effective teaching strategies (even though the learning models themselves are inevitably never perfect). Indeed, as far as it goes, the method can hardly be quarrelled with. The trouble is that it cannot be taken very far because only in a few special cases do we understand the learning processes well enough to be able to express them in the required mathematical form. We doubt in fact whether the language of mathematics is an appropriate one for describing general learning processes. We agree with Laubsch (1975) himself: 'the traditional approaches . . . using decision theory and stochastic learning models have reached a dead end due to their oversimplified representation of learning. The reason for stochastic learning models failing as models of instruction is their lack of representing the *content* to be taught.'

The TICCIT project

By the end of the 1960s, many of the computer-assisted learning projects which had blossomed forth were beginning to wilt. None the less, there remained a feeling that computer-assisted learning really ought to be effective, and in 1971 the National Science Foundation of America (NSF) decided, in an attempt to settle the question once and for all, to invest $10 million over five years in two demonstrations of computer-assisted learning: the TICCIT and PLATO projects. These two projects define two quite distinct approaches to computer-assisted learning, which will be described in this and the next section.

The directorship of the TICCIT (Time-shared Interactive Computer Controlled Information Television) project was entrusted to the MITRE Corporation which had been developing cable television systems. MITRE was to design and develop hardware and software for a computer-assisted learning delivery system. A related contract to develop course material was given to what became the Institute for Computer Uses in Education at Brigham Young University. NSF also provided for an evaluation of the TICCIT project by the independent Educational Testing Service.

The aim of the project was to demonstrate that computer-assisted learning 'can provide today better instruction at less cost than traditional instruction in community colleges' (Mitre Corporation, 1974). TICCIT was not designed to be used as an adjunct to regular classroom teaching, but to be used as the main source of the delivery of instruction ('mainline' computer-assisted learning, in TICCIT jargon). This choice seems to have been made not as a matter of principle, but as a practical expedient: the mainline approach was 'designed from the first for mass dissemination' (Mitre Corporation, 1976). This accords with their belief that neither lower cost, higher performance systems, nor improved theories of instructional psychology would get computer-assisted learning in the schools, but that 'the real problem is the making of a market' (Mitre Corporation, 1974).

One of the main characteristics of this approach is in fact its factory-like production of course material (Bunderson, 1974). Material is produced by a team, including an instructional psychologist, a subject-matter expert, an instructional design technician, an evaluation technician, and a packaging specialist. This division of responsibility follows from the TICCIT premise that the effectiveness of a particular learning strategy is independent of subject-matter (Bunderson, 1974), and hence that course content can be completely separated from both computer programming and teaching strategy. The particular model of instruction implemented on TICCIT is, naturally, based on 'instructional theorems having sound empirical footings where possible and theoretical integrity elsewhere' (Mitre Corporation, 1976). In practice, most learning is considered to involve concept learning and rule using,[10] and most teaching sessions are organised on the basis of presenting a general statement, examples of the generality applied to specific instances, and practice problems. A range of examples and problems are provided, and the learner is allowed to choose between them at different difficulty levels.

TICCIT lays great emphasis on the fact that its course material is learner-controlled: 'the coursework is controlled by the student by means of a high level command language — a characteristic of man-machine symbiosis' (Mitre Corporation, 1976). Figure 3.4 shows the reality. The keyboard includes a set of 'learner control buttons', as shown. The lower nine of these are the main ones by which the learner controls his own learning tactics. The OBJ'TIVE button accesses an illustration of the segment objective, MAP accesses the next higher level for status or survey, and ADVICE elicits advisor program comments on strategy. The HELP, HARD and EASY buttons are used in conjunction with the RULE, EXAMPLE and PRACTICE buttons (as shown in the dialogue

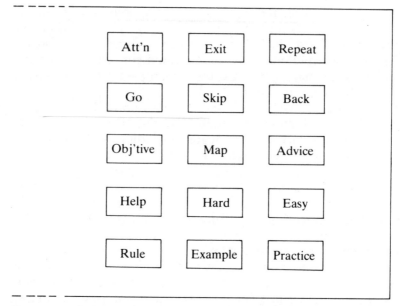

Figure 3.4   *TICCIT learner control buttons*

given in Figure 3.5). There is, of course, a default sequence of presentation built into the lesson material.

The student terminal includes a keyboard and a colour television set able to display alphanumerics and graphics in seven colours (not shown in Figure 3.5) and full-colour videotapes. A loudspeaker on each terminal may give prerecorded audio messages to the student, and the student may communicate with the program by the keyboard or, if appropriate, by light pen, a device permitting a student to point to a specific location on the television screen. Each TICCIT system has up to 128 such terminals, controlled by two standard minicomputers.[11] This use of relatively proven 'off-the-shelf' products was intended to result in a more reliable system and thereby to increase the chances of user acceptance.

Figure 3.5   *A dialogue with the TICCIT system* (from Mitre Corporation, 1976)

.
.
.

Map
[Student decides to ask for a map of lesson 6 unit 3]

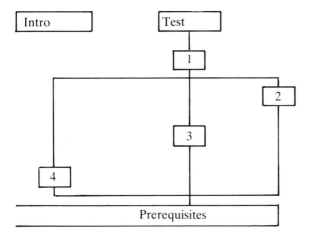

6.1 Correcting
      Dangling and
      Misplaced
      Modifiers
6.2 Interrupting
      Misplaced
      Modifiers
6.3 Misleading
      Misplaced
      Modifiers
6.4 Dangling
      Modifiers

1 Obj'tive
[To be given the objective of segment 1]
Given a sentence, you will
    1) mark the dangling or misplaced
        modifiers, if any . . .
    Screaming wildly, the cake fell to
    the floor
Rule
To correct a misleading misplaced
modifier:

1. Move it closer to the element it modifies,
2. Rewrite the sentence if the modifier is still awkward.

Example Easy
Going to bed late, a comet was seen.
The modifier in light blue above is a dangling modifier.
The sentence could be corrected like this:
As we were going to bed late, we saw a comet.

Help
I have never asked to, without deserving it, get a raise.
A sentence may have modification problems if it is in some way confusing, or if it is awkward to read.

Practice
Paul looked at the pie that was sitting on the table hungrily.
The sentence above may or may not have modification problems.
Mark each word in any dangling or misplaced modifiers. If there are none, just type enter.
.
.
.

Advice
[Student requests advice (on the strategy to follow) and is shown her status.]

EXAMPLE/PRACTICE	EASY	MED	HARD
You should see at least this many more items:	4	4	4
Current practice 'score' (pass 80, fail 20)	50	50	50

	Rule	seen
Rule/	Rule-easy	seen
Objective	Rule-help	not seen
	Objective	not seen

Enter
[To be given a suggestion on what to do next]
If you think you understand these items,
    Then press PRACTICE.
If you're not sure you understand,
    Then press EXAMPLE.
If you're having trouble,
    Then press HELP.
To get more information, press ENTER. (To get back to the page you were working on, press EXIT.)

.
.
.

The NSF-funded program was to implement TICCIT at two community colleges and to develop courses in pre-calculus mathematics (reviewing basic arithmetic and teaching intermediate algebra, logarithms, systems of linear equations, permutations and progressions), and English composition (teaching grammar, diction, sentence structure and paragraph development). In a mid-project report (Morrison, 1975), one of the college project directors wrote that the initial presentation to the college faculty was a 'total disaster': the emphasis on economies to be achieved and the assumption of a 'position of hard sell laced with tactless humour' turned faculty away. In addition, the development of course material, particularly in English composition, caused problems: 'differing factions became embroiled in interminable debates around both content and methodology'. Since it was also

91

said that 'the effort required for software development was grossly underestimated', it is not surprising that the actual demonstrations began later than planned.

The final NSF evaluation has been available in draft form since 1977, but seems not to have been published in full: Alderman (1979) gives the summary and conclusions section only. The main conclusion reached was the TICCIT exerted a significant positive impact on student achievement in both mathematics and English composition. Students who completed courses under the TICCIT programme generally attained higher post-test scores than similar students in lecture-discussion classes. This positive result warrants underlining, for it is in fact an unusual one for any educational experiment.

Some disquiet was expressed in the evaluation over the number of students who did not complete TICCIT courses. TICCIT had a negative effect on completion rates in all but one of seventeen analyses. In mathematics the completion rate was 16 per cent compared to 50 per cent for non-TICCIT courses. The evaluation argued that this may have been because TICCIT itself favoured high ability students to the detriment of students of low ability: 'programs that allow each student to proceed at his or her own pace risk losing students unable to manage their own instruction'. Jones (1978) has attributed the low completion rates to an insufficient degree of instructor involvement in managing student progress. It would seem that learner control and self-pacing, if it increases motivation at all, does not do so enough. The system features were not much appreciated by students, only the PRACTICE button receiving high ratings: 'the practice problem appeared to be the cornerstone of the TICCIT system'. There was no evidence given that the implementation of learner control and advisor programs did achieve the hoped-for student growth towards 'approach rather than avoidance, improved strategies and responsibility' (Bunderson, 1974).

The faculty response to TICCIT was lukewarm. A new role had been proposed for a teacher as 'a tutor-advisor/diagnostician and problem solver for individual students' (Mitre Corporation, 1976). Even after several terms, faculty were uncertain that TICCIT had affected their duties and were 'less certain that computer-assisted instruction, particularly the TICCIT program, would benefit them in fulfilling their instructional responsibilities' (Alderman, 1979).

The evaluation concluded that 'the TICCIT program has confirmed the potential of computer-assisted instruction as an effective resource in student learning'. (Note the persistence of the word 'potential'!) Subsequently, both community colleges have continued to use TICCIT, but there is no sign of widespread adoption of TICCIT by other educational institutions. Two more recent applications of TICCIT have been in special education (for example, in New York TICCIT is used in the first project to attempt large-scale delivery of computer-based instruction to homes to teach homebound handicapped children), and in military training (for example, to train Viking air crews in procedural skills before using costly simulators).

The PLATO project

The second of the two NSF-funded projects was one based on the PLATO (Programmed Logic for Automatic Teaching Operation) system of the Computer-based Education Research Laboratory at the University of Illinois, Urbana-Champaign. The PLATO system has a long history: from the 1960 one-terminal PLATO I to the NSF-funded PLATO IV with about 950 terminals located at about 140 sites and about 8000 hours of instructional material contributed by over 3000 authors.

The aims of the PLATO IV project, as listed by Alpert (1975), included the following:

> to demonstrate the technical feasibility of a truly novel computer-based education network;
> to prove that the system is manageable, economically viable, and capable of serving a variety of institutions at any educational level;
> to develop curricular materials for the new medium;
> to develop acceptance by instructor-users and students of a new medium designed for increasing the effectiveness and productivity of the instructional process.

But the PLATO approach to computer-assisted learning cannot be understood without appreciating the implicit aim permeating PLATO literature, which is that PLATO systems should become ubiquitous. A favourite pastime of PLATO enthusiasts is to derive cost estimates for PLATO education, and these tend to make assumptions such as that every school in America will have at least one PLATO terminal. Without such assumptions, proposals for 1-million terminal PLATO V systems (Bitzer, 1976) would make no sense, and comments such as 'a national or international educational network could begin to introduce a new dimension of learning for world citizenship' (Alpert, 1975) would be dismissed as pretentious dreaming.

The PLATO approach is intriguingly different from that of TICCIT. In particular, PLATO designers believe in very large networks of terminals and the latest in technological development, while TICCIT uses a modest minicomputer-based system with mass-produced components. Also, the preparation of course material for PLATO does not follow the organised pattern of TICCIT's production teams. There is no organisation of PLATO authors at all: teachers may use the PLATO system how and as much as they wish (subject of course to timetabling constraints). As a result, PLATO material is of variable quality.

One attempt to assist the author in writing material is the provision of the TUTOR author language, a short sample of which was given in Figure 3.1. As indicated, TUTOR programs consist of a series of statements, each of which has a command and a so-called tag (corresponding to the input of a Logo procedure). There are over 160 commands for display (e.g. arrow, at), control (e.g. next, goto), calculation and judging (e.g. answer, wrong). The judging commands attempt to process the student's answer, allowing for misspelled words or words out of order.

The student interacts with a PLATO program by means of a terminal, consisting of a keyboard and plasma display panel, Bitzer (1976). The important properties of the plasma panel are that it is transparent (enabling colour slides to be projected onto the back of the panel, and superimposed on computer-generated graphics) and has inherent memory (meaning that it does not need refreshing, and is free of flickers, unlike a cathode-ray tube). The addition of a touch panel enables the student to communicate with the program by touching the screen, for example, to select one of several words displayed on the screen. Such a capability is especially important for those such as children who find typing difficult. Other devices may be added to the terminal, such as random access audio and slide selectors, music synthesisers, film projectors and laboratory apparatus.

While no one PLATO program can be typical since the system does not aim to impose a pedagogical structure on material, the fruit fly program, shown in Figure 3.6, captures much of the spirit of PLATO.[12] The program demonstrates the genetic rules for fruit fly breeding. A student begins with two stocks of fruit flies and can

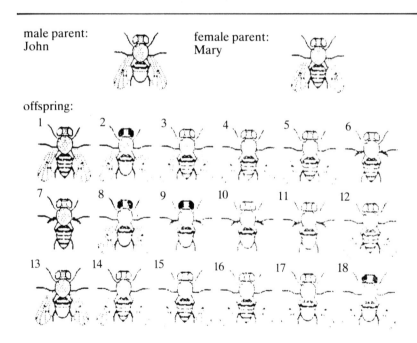

if you want to use any of these offspring, you must save them now. What do you want to do?

>

Figure 3.6   *The fruit fly program* (from Bitzer, 1976)

specify which of the flies he wishes to cross. The results of the mating then appear on the screen. The program includes procedures which define the genetic rules, and by executing these procedures the genes of the offspring can be determined. It perhaps needs emphasising here that this use of graphics is not an optional frill: the characteristics of interest are visual, and any other mode of presentation would be unnatural.

The operation of hundreds of graphics terminals simultaneously at various distances from the main computer necessitates a complicated but highly efficient system architecture.[13] That such a system can be built to deliver interactive teaching is unequivocally confirmed by the NSF-funded evaluation of the PLATO IV project (Murphy and Appel, 1977). However, the originally-planned 4000 terminals per PLATO IV system had to be dropped to 1000 mainly because it was found that more lessons were in use at any time than were expected (causing more transferring between memories), and because authors tended towards more sophisticated response processing and simulations than expected.

The evaluation of PLATO IV is less categorical about the effectiveness of PLATO teaching, as one could expect given the inevitable variation in quality of material and the difficulty of setting up comparison groups for a system which relies on voluntary participation. As with TICCIT, it appears that the preparation of course material turned out to be more difficult than planned and the demonstration period began a year late. Even so, by the end of the five-year project, the evaluators had managed to accumulate an impressive volume of data, which 'taken together and in perspective, provide no compelling statistical evidence that PLATO had either a positive or negative effect on student achievement'. It was also deduced that 'the PLATO system had no significant impact on student attrition', i.e. on drop-out rates.

Inevitably, the evaluators then turned towards more subjective evidence, such as questionnaires. It seems that the PLATO system was generally popular with student users. For example, 70 per cent or more of students continued to use PLATO outside their class period, and similar large percentages reported that they would use PLATO for another course if given the opportunity. While the evaluation considered that 'PLATO students showed much more favourable attitudes towards computers and computer-assisted in- struction than non-PLATO students', their enthusiasm was not blind: 19 per cent felt that 'computers are not good for instruction because they are always breaking down', 27 per cent agreed that 'computers are too impersonal for student instruction', and 83 per cent 'would not want to have the whole course taught on PLATO'. Teachers also seemed favourably disposed towards PLATO. For example, 88 per cent of them definitely or probably intended to use PLATO again. The authors of the evaluation report speculated on the reasons for this high acceptance in the absence of clearcut performance advantages: they considered that it resulted mainly from the fact that teachers perceived that they retained control over how PLATO was used, and that the system was therefore not a threat to their current procedures.

The evaluation includes some comment on the teachers' reactions to the TUTOR author language. Only 10 per cent of the sample found TUTOR 'not difficult at all', and 57 per cent did not even use the language. According to Denenberg (1978),

while it is very easy for anyone to create a simple TUTOR program in very little time, it is extremely difficult for anyone to write a moderately complex program using the structure afforded by the TUTOR programming language. . . The more useful lessons require a degree of expertise not commonly found even in many professional programmers.

The pedagogical neutrality of PLATO is, in fact, an illusion for the philosophy underlying its design is that students will be content to use pre-written material and will not want, for example, to do much programming themselves, and that teachers will write straightforward teaching programs which will not impose process- ing demands which will reduce the system's response times. These assumptions lead to severe time and space constraints for PLATO programs, which necessarily limits their capabilities (see, for example. Wilcox, Davis and Tindall (1976)).

The evaluation did not deal with the technical aspects and costs of the PLATO implementation and demonstration. The PLATO project itself, however, has always been very cost-conscious. The target cost for PLATO IV was $0.35-70 per hour of instruction (1972 prices), but in the event Bitzer (1976) gives a figure of $1.17 per hour. Without a lengthy description of the assumptions from which these figures are derived, the actual figures are almost worthless, but the relative values do indicate that a drop by a factor of about three is needed to make PLATO an equal-cost alternative to more traditional teaching methods.[14] Despite doubts about current costs, both PLATO and TICCIT are now being commercially marketed, PLATO by Control Data Corporation and TICCIT by Hazeltine Corporation.

We cannot leave a description of the PLATO and TICCIT projects without mentioning that the ground rules of this particular game have changed considerably since NSF decided to invest their $10 million. It is no longer true that bigger systems imply more economic systems: cheap minicomputers are now a much more attractive proposition, and the developments in microcomputing open up many possibilities in the personal computer field. The fact that communication costs have not been decreasing recently while hardware costs have dropped steeply also reduces the appeal of large educational networks. It has also been recognised, for example, as in the plans for PLATO V, that it is unlikely to be sensible to dedicate such a system to education: it will need to provide more general services, such as mail delivery, information retrieval, computation and game-playing. The future of PLATO-like systems is discussed further in Chapter 7.

Simulations

The PLATO fruit fly program mentioned above is an illustration of one of the most widely used techniques of computer-assisted learning: that of simulation. Here a program which models some process or system is made available to the student in the hope that by studying the performance of the program the student will gain insights into whatever process or system is being modelled. The student role is usually more than that of mere spectator: often he is responsible for providing inputs for the program, after deciding on some strategy of use, and thereby is able to experiment with the modelled system. Sometimes, but more rarely since it presumes programming competence, the student may modify the program itself to investigate the consequences.

The advantages of simulation as an approach to learning are of course well appreciated outside computer-assisted learning. The computer's particular advantages arise simply from the fact that it is a different, powerful and flexible device for controlling simulations. The physical sciences are largely concerned with the development and use of mathematical models, the complexities of which are often beyond the ability of a student. Computer implementations of such models make them usable by a student, who may thereby gain some understanding of the principles underlying them. Often a computer simulation may serve to remove complications which could obscure the more important principles to be understood. For example, the fruit fly simulation, where the intention is for the student to discover the genetic rules, dispenses with many of the problems which would be associated with conducting the actual laboratory experiment and also adjusts the time-scale to a more convenient one. A computer simulation may be the only way to provide a student with a safe, inexpensive view of certain phenomena, such as nuclear reactions, or space travel. Such simulations may be made more effective by capitalising upon the computer's ability to generate special displays, and to engage in an interactive conversation in order to impress salient features upon the student. One particular adaptation is to turn the simulation into a game in which the student has to specify inputs to reach some goal, either in competition with the program itself or with other students.

Imagine, for example, that we had a program able to show on a visual display unit the moon's orbit about the earth, such a program incorporating the law of gravitation, from which the orbit may be calculated. A student might be provided with the opportunity of changing the moon's mass in order to see what difference it makes to the orbit (he might be asked, for example, to find the maximum mass the moon could have and yet stay in orbit around the earth). Playing God in this way fascinates children and adults alike.

Figure 3.7 illustrates a typical simulation, that of cardiac output in biology (McKenzie, 1977). In the laboratory, some dye would be injected into the blood stream and samples of blood repeatedly taken to determine the dye concentration. The computer simula-

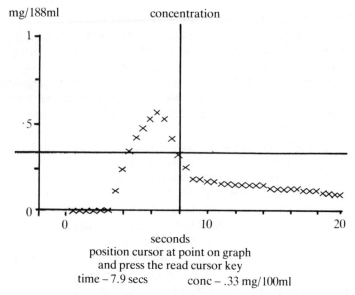

Figure 3.7   *Screen display from Dye simulation* (from McKenzie (1977).

tion plots the concentration against time and permits a more rapid and reliable sampling than would be possible in real life. The student can steer a cursor to any point on the curve to find the exact coordinates of a point. During the simulation, no programming expertise is required of the student and he is in general expected to make his own decisions about how to proceed. The implementation of such a simulation program is straightforward, involving largely standard numerical programming and for which author languages are not appropriate.

This particular simulation formed part of one project in the United Kingdom's National Development Programme in Computer-Assisted Learning (NDP), a five-year £2.5 million, government-sponsored program which began in 1973. Since most NDP funding was devoted to the development of simulation programs ('prewritten programs for use by students in "laboratory mode" ', according to Hooper (1977)), it is appropriate to discuss the aims and achievements of this programme here.

The main aim of the programme was 'the institutionalisation of computer-assisted learning and computer-managed learning', which, after insufficient apology for the assault on the English language, was defined as follows: 'to develop and secure the assimilation of computer-assisted and computer-managed learning on a regular institutional basis at reasonable cost'. During the five years, an assortment of twenty-nine projects were supported, involving some 700 teachers in forty-four different institutions, with a bias towards science teaching in the tertiary sector of education.[15] In December 1977, as promised, NDP funding stopped, and projects were left to be institutionalised or die.

The final report (Hooper, 1977) estimated that thirty-two of the forty-four project institutions were planning to continue funding. This figure has never been confirmed or amended. A secondary aim, which was to 'promote the spread of experience, new ideas and teaching materials', was considered met by transferring material to over 125 other institutions in the United Kingdom, and to twelve other countries by the end of the program. Subsequent use of NDP material has not been fully documented, although various 'programme exchanges' and 'information services' have been set up to aid its dispersal.

But, as usual, there is more to be learned from the shortcomings than from the successes of the enterprise. The 'institutionalisation' aim led naturally to the selection of projects which were more likely to be accepted by the host institution. Projects tended to play safe by attempting to implement existing educational objectives, and to avoid significant innovatory developments, knowing that in only five years or less they were unlikely to bring about major changes in the educational system itself. Projects were led away from research to applications, the NDP being explicitly a development programme with no research policy. The idea that in 1973 there existed a body of knowledge about computer-assisted learning which it was worth developing without further associated research seemed at the time fanciful, and in retrospect absurd.

The absence of a proper experimental design resulted in a proliferation of 'case-studies', the significance or success of which is virtually impossible to determine. The actual developments embodied in the projects were marginal in relation to existing knowledge, for, despite the attempt in the final report (Hooper, 1977) to distinguish between the NDP approach to computer-assisted learning and 'computerised programmed instruction', described as the American tradition, there were, even in 1973, plenty of projects which emphasised the laboratory or simulation mode of use.[16]

Technologically, the NDP projects were unadventurous. They made use of general-purpose computer systems, typically mini-computers, not specifically designed for computer-assisted learning and almost all the teaching material was written as small programs in FORTRAN and BASIC, two languages whose design reflects their vintage, but which do alas provide the desired trans-ferability since almost all computer manufacturers have felt obliged to provide compilers or interpreters for them. Some material, such as some of the CALCHEM project which was mentioned earlier in this chapter (Figure 3.2), and which was funded by the NDP, was written in a conventional author language. This uninspired use of available technology may help to explain the final report's pessimistic conclusions concerning the technical aspects of computer-assisted learning. Apparently, 'computing technology, both as regards hardware and systems software, is still very unreliable', a conclusion in contrast with that of the evaluators of the PLATO system, a system considerably more sophisticated than any used in the NDP projects. Moreover, the NDP report considered that computer-assisted and computer-managed learning are 'extremely high cost technologies and are the most expensive tools yet introduced into the teaching process, however one costs them', and concluded that computers in education must be regarded as an 'add-on cost'.

During its five years, the NDP took upon itself a further aim which was to make recommendations about the future of computer-assisted learning in the United Kingdom. In view of the poor experimental design of NDP projects, it will be no surprise that a moratorium was proposed, a further three-year period to 'test the strength of computer-assisted learning' (as embodied in the NDP projects) and during which there would be no new development. In the event, the NDP has been submerged under the wave of microcomputers, of which there is no mention in the final report. The report's conclusions on technical matters have thus been rendered obsolete and much of the original 'development' work is now seen to be irrelevant. By design, the NDP has left little of fundamental, lasting value, only a handful of small programs, hastily modified to run on present microcomputers.

Games

A 'computer game' is a computer-based activity which leads its participants to leap joyfully (from the Indo-European 'ghem', to leap joyfully). This is as good a definition as we are likely to get – it does distinguish games from all the other activities we have described! There have been games on computers almost as long as there have been computers, but the advent of cheap micro-computers in the last few years has now made them widely available. Most public places, it seems, have been taken over by the aptly-named 'space-invaders'-type games; we can buy 'chess challengers' for Christmas presents; personal computers are delivered with a set of demonstration games. Computer games are undeniably popular – our question is whether they can contribute to learning.

First; how do computer games differ from other games? Banet (1979) has listed features that make for successful computer games, and from among them we may isolate those that seem particularly to derive from the computer's special properties:

1. Audio and visual effects are used to reward success and to present the game situation.
2. The game can increase in its ability to challenge the player; it need not become boringly simple.
3. The game incorporates fantasy elements (e.g. piloting a spaceship).
4. The computer can time the player's responses and calculate scores.

In order to investigate why computer games are so captivating, Malone (1980, 1981) surveyed children about their preferences concerning twenty-five computer games. He describes three

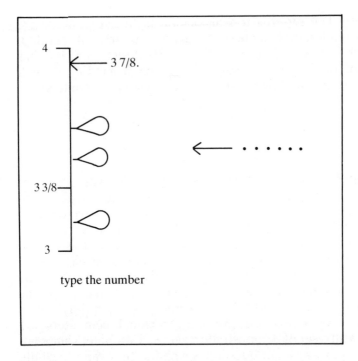

Figure 3.8   *Display format for the game of 'darts'* (from Malone, 1980)

characteristics of intrinsically motivating environments:
  1. *Challenge* – there is a goal whose attainment is uncertain;
  2. *Curiosity* – the player knows enough to have expectations about what will happen, but sometimes these are unmet;
  3. *Fantasy* – the games provoke mental images not present to the senses.

This Malone compares nicely with Piaget's theory: 'people are driven by a will to mastery [challenge] to seek optimally informative environments [curiosity] which they assimilate, in part, using schemes from other contexts [fantasy]'. The survey showed that there were big differences in children's preferences, but there were one or two interesting findings. For example, the most common reasons given for not liking a game had to do with the difficulty level – which is one area where computer games should excel. Also, it was found that games were liked mainly for reasons to do with fantasy, and yet fantasy was not correlated with game ratings – presumably, different children prefer different fantasies.

Let us now look at two computer games which seem to have more academic relevance than most. The first, called 'darts', is described by Malone as follows:

A game designed to teach elementary students about fractions. Three balloons appear at random places on a number line and students try to guess where the balloons are. They guess by typing in mixed numbers, and each time they guess an arrow shoots across the screen to the position specified. If the guess is right, the arrow pops the balloon. If wrong, the arrow remains on the screen and the player gets to keep shooting until all the balloons are popped. Circus music is played at the beginning of the game and if all three balloons in a round are popped in four or fewer tries, a short song is played.

In order to explain the appeal of the game, Malone distinguishes between extrinsic fantasy and intrinsic fantasy: the former is an arbitrarily interchangeable fantasy (e.g. hanging a man, stepping towards a cliff edge); the latter depends crucially on the skill being used. He then argues that intrinsic fantasies are more instructional and more interesting than extrinsic ones. Darts is a game with an intrinsic fantasy, since the relative sizes of numbers are intimately related to the positions of the arrows and balloons. Malone experimented with various features of the game and found (among other things) that whenever boys liked a feature, girls disliked it: thus may attitudes towards mathematics and other subjects be unintentionally perpetuated. As regards the game's contribution to learning, Malone found – yes, you've guessed it – none (but then no serious effort was made to do so).

Our second game is 'How the West was Won', played on a game board like that in Figure 3.9. The object of the game is to get to the last town on the map (position 70). On each turn a player gets three spinners. He can combine the values of the spinners using any two different arithmetic operates ($+$, $-$, $\times$, or $/$). The value of the expression he makes is the number of spaces he gets to move. (He must also say what the answer is.) If a player lands on a shortcut, he moves to the other end; if he lands on a town, he goes on to the next town; if he lands on his opponent, the opponent retreats two towns.

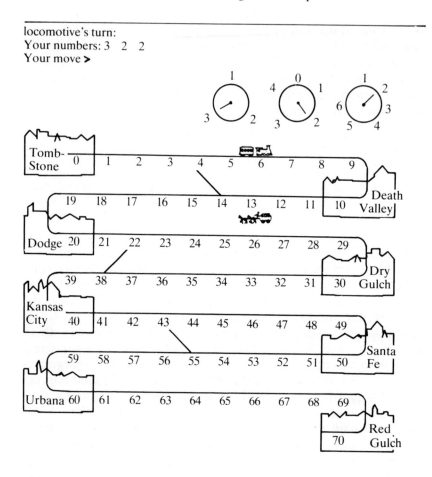

locomotive's turn:
Your numbers: 3 2 2
Your move **>**

Figure 3.9   *Screen display for 'How the West was Won'* (from Bitzer, 1976)

   The game is therefore a camouflaged arithmetic drill-and-practice. Apart from the aim of reviewing basic skills, the game may also introduce new ideas – for example, the idea of maximisation. A good version of this game could also try to determine whether a player has specific skills, e.g. that of using brackets when appropriate, and, if not, give him some advice. A player has to develop some strategy for playing the game and this is basically one of three kinds: maximise the value without rearranging the given order of numbers, rearrange to maximise the value, or maximise the gain over the opponent (using shortcuts or 'bumps' if possible). Resnick (1975) found that although a child would play the game for hours, he usually latched onto a limited strategy and continued with it regardless. He therefore missed much of the point of the game, whose effectiveness as an arithmetic drill is much reduced since the child is performing only one calculation per move instead of the dozens required to carry out an ideal strategy. There is clearly considerable scope for more sophisticated programming of computer games, and a desperate need for experimental studies of their educational effectiveness.

Problem-solving

The 'computer programming game' is one of the best computer games of all. It is rich in challenge (getting a program to work better), curiosity (finding unexpected failures), and fantasy (controlling a responsive entity). The problem-solving approach to computer-assisted learning is based on the hypothesis that the thought required to write a computer program aids the development of general problem-solving skills. It differs from simulation in that the activity of programming, rather than the specific subject of the program, is considered central. In simulation, the student is given the programmed model to use, not asked to write or change this program. The underlying educational philosophy of the problem-solving approach is a belief in what may be summarised as 'learning by doing', as opposed to simulation's 'learning by seeing'.

Problem-solving is an important high-level skill – indeed Gagné, in his listing of the varieties of learning (Gagné, 1977), regards problem-solving as the most complex of learning activities – but there has been little significant analysis of the skills involved. In general, students are expected to develop these skills by some ill-defined process involving illustration and performance. The role that programming might play in this is that computers enable students to develop, investigate and experiment with their own ideas and theories in a relatively enjoyable and informative fashion. Such arguments will be discussed and explained further in Chapter 5: for now we are concerned mainly with summarising the history of these developments.

The problem-solving and programming movement is most closely associated with the LOGO project, the name deriving from a programming language devised at Bolt Beranek and Newman in 1967, and subsequently developed by the Artificial Intelligence Laboratory at the Massachusetts Institute of Technology. According to Papert (1973), the theory underlying this work 'draws on ideas from the Piagetian tradition of thinking about children and from those aspects of artificial intelligence concerned with thinking about thinking in general'. The origins and philosophy of this approach therefore contrast strongly with those of the computer-assisted learning approaches derived from behaviourism and, certainly in the early days, LOGO proponents vociferously opposed the contemporary computer-assisted learning activities which they saw as attempting to introduce computers into education without major changes to the education system. Instead they suggested 'more radical experiments in the global re-design of learning environments' (Papert, 1973).

One enterprising emphasis of the LOGO project was that it was oriented towards young children of about ten or eleven. These children were expected to be able to write computer programs at an early stage in their development of mathematical, logical and problem-solving skills: an expectation based on the LOGO premise that programming helps to develop these skills and not merely to exercise them. For this to be possible in practice several conditions need to be satisfied:

1. The programming language to be used must be well-designed: its underlying concepts should be clear and consistent, seem 'natural' to the child, and be without arbitrary restrictions.
2. The computer environment should be a friendly one: for

example, the language interpreter should not abuse the child for trivial syntactic errors, the child should never be baffled by technical jargon, and the actual use of the system should be straightforward.

3. There should be interesting programs for the child to write: in the case of the LOGO project, this has been helped by the design of a 'cybernetic zoo', including turtles, worms and spiders, which are devices which can be programmed to perform various activities.

The essence of the LOGO project is best conveyed by an example (adapted from Papert, 1973). A 12-year-old boy tried to write a program which would enable a touch-sensitive turtle, initially facing north, to move to the north wall of a room, moving around any objects encountered on the way. He had already written a procedure for moving all the way round any object:

```
W: BUILD 'CRAWLROUND
CRAWLROUND
    1 IF LEFTTOUCHINGQ THEN RIGHT 1 ELSE LEFT 1
    2 FORWARD 1
    3 CRAWLROUND
```

where LEFTTOUCHINGQ, RIGHTTOUCHINGQ, FRONT-TOUCHINGQ are procedures which return 'TRUE if the turtle is touching an object to the left, right or front respectively, otherwise 'FALSE.

The boy's outline solution was: when in the clear the turtle is to advance north; when contact is made with an object the turtle is to start to crawl round it; when the turtle has crawled enough, it is to advance again. First, then, he wrote

```
W: BUILD 'ADVANCENORTH
ADVANCENORTH
    1 IF NOT FRONTTOUCHINGQ THEN FORWARD 1
    AND ADVANCENORTH
```

The next step is to modify CRAWLROUND so that the turtle only crawls 'enough'. Enough is enough, but not for a turtle: it needs defining. So the boy suggested that the turtle be considered to have crawled far enough when it is again facing north:

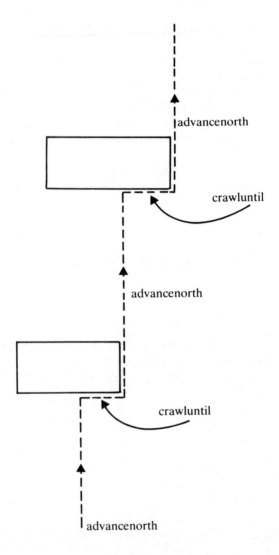

The turtle's orientation needs to be kept track of, and a variable ORIENTATION was introduced, initially 0, which was adjusted whenever the turtle turned left or right:

W: BUILD 'CRAWLUNTIL
CRAWLUNTIL
  1 IF LEFTTOUCHINGQ
      THEN RIGHT 1 AND
      MAKE 'ORIENTATION (ADD :ORIENTATION 1)
      ELSE LEFT 1 AND
      MAKE 'ORIENTATION (ADD:ORIENTATION −1)
  2 FORWARD 1
  3 IF NOT EQUALQ
      (REMAINDER :ORIENTATION 360) 0
      THEN CRAWLUNTIL

The solution then is (neglecting the problem of determining when the turtle has in fact reached the north wall)
  W: BUILD 'CROSS
  CROSS
     1 ADVANCENORTH
     2 TURNRIGHT
     3 CRAWLUNTIL
     4 CROSS
where TURNRIGHT was defined by
  W: BUILD 'TURNRIGHT
  TURNRIGHT
     1 RIGHT 90
     2 MAKE 'ORIENTATION (ADD :ORIENTATION 90)
This solution works in most cases, but fails for the 'turtle trap' shown in Figure 3.10. Since the answer to this particular problem will appear obvious to anyone who can read it in the next line, we have relegated it to an end of chapter note to encourage you to work it out for yourself.[17]

What is to be learned from such a session? In this case, the boy discovered an interesting result in topology unlikely to be available to him by any other means. More generally, he may have developed an appreciation of the concept of a 'state' and of 'feedback', both of which are fundamental to the sciences. And he has seen the virtue of giving a precise description of his ideas, of looking for mistakes and oversights (and not being ashamed or frightened of them), and of developing ways of removing such

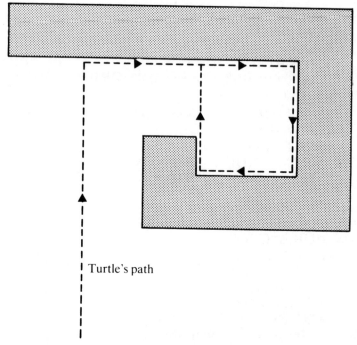

Turtle's path

Figure 3.10   *A turtle trap* (from Papert, 1973)

bugs. Further discussion of such points is left to Chapter 5.

A serious difficulty for advocates of the problem-solving approach concerns evaluation. Improvements in general problem-solving skills are not easy to demonstrate convincingly, especially if the improvements are only significant after a 'global re-design of learning environments' which is likely to occur only after a convincing demonstration. To attempt a direct comparison with alternative methods would be fruitless since, so the argument runs, this is a new approach to learning for which there are no alternative methods. But we can at least list some things which are going for the problem-solving approach:

The learning is individualised, for each student creates programs uniquely his own (as far as he is concerned).

Developing programs is a highly motivating activity, since there is a continual (if sometimes illusory!) feeling of making progress.

112

Errors come to be seen by the student as sources of enlighten-
ment not causes for despair.

The student regularly experiences the 'aha-phenomenon', for it
is not too much of an exaggeration to regard his program as his
own scientific theory to be developed by exploring cause-and-
effect questions.

Children enjoy it, and if LOGO activities are play so much the
better.

The LOGO laboratory is a foretaste of more sophisticated com-
puter-controlled learning environments with a 'high potential for
personal involvement, intellectual adventure and cognitive
enhancement' (Papert, 1973). Other projects are described in
Chapter 5, and since the advent of personal computers will renew
emphasis on this approach we shall return to it in Chapter 7.[18]

Emancipatory modes

Students may use computers to solve problems without necessarily
writing their own programs – they may use programs written by
someone else. One of the least controversial roles of the computer
in education involves requiring the student to use the computer
much like most other users – as a labour-saving device to perform
calculations, to plot graphs, to retrieve information, to manipulate
text etc., to tackle some given task. This mode, in which the
information-handling abilities of the computer are exploited to
improve the quality of the learning experience by taking the tedium
out of some kinds of tasks, has been called 'emancipatory' by
MacDonald (1977).

We shall look briefly at one example, that of information retrieval, in which the computer is used to search through a quantity
of information to find items of interest. The potential virtues of
such a use have long been recognised (see, for example, Hayes
(1967), who describes a vision of a computerised library) and
several large-scale information retrieval systems do exist, often
involving telecommunication links to libraries, to support the research scholar. These are, however, expensive and it is only

recently, with the advent of microcomputers and public information systems (such as the British Telecom Prestel system), that the widespread use of computers in education in this mode has become feasible. Small information retrieval systems are becoming available on microcomputers. For example, one called QUERY Lewis and Tagg (1981), developed at the Advisory Unit for Computer Based Education in Hatfield, is being used by the Open University in its Microelectronics in Schools course to show teachers how classroom activities may be based on such systems. One project involves using a database containing the 1851 census returns for the village of Ashwell. QUERY provides a simple 'query language' in which retrieval requests can be phrased, for example:

QUERY AGE LT 14
[Find the number of children under the age of 14.]
QUERY SEX IDENT 'F' AND AGE LT 20
AND CBI NIDENT ('HRT' OR 'CAM' OR 'BDF')
PRINT SCHED
[Print the schedule numbers of all households in which live females under the age of twenty whose county of birth was not Hertfordshire, Cambridgeshire or Bedfordshire.]

Such an information retrieval system may then be used in more open-ended projects, such as an investigation of the role of women in Ashwell in 1851, where the student has to decide what questions to ask and to interpret the information retrieved. In addition, this information may be used to support other classroom activities, such as statistical analyses and the use of maps.

In this mode, then, the computer plays the role of an unobtrusive assistant during conventional learning activities. As far as information retrieval systems are concerned the main limitations are technical ones. First, in organising the data in computer memory so that retrieval is acceptably speedy. Secondly, in providing unsophisticated users with a convenient means of expressing their requests. If the information retrieval system were to allow requests to be expressed in English, and were then to play a more active role in the conversation, we would be returning to the tutorial mode, which we shall now consider further.

Dialogue systems

As we saw, programmed learning and its computer implementation as branching programs led to rather regimented dialogues in which the computer asked all the questions and the student usually selected his answer from a small set of possible answers. Much of the subsequent development of computer-assisted learning can be seen both as a reaction to this regimentation and as a result of a more imaginative appreciation of what learning involves. There have been attempts to increase the amount of control which the student himself has over the course of teaching and an emphasis on simulation and problem-solving, leading ultimately to the view that the computer is best used as a tool by the student in an essentially undirected manner. The question remains, however, of whether it is in fact so difficult to program a computer to be able to engage in a sensible dialogue with a student that the best thing to do is to abandon the attempt, or whether it may be possible to understand more of the nature of a successful tutorial dialogue to help in the implementation of such a program. The 'computer as guru' vision appeals not only to 'science fiction fans'.

First of all, let us list some of the characteristics of a tutorial dialogue which tend to be missing from the computer dialogues described so far:

The language used by both participants is a natural one, such as English, and there is no presumption that one participant is restricted to short (one-word) utterances.

Both participants can ask questions at any time, and not necessarily specifically anticipated questions.

The questions asked may require some computation or reasoning before a sensible answer can be given.

The topic of conversation can be changed on either participant's initiative, although there are some subtle conventions about this.

The dialogue retains some overall direction, giving some predictability to individual contributions.

It is spoken. (We can dispose of this last point straightaway for speech-understanding by computer is nowhere near well enough advanced for a true student-computer dialogue. All the dialogues given in this book took place using a device such as a teletype.)

Since about 1970 several computer-assisted learning systems have been implemented which look at some of the problems which arise in trying to simulate a human tutor. In this chapter we shall consider only the first such system, SCHOLAR (Carbonell, 1970), and shall describe only what the system actually does: the implementation of SCHOLAR and other systems will be described in Chapter 4.

Figure 3.11 gives an extract from a SCHOLAR dialogue. SCHOLAR is intended to review the student's knowledge of the geography of South America. As can be seen, the student responds in English, sometimes with short answers of the kind we have seen with branching programs, but sometimes with apparently unrestricted sentences, for example, to ask a question. Since the questions cannot be anticipated by SCHOLAR, it has to be able to analyse them in order to determine what information it is that the student requires. In fact, SCHOLAR's language processing capabilities were rather limited, as will be explained in the next chapter.

Figure 3.11 *A dialogue with SCHOLAR* (from Carbonell, 1970).

.

.

.

Use one of the following:
Sucre
French
Argentina
Spanish
to answer the question:
What is the language in Chile?
Spanich
You should have written 'Spanish'.
Very good.

116

The capital in Chile is Santiago.
Correct or incorrect?
Correct
That's right.
Approx what is the area of Brazil?
2500000 square miles
Wrong.
Please indicate if the following statement is correct
or incorrect:
The area of Paraguay is approx 47432 square miles.
What is the area of Brazil?
The area of Brazil is approx 3600000 square miles.
Now answer the question you didn't answer before.
False
Rephrase your statement. I can't understand it.
Incorrect
Very good.
The area of Paraguay is approx 157000 square miles.
The language in Brazil is French.
Right or wrong?
Wrong
You are correct.
The language in Brazil is Portuguese.
Is it true that the capital of Brazil is Brazilia?
Yes
That's fine.
Approx what is the population in Brazil?
60000000
Approximately true, but a more exact value is 70000000.
What is Brazil?
Tell me something about Peru
Wait a minute. I'm checking my files.
Let's proceed now.
Peru is a country.
It is in South America.
The population is approx 7000000 people.
The capital is Lima.
Now answer the question you didn't answer before.

q/a
Do you want to change the general mode of the interaction
to q/a?
Please answer y or n.
y
Ok, Mr Jones. Let's go ahead.
Please, tell me more about Peru
The area of Peru is approx 480000 square miles.
The language is Spanish.
How many square miles are there in Brazil?
The area is approx 3600000 square miles.
What is the principal religion in Uruguay?
The principal religion in Uruguay is Catholicism.
The principal religion in Peru is—
I'm afraid I can't answer that.
Is it true that the area of Uruguay is 70000?
That's about right. The exact answer is 79000.
Could you please indicate the principal rivers in Argentina?
I don't understand your word 'indicate'. I'll give you
another chance.
The principal rivers in Argentina are —
The principal rivers in Argentina are the Rio de la Plate, the
Parana, the Uruguay river, the Salado, the Paraguay river, and the
Pilcomayo.
Mixinit
Do you want to change the general mode of the interaction to
mixinit?
Please answer y or n.
y
Ok, Mr Jones. Let's go ahead.
Where is Brazil?
.
.
.

Carbonell coined the term 'mixed initiative' to indicate that with
SCHOLAR both participants could take the initiative and ask

questions. In the dialogue shown, the student typed 'q/a' to change the mode of interaction to one in which he could ask questions and use SCHOLAR as an information-retrieval system. Typing 'mixinit' returns the system to the mixed-initiative mode. It is a premise of the design that the student ought to be able to ask questions, and at the time they occur to him.

It should be obvious that the SCHOLAR system does not find answers to questions by searching a long list of facts about South America. For one thing, it would take too long. For another, the particular fact required need not be stored at all. For example, the two facts 'Peru is in South America' and 'The capital of Peru is Lima', plus a little common sense, should be sufficient to enable the question 'Is Lima in South America?' to be answered. One can fairly easily provide a program with this specific piece of common sense, but the reader may suspect (rightly) that the general problem is a difficult one which SCHOLAR attempts to avoid by dealing only with straightforward facts.

SCHOLAR is a generative system, in that it constructs questions and responses from the information it has stored and does not have them pre-specified, but it differs from the kind of generative system described earlier by attempting to deal with rather ill-defined verbal knowledge. As Figure 3.11 indicates, the questions follow certain stereotypes, with particular topics being selected on an essentially random basis. There is no teaching strategy, and in this respect SCHOLAR compares unfavourably with branching programs such as CALCHEM (Figure 3.2). SCHOLAR seems to flit from one thing to another, and there is no systematic attempt to develop the student's knowledge in any particular direction. In the next chapter we shall describe some attempts to improve SCHOLAR's tutorial strategies.

There are two additional problems with dialogue systems such as SCHOLAR which are not obvious from looking at the dialogues themselves. First, a program may take a considerable time to understand an English sentence and to compute an appropriate response, and this may well reduce the effectiveness of the tutorial interaction. Secondly, writing a program like SCHOLAR to simulate a human tutor is not a trivial task: it is not one to be tackled by those teachers for whom author languages were intended, for it requires man-years of expert programming.

None the less, systems like SCHOLAR do demonstrate that there is at least a possibility of achieving the goal of developing programs able to engage in meaningful tutorial dialogues, for which the venerable dialogues of Socrates have served as something of an ideal and inspiration. But this goal will not be achieved easily if at all because it requires solutions to problems which we know to be difficult from studies in artificial intelligence, namely, how do we enable a computer to converse freely in natural language, even within a limited domain? How can a computer develop, and modify if necessary, a plan of action, for that is what a teaching strategy is? How do we represent a body of knowledge so that it can be discussed with a student? How can a program use this knowledge representation to answer questions? How can a program represent what the student knows so that its comments and actions are appropriate to him? Naturally, people attempting to implement intelligent computer tutors have been turning to artificial intelligence for help, and so shall we in the next chapter.

Summary

The 'learner as bucket' philosophy, summarised at the beginning of this chapter, still dominates the computer-assisted learning field. Approaches derived from programmed learning are unfortunately too easy to implement on a computer. However, as we have seen, there are alternatives and these, on the whole, demonstrate a trend from a behaviouristic to a cognitive approach to teaching and learning in that they view computers as devices for implementing not rigid, mechanistic, statistically-based teaching systems, but ones which treat the student as a thinking, understanding and contributing individual. It may seem paradoxical that computers, symbols of the mechanised society, will in the end help to make education less mechanised. Artificial intelligence (upon which computer-assisted learning systems will increasingly be based) does not presuppose a dehumanising view of man (see Boden, 1977). On the contrary, the emphasis in artificial intelligence on symbolic processing acknowledges that each of us thinks and lives within our own individual representation of reality.

To some extent, the developments from linear programming were inevitable, for computers could obviously do so much more. Branching programs and simulations are natural though sometimes uninspired applications of the computer. The two relatively form-alised approaches, generative computer-assisted learning and the use of mathematical models of learning, have both reached the end of the line, as originally conceived, for they presuppose well-structured problems and the existence of suitable learning models.

The two NSF-funded projects will probably have to be considered failures by their own criterion – that of commercial profit-ability. There is currently no evidence that TICCIT or PLATO will establish a sizeable market. Their emphasis on technological issues was misplaced, and they have not solved the more fundamental problem of producing worthwhile teaching material.

Most methods of computer-assisted learning have their merits. Straightforward arithmetic drills or simulations, for example, are quite unobjectionable, but they are fundamentally limited. They do not aim to make more than a marginal contribution to educa-tion. The two approaches for which the limitations are least clear at the moment (and which offer the best hope for radically enhancing the educational process) are those most concerned with methodo-logical issues: problem-solving and dialogue systems. The former regards the computer as a tool to be used for developing the student's problem-solving skills; the latter considers that the computer can be used to tutor intelligently provided it can be programmed to know about the subject being taught, the student being taught, and how to teach him. Both emphasise that teaching and learning need to be understood and represented as intellectual processes. Both emphasise the learner himself, his activities, his interests and his contributions to the conversation. There is a common belief in a cognitive representation of learning. Both approaches are expressly based upon the subject of artificial intelligence. In the next two chapters we shall explain how ideas from artificial intelligence help in the implementation of dialogue and problem-solving systems.

121

Notes

1. Skinner has remarked that 'a simple programmed workbook will do what the computer can do at one-tenth the cost'! (Zinn, 1970). Skinner (1938) contains the basic ideas of his learning theory, derived largely from experimental studies of the behaviour of pigeons. The implications of this theory for teaching machines were not followed through for almost twenty years (Skinner, 1954, 1958, 1965). There are now few rigid adherents for, as McKeachie (1974) writes, 'each of the principles confidently enunciated by Skinner (1954) now turns out to be untrue – at least in as general a sense as he believed at the time'.

2. Some experimental studies supporting this conclusion are described by Gilman (1969), Guthrie (1971), Anderson, Kulhavy and Andre (1972) and Tait, Hartley and Anderson (1973). Kulhavy (1977) concludes that feedback aids learning unless the teaching material is too difficult or the feedback is too easily available to the student. A further result, opposing the feedback-as-reinforcer belief, is the 'delay retention effect' by which delaying the presentation of feedback for a day or more may lead to significant increases in what students remember (Sturges, 1978). A possible explanation is that immediate feedback may cause interference between correct and incorrect responses, whereas the latter may tend to be forgotten if the feedback is delayed.

3. Conference proceedings edited by Galanter (1959), Lumsdaine and Glaser (1960), Coulson (1962) and Gerard (1967) give some idea of early computer-assisted learning. The position after the first flush of enthusiasm is revealed by Atkinson and Wilson (1969), Zinn (1970) and Oettinger (1971).

4. TUTOR is the author language provided for the PLATO system described later in this chapter. Other author languages include COURSEWRITER, supported initially by IBM; PILOT, now available on many microcomputers; NATAL (Westrom, 1974), intended to be a common author language for computer-assisted learning in Canada.

5. The first clear statement to this effect was made by Naur (1963). The concept of structured programming (Dahl, Dijkstra and Hoare, 1972; Wirth, 1973), which has been central to the development of computer programming recently, has sometimes been equated with that of 'GO-less programming', although this is an over-simplification. The liberal use of GOs leads to all sorts of structural irregularities, making programs hard to understand and hard to modify. The essential reason that such programs are hard to understand is that the program text does not reflect the dynamic structure of processes occurring at execution time.

6. Earlier generative systems include those by Uhr (1969), teaching addition; Uttal, Pasich, Rogers and Hieronymus (1969), analytic geometry; Peplinski (1970), simple algebra; Wexler (1970), arithmetic; Siklossy (1970), basic set theory; Koffman (1972), computer science concepts; Gilkey and Koffman (1974), high school algebra. The Stanford arithmetic drill program, one of the most well-known in computer-assisted learning, is described in Suppes, Jerman and Brian (1968) and Suppes and Morningstar (1972).

7. Earlier descriptions of the application of mathematical models of learning to computer-assisted learning are given by Laubsch (1970), Van der Veer (1970), Smallwood (1971) and Atkinson (1972). These mathematical models can also be used for purposes other than the moment-to-moment determination of teaching actions. For example, Atkinson (1972) describes how the definition of different objectives influences the optimal strategy for allocating a fixed amount of instructional time among a set of students. Chant and Luenberger (1974) show how a general learning model can be used to derive an optimal pace of instruction for a heterogeneous group of learners.

8. The details of Laubsch and Chiang's model are as follows. At any time, each word is assumed to be in one of three states, called L, F and U. The model says that, between sessions, words in states L and U stay there, but words in F either stay in F (with probability d) or transfer to state U (with probability 1-d). If the student is asked a word which is in L or F, the model says he will respond correctly, but if the word is in U he will respond incorrectly (except by a wild guess). Informally, then, words in L are 'permanently learned' words, words in F are 'temporarily learned', i.e. 'forgettable' words, and words in U are 'unlearned' words. What happens between teaching sessions can be represented diagrammatically:

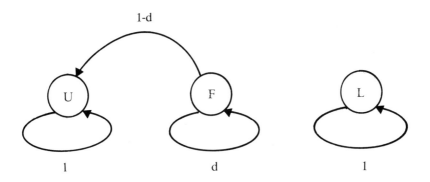

where the circles represent states and the numbers on the arrows from one state to another represent the probability of words transferring between these states. The model says that when a word is actually presented to a student during a teaching session, the following transitions between states are possible:

123

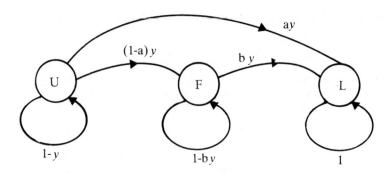

Here y is the probability that a student is paying attention, and a and b are the probabilities of permanently learning words previously in U and F respectively. From these it is possible to work out P(w,s,t), the probability of a word w being in a state s immediately after session t, in terms of P(w,s,t-l), i.e. the probabilities after the previous session, as follows:

Let P^1 (w,s,t) be the probability that w is in s immediately before session t. Then

$$P^1(w,U,t)=P(w,U,t-1)+(1-d)*P(w,F,t-1)$$
$$P^1(w,F,t)=d*P(w,F,t-1)$$
$$P^1(w,L,t)=P(w,L,t-1).$$

If w is not presented during session t then

$$P(w,s,t)=P(w,s,t-1)$$

assuming that the time taken by the session is much shorter than that between sessions. If w is presented during session t then

$$P(w,L,t)=P^1(w,L,t) + by*P^1(w,F,t) + ay* P^1(w,U,t)$$
$$= P(w,L,t-1) + (byd + (1-d)ay)* P(w,F,t-1)$$
$$+ ay * P(w,U,t-1)$$

and similarly for P(w,F,t) and P(w,U,t).

9. Let Q(r,s) be the probability that a student will give response r (right or wrong) to a word in state s. For our model, Q(right,L)=Q(right,F)=1 and Q(right,U)= g, the probability of guessing correctly. Then

$$P(w,s,t)=\frac{\text{Probability (state is s at t and r is given)}}{\text{Probability (r is given)}}$$

$$= \frac{\sum_{\mu}P(w,\mu,t-1)*T(\mu,s)*Q(r,\mu)}{\sum_{\mu} P(w,\mu,t-1)*Q(r,\mu)}$$

where $T(\mu,s)$ is the probability that a word makes the transition to state s, given that the word was in state μ and was present in session t. $T(\mu,s)$ is given by the diagrams in note 8.

10. The particular instructional theorems upon which TICCIT is based are given in Merrill (1974). The implication that concept learning and rule using are well understood would be disputed by many experimental psychologists. Contemporary surveys of concept learning theories are given by Millward and Wickens (1974) and Levine (1975), and it is apparent that they are well-developed only for specialised, unrealistic learning situations.

11. The basic TICCIT configuration employed two Data General 800 series computers, one for handling the terminals and the other for the main processing activities. Technological advances have enabled the present TICCIT system to be supported by only one minicomputer. All the courseware for the courses developed for the project is stored on two large discs, one mainly for graphic material and the other for educational text. The cost of the hardware for the full TICCIT system was put at nearly \$0.5m (1974 prices). The courseware development costs were about \$1.5m but 'if only two percent of the nation's 1000 community colleges procured TICCIT systems, and used this program's four courses for a five-year period, the prorated cost per contact hour for courseware alone would be about 15 cents' (Mitre Corporation, 1976). 'If only', indeed.

12. Published descriptions of PLATO programs include the following: Francis (1973), qualitative inorganic chemistry; Obertino (1974), elementary reading; Boast (1975), agronomy; Maggs and Morgan (1975), law; Curtin, Dawson, Provenzano and Cooper (1976), Russian; Montanelli (1979), computer science; Sorlie and Essex (1979), medical sciences; Kane and Sherwood (1980), classical mechanics. The 1980 catalogue of PLATO courses lists about 700 offerings in subjects from astronomy to veterinary medicine. CERL (1977) is an internal report on the PLATO IV project.

13. The PLATO IV system was based on two computers, a CDC Cyber 73-2 and a CDC 6500, with ten peripheral processing units acting as minicomputers to handle input and output to the terminals. Discs were used for bulk storage of teaching material, and the material actually in use was transferred to a 2 million word extended core storage, from where it was transferred to the high-speed 65,000 word main memory for processing. In this way, the average response time for each terminal was kept down to about 1/8 of a second. Binding the system together was a complex communications network. Output data for all terminals were transmitted over standard television channels or microwave links to site controllers which recovered the data for each terminal and transmitted it over standard telephone lines. Communication from terminal to computer was exclusively by telephone line (Bitzer, 1976). Much of this is now obsolete for the latest PLATO terminals are based on microcomputers, to which teaching material is transferred from a central computer. Thereafter communication with the central computer is needed only to update any records associated with the use of the material.

125

14. The figure of $1.17 per hour was accumulated from $0.67 for initial capital investment, $0.30 for operating costs, $0.20 for lesson material and nothing for communication costs (which can however be $1.00 if the terminals are 1000 miles from the computer), all in terms of costs per hour of instruction (Bitzer, 1976). Alpert (1975) derived a figure of $2.50 per hour. It is tempting to make too much of these figures. For example, Rockart and Morton (1975) quote cost figures in the very first paragraph of their book on computer-assisted learning. The conclusions of earlier studies, for example that of Kopstein and Seidel (1969) that 'compared to hardware costs, the remaining categories are minor', soon seemed out-of-date, and no doubt the same will be true of more recent studies.

15. A brief summary of all NDP projects is given by Hooper (1977), with more detailed descriptions of some of these projects being available in McKenzie (1978), Beech (1979) and Tawney (1979). The Dye simulation formed part of the Computers in the Undergraduate Science Curriculum project. Other projects making heavy use of simulation were the Engineering Sciences Project, the Computational Physics Teaching Laboratory and the Management Decision-Making project. The financial evaluation of the NDP projects is given by Fielden and Pearson (1978).

16. For example, some of the PLATO programs at Illinois, computerised games such as economics-based simulations at the Division of Instructional Systems, Philadelphia (Charp and Woolson, 1969), the University of California at Irvine physics programs (Bork and Robson, 1972), and the University of Pittsburgh's Project Solo (Dwyer, 1971).

17. The difficulty arises because ORIENTATION is being used only to tell us when the turtle is facing north, whereas we should take account of how the turtle got into this position. When the turtle changes from its initial orientation (i.e. 0) it should in fact continue CRAWLUNTILing until its orientation has returned to this initial value. In other words, line 3 of CRAWLUNTIL should read

    3 IF NOT EQUALQ :ORIENTATION 0 THEN CRAWLUNTIL.

18. There are other reasons for encouraging students to write computer programs which it is beyond the scope of this book to discuss in detail. They are essentially the arguments put forward by those who propose to expand computer science teaching in schools and universities – in short, that nowadays all students ought to be exposed to computers and how they are used. As the director of the Dartmouth College project which began developing the language BASIC and a large time-sharing system as long ago as 1964, put it: 'if the computer is so powerful a resource that it can be programmed to simulate the instructional process, shouldn't we be teaching our students mastery of this powerful intellectual tool' (Luehrmann, 1972).

4. COMPUTER AS TEACHER

Both the processing and the uses of information are undergoing an unprecedented technological revolution. Not only are machines now able to deal with many kinds of information at high speeds and in large quantities, but also it is possible to manipulate these quantities of information so as to benefit from them in entirely novel ways. This is perhaps nowhere truer than in the field of education. One can predict that in a few more years millions of school children will have access to what Philip of Macedon's son Alexander enjoyed as a royal prerogative: the personal services of a tutor as well-informed and responsive as Aristotle. (Suppes, 1966)

The computer as a surrogate teacher has been a remarkably persistent mirage. The vision of the Aristotlean tutor still tantalises despite the manifest delay. But while one may despair of reaching this particular oasis, the journey itself is full of interest. The terrain will be surveyed in this chapter. We shall describe several recent dialogue systems, explaining how they were implemented. All these systems are working ones in the sense that they are able to sustain the conversations given, although in some cases the systems serve only as demonstrations for they have not been used with real students. As always, extracts of student-computer dialogues need to be read with some caution or even scepticism for they should be appreciated only to the extent that they fairly reflect the program's ability to sustain such dialogues in general. We shall therefore concentrate on the principles underlying a program's implementation.

A tutorial comprises three interacting components: the subject, the student and the teacher – the 'what, who, how' components (Self, 1974). Similarly, a computer program to conduct a tutorial should have representations of what is being taught, who is being taught, and how to teach it to him. The first three sections of this chapter are concerned with these respective representations:

program competence, student models and tutorial strategies. These issues are of concern more to the implementer than to the user of computer-based tutorial systems. The last section of this chapter considers the problem of communication, the only aspect of tutorial systems with which a student is directly concerned.

Program competence

Computer tutors should know what they teach. This slogan has been shouted so often recently that there is a danger of inducing inattention.[1] The message is that whatever knowledge is supposed to be gained by the student during a tutorial, ranging from simple facts such as 'Lima is the capital of Peru', to complicated procedures such as how to find out what is wrong with a faulty electronic circuit, this knowledge should be available to the tutor itself during the tutorial. Only then could a computer tutor answer unanticipated questions about the subject under discussion. In addition, it is possible that the tutor could use its own knowledge to generate explanations as appropriate, and could understand a student's difficulties by some analysis of the knowledge involved.

There are, of course, degrees of knowing, and all the slogan amounts to is a plea for computer tutors to be given a deeper knowledge than in present programs. The difficulty can be traced back to the philosophy behind programmed learning. Skinner (1954) wrote as follows:

Mathematical behaviour is usually regarded not as a repertoire of responses . . . but as evidence of mathematical ability. . . . The techniques which are emerging from the experimental study of learning are not designed to . . . further some vague 'understanding' of mathematical relationships. They are designed, on the contrary, to establish the very behaviours which are taken to be the evidence of such mental states or processes.

The emphasis then was on the analysis and manipulation of responses, with consideration of any response-producing processes being labelled as unscientific. And so tutorial systems implemented using author languages know only a repertoire of responses, and only those responses explicitly specified by the authors of programs. Any tutorial with an author language program deals with a subset of the stimulus-response situations anticipated by the author, for there is no mechanism for such systems to use their knowledge in any other way. For a tutorial program to be able to respond to unanticipated situations, more general and flexible methods of representing and manipulating knowledge are needed.

The SCHOLAR system (Carbonell, 1970) which we introduced in the previous chapter uses a representation of the knowledge under discussion, the geography of South America, in which facts, concepts and procedures are organised as a data structure in the form of a network. The elements of this network are related systematically to other elements in the network. Figure 4.1 is a pictorial simplification of part of such a network. Each node in the network denotes some concept, and the lines pointing to other nodes denote relationships to other concepts. For example, two of the lines in Figure 4.1 might be understood to represent the knowledge that 'Argentina is located in South America', and 'the latitude of Argentina ranges from -22 to -55'. For the SCHOLAR system itself similarly to appreciate the significance of the structure of the network it is necessary to have a program which interprets the network in the required manner. To the extent that we can write such a program we could say that the 'meaning' of a node is represented by its relations to other nodes, their relations to other nodes, and so on. For this reason, such networks are commonly called *semantic networks*.

In SCHOLAR, the semantic network is used in two ways: to help determine tutorial actions, and to answer questions. Discussion of the former will be postponed until we look at the general problem of determining tutorial strategies. To answer a specific question, such as 'What is the latitude of Argentina?', SCHOLAR must find a node ('Argentina') in the network, and then find the relevant relationship (to 'latitude'). For South American geography it is not very difficult to organise the network so that a systematic search will locate required nodes sufficiently quickly. We should notice also that SCHOLAR can deal sensibly with questions which require enumerating the members of some set, for example 'What are the bordering countries of Argentina?', questions which would present great difficulty to author language

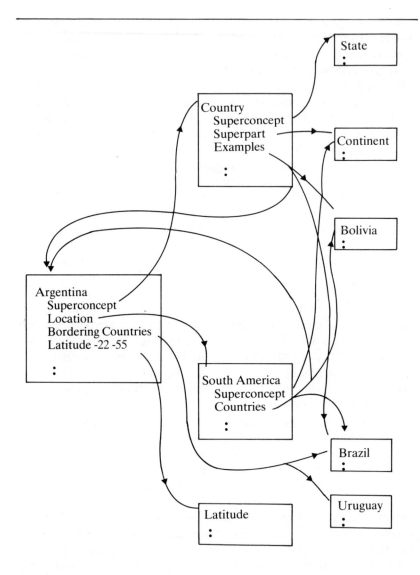

Figure 4.1   *A representation of part of a network on South America* (adapted from Carbonell, 1970)

programs expecting exact matches between the correct answer and the student response. SCHOLAR can ignore the order in which the members are mentioned, and can point out differences in the membership of the student's set and the set determined by searching the network.

As indicated in Figure 3.11, SCHOLAR can also respond to student requests to 'Tell me about . . . '. In a semantic network, the distance between two nodes (that is, the smallest number of lines along which one could get from one node to the other) is an approximation to the irrelevance of the represented concepts to one another. So, to provide relevant information, SCHOLAR will first mention properties near to the mentioned node. In SCHOLAR, in fact, these properties have a 'relevancy tag' associated with them to indicate their subjective importance, and obviously only the most important properties will be mentioned first. A 'Tell me more about . . . ' request will lead SCHOLAR to mention less important and more distantly related properties. While the SCHOLAR mechanism may seem unsatisfyingly arbitrary, it does serve to illustrate that programs can sometimes be written to respond sensibly without complicated processing being necessary.

But so far all questions have required that SCHOLAR behave as an information retrieval system since it has been necessary only to find facts actually stored in the network. The real power of the semantic network approach comes by recognising that it is possible to answer questions for which the answers are not stored. For example, we need not store in the network that 'Buenos Aires is in South America' provided that the program which interprets the network can make the relevant inference. In other words, the program must know something about the properties concerned, 'location' and 'capital', in particular, that if x is the capital of y and y is located in z then x is in z – a rule of inference.[2]

As Carbonell emphasised, SCHOLAR was a first attempt to develop a tutorial system to teach 'the same way human teachers do'. Clearly, human teachers do not often recite specific questions, as branching programs do, but act on the basis of their knowledge of the specific subject at hand and of more general knowledge. The semantic network representation was adopted because it was felt

131

that it enabled the relevant knowledge to be expressed in a form which reflected the assumed conceptualisations of a human teacher. Semantic networks are to some extent general-purpose representational schemes since other kinds of knowledge could be expressed in them. For example, SCHOLAR could be adapted, with increasing difficulty, to teach, say, the geography of Africa, the anatomy of the circulatory system, or aspects of analytic geometry, mainly by changing the contents of the semantic network and not the program itself.

The difficulty increases as the subjects become less about facts and more about procedures. To teach the geography of Africa we would need to change only the entries in our semantic network, the structure of the network and the rules of inference remaining largely unchanged. But, as we are sure the reader has noticed, SCHOLAR only deals with a small part of what is normally covered by 'geography': it cannot, for example, explain processes (e.g. how an ox-bow lake is formed) or interactions between systems (e.g. wind, sea and cloud). However, the fact that some of SCHOLAR, at least, could be carried over to a new topic is an improvement on an author language program to cover the same material. This would need virtually complete rewriting, since all the messages to the student would need changing.

The definition of a semantic network as concepts of various kinds related to one another is wide enough to apply to any conceivable knowledge representation. In practice, the term 'semantic network' is usually reserved for the kind of hierarchically-organised, factual representation illustrated by Figure 4.1. As such, there are limitations on the knowledge which can be satisfactorily represented in a semantic network and on the extent to which the representation is a psychologically valid one.[3] Alternative representational schemes have been the subject of much debate in artificial intelligence, where the 'representation of knowledge' question has assumed central importance. Formal logic, which at one time was presented as an opponent of semantic networks, has fallen into disfavour because general deductive schemes, in which of course logic specialises, are computationally inefficient and an unrealistic model of human thought processes. Production systems, which we introduced in Chapter 2, have a long history in artificial intelligence, and have retained their enthusiasts, as illustrated by some of the systems described later in this chapter. But rather than pursue an abstract discussion of particular representational schemes it will be easier to describe their merits with respect to particular concrete examples. However, one conclusion of the debate seems to be that the search for a general-purpose, all-powerful method for representing knowledge in computer programs should be suspended: different methods have different advantages which we must balance and combine.

Correspondingly, in designing artificially intelligent computer tutors there is little concern now with making as much as possible of the system subject-independent (as there was with SCHOLAR). Instead, systems teach specific skills using whatever specific techniques seem appropriate. To take an example: imagine trying to develop a program to teach students how to determine molecular structure from nuclear magnetic resonance spectra. Following our introductory slogan, we would expect our program to have to be able to solve such problems itself. How can we get it to do this? Well, we could go and ask an expert how he solves these problems. This may not be very helpful,[4] even if we greatly simplify matters by assuming that we are dealing only with linear saturated molecules. Let us then make up a method. If the molecule is linear, we can guess groups one by one from one end of the structure. At any stage, there may be none or more groups consistent with the known molecular formula and spectral peaks. If there are more than one, we arbitrarily select one and proceed. If there are none, then the previous arbitrary selection must have been incorrect so we return and make another selection. If there are no previous selections to return to there is no solution. If we reach the other end of the molecule we have found a solution.

In artificial intelligence, such a method glorifies in being called a depth-first search with backtracking. It forms the basis of a program capable of the dialogue shown in Figure 4.2 (Sleeman, 1975). The program's response to the student's request to 'explain' is merely a description of its unsuccessful attempt to complete the depth-first search. It should also be noticed that a solution strategy has been imposed on the student, and moreover that it is a strategy which, with the assumption that the molecule is linear, ensures that at each stage there is a single correct next step, thereby enabling the system to rap the student over the knuckles as soon as he types in an incorrect step.

Figure 4.2 *A dialogue discussing an n.m.r. spectrum* (adapted from Sleeman, 1975)

.

.

.

Join CH₂ corresponding to peak (2,2)
Correct
Help
So far you have identified $CH_3CH_2CH_2CH_2$.
Also we know that the peak for the last group is (2,2). The previous group has 2 interacting protons: therefore the next group must have 0 interacting protons: choose appropriate groups from those remaining.
Join O corresponding to peak (0,0)
No
Explain
We will now attempt to build such a molecule.
No peaks left in spectra. Spectrum of molecule is ((3,2) (2,5) (2,4) (2,2) (0,0) (2,3) (3,2)).
Molecule built was $CH_3CH_2CH_2CH_2OCH_2CH_3$.
Spectra still to be explained is nil.
Remaining molecular formula C.
Search was unsuccessful.
Join CO corresponding to peak (0,0)
Correct
Help
So far you have identified $CH_3CH_2CH_2CH_2CO$.
Also we know that the peak for the last group is (0,0).
The last group had no interacting protons − in view of the mf remaining and the spectra still to be explained we are limited to the following group(s)
CH_2

.

.

.

Figure 4.3   *A dialogue with Kimball's integration tutor* (from Kimball, 1973)

Our integral is∫x*log(x) dx
What shall we do to solve it? :*sub*
Can you think of a substitution?   (yes, help or exit)
yes
Let u = *log(x)*
Ok, Ruth, we will let u = log(x).
Thus x =e^u and dx =e^u du
which we substituted into the integrand.
Our new integral is now∫u*e (^{2*u}) du.
Please type good, bad or giveup.
bad
Can you think of a substitution? (yes, help or exit)
help
I can't find a suitable substitution! Will exit . . .
Ok, Ruth, our integral is∫x*log(x) dx
What shall we do to solve it? :*help*
I suggest you try integration by parts
What shall we do to solve it? :*parts*
Integration by parts!
We will use the notation∫udv = u*v −∫vdu
Can you think of a choice for u? (yes, help or exit)
help
How about letting u = log(x).
Can you think of a choice for u?
yes
Let u = *log(x)*
Ok, Ruth, we will let u = log(x).
Thus dv = xdx
hmmmm . . .
[program now finds the integral of dv]
An intriguing choice!
Thus v =$\frac{x^2}{2}$and du =$\frac{1}{x}$
We now have x*log(x) dx =$\frac{x^2*\log(x)}{2}\int-\frac{x\,dx}{2}$

135

Please type good, bad, again, solve or giveup.
Good
Ok, Ruth, our integral is now $\int x \, dx$ times $-\frac{1}{2}$.

What shall we do to solve it? :*known*
Very good!

.

.

.

A program's systematic search for a solution to a problem can however form the basis for a more flexible monitoring of a student's attempt to solve the same problem. In many cases, the student is expected to proceed by recognising that a problem may be solved by transforming it into one or more sub-problems, one or more of which must then be solved for the original problem to be considered solved. The sub-problems may in turn need to be transformed into sub-subproblems, and so on. The student's difficulty is in deciding which sub-problem to tackle first. For example, students are usually taught to solve symbolic integration problems by selecting from a small set of standard transformations one which it is hoped will turn the problem into one or more simpler integration problems. If the transformation does not lead to a solution, the student is expected to return and select a different transformation to try. Kimball (1973, 1982) wrote a program which monitored a student trying to solve integration problems along these lines (see Figure 4.3).

This program compromises neatly between the options of trying to ensure that the student follows a recommended pre-stored solution path for each problem, and of allowing him to follow whatever path he wishes. The program does indeed have access to a solution, but this is not used directly; neither does the program make use of a general symbolic integration procedure, since this would be computationally expensive. Instead, the program can provide help to the student by recommending a transformation

136

which, according to the archive of problems and solutions, is most often useful for problems similar to the one facing the student. Such a technique is also applicable to problems suggested by the student, for which of course there are no archived solutions. For problems in the archive, the program can and does interrupt the student when his solution process seems excessively long, i.e. his number of transformations exceeds that of the archived solution by some arbitrary amount. Therefore, the appealing features of Kimball's system derive from the way in which its admittedly sketchy knowledge of how to solve symbolic integration problems is used to support a more subtle control of the tutorial dialogue.

Programs such as those of Sleeman, Kimball and others[5] which try to teach by discussing with the student his attempt to solve a problem differ in important ways from those which we described in the previous chapter as generative systems and branching programs. We are not now concerned with merely rehearsing some previously taught skill or with teaching specific solutions to specific problems (e.g. that the integral of x log x is $(2x^2 \log x - x^2)/4$) but with teaching how problems of a certain kind are solved in general. It is therefore not simply a matter of checking the student's answer but his process of getting an answer. Moreover, the problems are usually such that there are alternative ways of obtaining a solution and therefore an intermediate step cannot be said to be right or wrong in itself, but only in the context of the solution as a whole. It is not sensible therefore to pre-store anticipated correit responses from the student.

If a program does not have access to a stored description of an 'ideal' solution, including of course the intermediate steps, and it is supposed to comment sensibly upon a student's attempt, then it is clearly desirable that the program should itself be able to solve the given problem and to compare its solution with that of the student. As we have seen, this problem-solving ability supports the more advanced features of these newer systems, such as the provision of explanations of why a proposed step is or is not appropriate and of suggestions about a good next step to try.

The general approach towards the design of computer-assisted learning programs exemplified by Figures 4.2 and 4.3 is, then, to take a problem-solving mechanism for some specific task (a 'performance program') and to compare its solution steps with those of a student. While it is of course possible to teach without understanding what a student is trying to do – it happens frequently in the classroom – it seems reasonable to believe that any such understanding possessed by a program may enable it to teach more intelligently. The main difficulty is in balancing the desires to allow the student to explore his own solution methods and yet to maintain some understanding of them (as we will explain further in the next section).

The reader may well be wondering whether it is possible to commandeer *any* existing performance program, and to build a teaching program around it. Certainly, artificial intelligence researchers have recently developed several 'expert systems', i.e. systems which try to solve practical problems which would otherwise require considerable human expertise,[6] and it is a requirement of such systems that they be able to explain the reasons for the answers they give, so that a human user can determine what reliance to place upon them. These expert systems would seem well-suited for turning into teaching programs since the extent to which this is possible for any performance program is determined largely by how comprehensible to a student its solution processes are, and of course by how close they are to what the student is to learn.

For example, the MYCIN program which we introduced in Chapter 2 has been developed as a teaching program called GUIDON (Clancey, 1979a and b). MYCIN is a program which engages in consultations to determine the causes of infectious diseases, and to provide antibiotic therapy. The aim of the GUIDON project is to see whether the expertise of the MYCIN system can be transferred to a student by engaging in a tutorial dialogue about a particular case diagnosis. During a GUIDON tutorial the student plays the role of a consultant who, after being given general information about a case, is expected to ask relevant questions to enable him to arrive at a diagnosis. GUIDON compares the student's questions with those that would be asked by MYCIN in the same circumstances and comments upon them on this basis.

138

Figure 4.4 *A dialogue with the GUIDON system* (from Clancey, 1979a)

.

.

.

You should now proceed to ask questions that will enable you to make a hypothesis about the organisms (other than those seen on cultures or smears) which might be causing the infection.

[The student may ask for more data, make a hypothesis, or use a special option.]

How is the fact that the patient is burned relevant?

The fact that patient-326 is seriously burned will be used to conclude that pseudomonas-aeruginosa is one of the organisms which might be present (in addition to those seen on cultures or smears) Rule 578.

Help

Try to determine the type of the infection: bacterial, fungal, viral, or Tb.

[To provide help, GUIDON chose a rule to discuss and a method of presentation.]

What is the patient's wbc?

[GUIDON observes that this question is relevant to the new topic and provides the requested data]

.

.

.

In order to be able to carry on a dialogue such as that shown in Figure 4.4[7] GUIDON needs to know something about the nature of tutorial dialogues in general, and of the student's competence and interests: these aspects of GUIDON we shall describe later. For the moment, we are concerned mainly with showing how the performance program itself may be made use of. As described in Chapter 2, the expertise of the MYCIN program is expressed by a few hundred production rules, each of which consists of a set of preconditions and a conclusion, such that the conclusion (or goal) is justified if the preconditions (or subgoals) are all true. To establish a particular conclusion, then, MYCIN may try to establish the preconditions of any production rule with this conclusion. Each precondition may in turn necessitate a search through the rules. Figure 4.5 represents this process by an 'and/or tree', so-called because the conclusion is proved by rule 1 or rule 2 or . . . rule n (these are all rules which have the conclusion on their right-hand sides) and each rule is successful if precondition 1 and precondition 2 and . . . precondition m all hold. The MYCIN system is able to explain itself (e.g. to give reasons why particular data is asked for) by expressing the relevant part of the and/or tree in English.

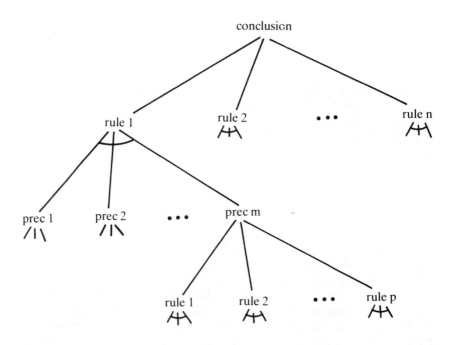

Figure 4.5   *An and/or tree representing MYCIN's general method of searching for solutions*

Such explanations may themselves be of educational value, but scarcely constitute a tutorial: they are not tailored to the student's competence, and the student himself has no opportunity to participate in the reasoning process. GUIDON's problem then is how to use MYCIN's and/or tree to monitor a student's attempted solution. Medical diagnosis, like symbolic integration and most other intelligent activities, is not a precise science: there are no foolproof procedures to follow, and a teaching program should be flexible enough to recognise this. The method adopted by GUIDON can be illustrated by looking at Figure 4.6, which is a simplified version of the and/or tree which might be created by MYCIN in dealing with the case discussed in Figure 4.4. 'Coverfor' signifies the goal of determining organisms which must be covered by a therapy recommendation. Production rule 578 is relevant to this goal since it may conclude that a particular organism is present. 'Burned' and 'type' denote two of the preconditions on the left-hand side of production rules which contain 'wbc' and 'csf-findings' on their left-hand sides.

We can see that the student's first question is answered by finding in the tree the goal for which 'burned' is a subgoal. GUIDON provides 'help' by finding, from MYCIN's solution, a subgoal ('type') for the goal under discussion which the student has not yet investigated. The order in which subgoals are attempted does not matter, and GUIDON therefore does not insist that the MYCIN tree is worked through in any particular order. When a student requests information, as in the last question of the extract, GUIDON checks that the question is relevant by seeing if MYCIN asked the same question ('wbc') to achieve the required conclusion. If it were not relevant, then GUIDON would have to decide whether to interrupt or not. Considerable further experimentation, however, is required before GUIDON gets an appropriate balance in its decisions about when to say something and what to say in, for example, avoiding annoying students by too many interruptions with tedious monologues. It is one of the virtues of the GUIDON approach that the division between medical and teaching expertise enables experiments to be carried out with the latter relatively easily (as compared, for example, with author language systems).

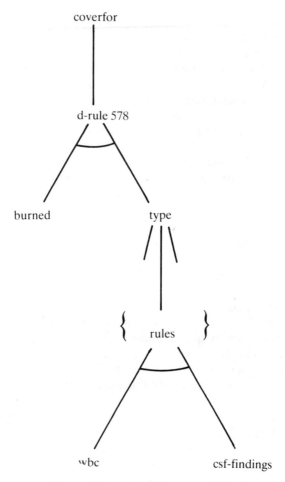

Figure 4.6   *A simplified version of part of the and/or tree corresponding to the case dialogue shown in Figure 4.4* (from Clancey, 1979a)

GUIDON's teaching expertise is to a large extent independent of the subject matter of MYCIN. We might hope that GUIDON could be used to teach some other subject by simply replacing the MYCIN production system by one for some other expert system (c.f. SCHOLAR's subject-independence). An experiment along these lines was carried out: MYCIN's production rules were replaced by those used in PUFF, a consultation system for diagnosis of pulmonary function, and SACON, a system for suggesting a structural analysis regime. The resultant tutorials, however, were too verbose, partly because it was assumed that the student was a complete novice, but mainly because the solutions proceeded differently, especially with SACON. Whereas MYCIN's and/or trees tend to be shallow and broad, SACON's tend to be deep and narrow, reflecting the fact that SACON's task is more algorithmic. Since GUIDON discusses single rules or goals but has no overall picture of the solution, the SACON tutorial tended to degenerate into a lengthy description of one branch of the tree. The production system representation is unlikely to be universally ideal.

Student models

Teachers have always appreciated that students learn differently from one another. Long before the advent of computers, psychologists were concerned with demonstrating, for example, that students respond differently to praise or blame, and learn more if a teacher understands their behaviour.[8] And yet in computer-assisted learning it has been an uphill struggle to establish how important it is that a teaching program should determine its actions from its understanding of the student's needs. Again, computer-assisted learning was set off in the wrong direction by Skinner's insistence that in linear programs the student's responses could be ignored.

A student model is any information which a teaching program has which is specific to the particular student being taught. The reason for maintaining such information is to help the program to decide on appropriate teaching actions. The information itself could range from a simple count of how many incorrect answers have been given, to some complicated data structure which purports to represent a relevant part of the student's knowledge of the subject.

Author languages typically provide the author with a set of variables which he is expected to use to count errors, to set flags indicating that particular concepts have been understood, and thus to enable his program to decide between alternative teaching strategies. TUTOR, for example, provides 150 such variables. This may seem ample, but in fact it has proved very difficult to use these variables effectively. Hartley (1978), writing with reference to the tutorial programs of the UK's National Development Programme, remarks that 'the records of a student's performance are sparse and there is little attempt to build up a representation of his knowledge and skills. So the programs are content-centred, and not based on adequate student models; in consequence the teaching is primitive in accommodating individual differences since the decision rules are largely based only on the last response of the student.'

The problem for the author of such a program lies in enabling the program to make sense of what is, after all, merely a series of numbers. Sometimes the numbers can be interpreted with respect to a mathematical model of learning, and their use to determine teaching actions may then proceed as described in Chapter 3. Kimball's symbolic integration program similarly maintains a set of numbers $P(i,j)$ intended to represent the probability that the student will choose transformation j if he is in state i, one of a set of possible problem-solving states. As usual with mathematical learning models, the Markov assumption – that the state transition probabilities depend only on the state i (and not on how this state has been reached) – is made. With symbolic integration problems this assumption is untenable, as Kimball admits, without the introduction of the concept of a 'failure state'. When a student in a particular problem-solving state selects a transformation which turns out to be unsuccessful, Kimball's model assumes that the student returns to a failure state similar to the initial state, but with a reduced probability of selecting the unsuccessful transformation. Kimball also had difficulty in coping with another assumption of the mathematical learning model approach, that a student's learning takes place continuously and therefore can be modelled by small adjustments of the numbers. As Kimball writes, 'unfortunately . . . students changed their problem solving patterns suddenly and at unpredictable intervals'.

144

The hope that one can represent a student by a set of numbers and his learning by twiddling with those numbers has been abandoned in artificial intelligence work. There is just too large a distance between the numbers and what they represent for a program to be able to cross.[9] Instead, one must expect to need representations much closer to what is being represented: complex symbolic data structures to represent what the student is supposed to know and modifications to these structures to represent learning. This is undeniably difficult but some existing programs do show what is involved and what benefits should result.

Carbonell's SCHOLAR, as we saw, adopted a semantic network representation because it was thought to be close to the teacher's conceptualisation of the knowledge. By implication, the network also represented the desired student's conceptualisation. So SCHOLAR could associate flags with each node of the network to indicate whether the student was thought to know the information represented by that node. More ambitiously, Carbonell proposed to model student errors by introducing small 'perturbations' to the network (although this proposal was not followed up in the SCHOLAR system).

In GUIDON, Clancey makes use of an 'overlay student model',[10] where the student's knowledge is modelled in terms of a subset and simple variations of the expert's (MYCIN's) knowledge. Whenever MYCIN reaches some conclusion, GUIDON attempts to decide whether the student has reached the same conclusion. This decision is based on information such as the inherent difficulty of the relevant rule and the student's background and competence. Thus, GUIDON attempts to maintain an and/or tree to model the student's current knowledge. GUIDON also keeps a 'focus record', a record of goals and topics which have been discussed, to help maintain continuity during the dialogue. Such information may be used in fairly complex tutorial strategies. For example, referring to Figure 4.4, when the student requests 'help', GUIDON responds by applying a rule which may be paraphrased in English as: 'if the recent context mentioned a deeper subgoal relevant to the current goal then suggest that the student finish any incomplete subgoals mentioned in the last rule focused upon'.

An overlay model assumes that the student's knowledge can be related to the knowledge embedded in the performance program of the whole teaching system. Thus, GUIDON estimates the probabilities of a student knowing a rule (that is, of his being able to answer a question about it), and of his having used the rule during the tutorial. In revising this model no clear distinction is drawn between the recall and the use of rules. But a good student model should tell us more than what the student knows − it should tell us something about what he is doing and thinking. GUIDON's and/or tree provides this to some extent, but single steps of the solution are discussed without any appreciation of overall strategies. Also, since it is assumed that the student's performance is sufficiently expert that it can be modelled as a variant of MYCIN's performance, GUIDON is not suitable for beginners. There is no attempt to understand and clarify misconceptions or to follow other reasoning paths.

A simpler version of an overlay model has been grafted onto the 'How the West was Won' game described in Chapter 3. Untutored children fix on a simple strategy and miss the potential richness of the game. Burton and Brown (1979) describe how a tutor can be programmed to interject comments and suggestions to improve a child's play. First, they identify the set of skills the child has to master. Then a performance program is written to determine good moves. Now, when a child makes a move, the tutor compares the skills needed to derive the child's move with those used by the performance program in deriving the best move. The differences form the basis for tutorial advice, as the similarities do for encouragement. As Burton and Brown elaborate, these interruptions need to be made with tact. They report that children preferred playing the 'game plus tutor' to playing the original game.

The general line of argument that seems to be developing is that one should represent a body of knowledge in some appropriate manner and then model the student by introducing modifications to this representation. This student model is intended to explain and predict student performance. Teaching decisions are guided by comparisons between the student model and the original body of knowledge. Learning by the student is represented by changing the student model. This all seems a more realistic view of the teach-

---

PROCESSCOLUMN→TAKEDIFF; NEXTCOLUMN
RESULT =x → WRITE =x
NEXTCOLUMN → SHIFTLEFT; TAKEDIFF; STOP
S GTR M → BORROW
S EQ M → RESULT 0;NEXTCOLUMN
BORROW → CROSSOUT
BORROW → DECREMENT
BORROW → ADTENTOM
PROCESSCOLUMN → COMPARE
TAKEDIFF → DO TAKEDIFF

Figure 4.7 *A production system for subtraction by the method of decomposition* (adapted from Young and O'Shea, 1981)

ing/learning process than that embodied in most existing computer-assisted learning systems.

The art of student modelling is in its infancy and present tutorial systems do little more than introduce the problems. We can get a deeper understanding of what is involved by looking at some programs which concentrate on student modelling at the expense of other components of a complete tutorial system.

From the heady heights of symbolic integration, the interpretation of spectra, and medical diagnosis let us return to the basics. Consider this problem

$$\begin{array}{r} 74 \\ -28 \\ \hline \end{array}$$

One way to solve this is by the 'method of decomposition', whereby you proceed from right to left, 'borrowing' when the lower digit is greater than the digit above it and paying back the ten by decrementing the top digit in the column to the left. The process can be described a little more precisely by the production system shown in Figure 4.7: we ask the reader to trust that this is so, as the details do not need to be fully appreciated now.

Such a production system is important not as a problem-solving system (computers are built to do subtraction, anyway), but as a model of the psychological processes involved.[11] Each production rule is a relatively independent piece of knowledge about the subtraction process which could plausibly have been learned in the context of school mathematics. When a child makes a mistake in subtraction it is not always because of an error of recall or lapse of concentration, but is often the result of an error in the process of executing the subtraction. Young and O'Shea (1981) show that many of the incorrect strategies used by children can be modelled as the consequences of simple changes to the above production system, such as the omission of individual rules or the addition of rules appropriate for other arithmetical tasks. For example, the most common error, that of simply taking the smaller digit from the larger (so $74-28=54$) can be accounted for by omitting the comparison rule (processcolumn $\rightarrow$ compare).

If a computer-assisted learning system for teaching subtraction had access to such a student model it could conceivably be used to help generate more appropriate remediation and practice problems than is possible with the generative systems described in Chapter 3. For example, if a particular production is deemed to be missing after comparing the teacher and student production systems, then a problem could be generated which would draw the student's attention to the fact. We would of course still have the considerable task of guessing what the student model should be on the basis of his attempts to solve problems and of deciding when and how it should be changed.[12]

Let us now turn to two programs which are concerned with teaching students how to write computer programs. If a student model is to be interpreted to explain and predict student behaviour then it has to be seen as a kind of computer program, for that is all a computer can interpret. Computer-assisted learning tutorial systems are faced with the problem of hypothesising this student model/program. But if the subject is itself computer programming then the student's attempted solution, his program, may serve as a kind of student model. The programs of Koffman and Blount (1975) and Ruth (1976) help us to see what use might be made of a detailed student model.

The former program, called MALT, tries to teach machine language programming, i.e. programming in a language which the computer was built to understand (as opposed to a 'high-level

Figure 4.8 *A dialogue with the MALT system* (from Koffman and Blount, 1975)

Your problem is to write a program which will:
Read in 10(octal) 1-digit numbers and store their value starting in register 205. Is this problem OK?
yes
Here are the sub-tasks for the 1st line:
(1)   Initialize a pointer to register 205.
(2)   Initialize a counter with the value of − 10(octal).
(3)   Read a digit and mask out the left 9 bits.
(4)   Store it away using the pointer.
(5)   Update the pointer.
(6)   Update the counter and if it's not zero, jump back to start of
       loop.
Sub-task 1:
Use M377 to store the pointer value, and M376 as the pointer.
M377:
[What is in M377?]
105
Wrong! '0205' is the correct ptr value.
M001:
[User program starts in register 1]
7200
[Clear the acc.]
M002:
1377
[Get the value of the pointer]
M003:
3376
[Deposit into pointer]
Sub-task 2:
Use M375 to store the counter value and M374 as the counter.
M375:
0012
'0012' can't be used as the counter value. It should be either '0010'
or '7770'. Try again!
7770

Now set the counter value into the counter.
M004:
7200
[Clear the acc.]
You don't need a 'CLA' here but it's ok.
M005:
1375
M006:
3374
[Set up the ctr]
Sub-task 3:
You'll need 3 instruction to read a character.
M007:
6031
[Check the keyboard flag]
M010:
5007
[Jump to M007)
M011:
6036
[Read a keyboard character]
Let's store the mask in M373.
What number should we use as a mask?
M373:
0077
Wrong! '0007' is the correct mask because it should contain a '1' corresponding to every bit of the Accumulator we would like to keep. Now, 'AND' the acc. with the mask.
M012:
0373
['AND' the acc.]
Sub-task 4:
.
.
.

language' like Logo which requires a compiler or interpreter). Figure 4.8 gives a dialogue with MALT, with the comments in brackets added for those interested in the gory details of the instruction set. Ruth's program is concerned with the problem of understanding high-level programs well enough to be able to identify and describe any errors in them.

Two points about these programs are particularly worth looking at: the limited extent to which they enable a student to pursue his own methods of solution, and the manner in which they determine whether the student's solution is correct. MALT generates a complete problem from a set of twenty-six primitive problems (e.g. 'initialise a counter') for which solution schemes were pre-programmed. The problem is presented to the student in natural language, together with a list of logical subtasks. The student specifies (and MALT generates) each statement of a solution. The given subtasks impose a strategy upon the student (cf Sleeman's system for determining molecular structure) and generally enable each individual statement to be independently checked. The only freedom that exists for the student is in the selection of statements to accomplish the subtasks. Ruth's program, on the other hand, does not expect the student's solution to approximate a given 'best solution': it expects first to have to determine the student's method of solution by using broad outlines of possible strategies provided by the teacher. The system assumes, then, that the student will adopt one of a small set of pre-specified strategies. (In fact, in the only experiment described by Ruth, only two strategies were given.)

It follows that a student's program will almost certainly not be identical to any recommended solution. We could, as the MALT system does, run the student's program and compare its results with those of the generated solution, but it is quite possible to get the right answer for the wrong reason. If the results differ it may not help the student to be merely informed of the fact. MALT can trace the execution of the student's program but cannot isolate the location of any error in it. Ruth's program makes use of a motley collection[13] of sophisticated techniques in an attempt to locate and describe any errors in the student's program. The system's understanding is derived largely from a built-in body of knowledge about common programming constructs and errors. (The experiment mentioned resulted in the successful analysis of four out of five programs, but no details were given and the system has not been developed to face the acid test of having students let loose on it.)

In most of the computer-assisted learning systems we have been describing, where skills are to be learned by discussing their application to a specific problem, student models tend to operate on the wrong level: they provide information about the student's attempt to solve the specific problem but not directly about his understanding of the general skill involved. For example, in the MALT system the specific problem generated is incidental, but all the tutorial comments are concerned with this specific problem and not with the general skills of how to write machine language programs. While present tutorial systems aim to build up the student's knowledge of certain skills, it is often difficult to make this knowledge explicit enough for the system to be able to generate direct comments about it.

Criticism should not, however, obscure the fact that the philosophy behind these tutorial systems differs considerably from that of the earliest, and still prevalent, computer-based teaching programs. Students are no longer regarded as learning 'habits' and 'responses' by trial-and-error learning. Instead, they develop 'cognitive structures', hypothesised entities representing their perceptions or beliefs about something. The new approach is to model these cognitive structures as data structures in the computer, and to represent learning by appropriate changes. Correspondingly, there is more emphasis on problem-solving, on goal-directed behaviour, and on insightful learning.

Tutorial strategies

The tutorial strategy of a teaching program is that part of it which decides what to do next. It may range from simply following a sequence of actions which have been pre-specified by the author of the teaching program, as in linear programming, to executing a complex decision procedure which attempts to take into account a student model and the course objectives. It may, indeed, be non-existent, as in straightforward simulations or programs running under 'learner control', a concept to be discussed shortly.

The authors of branching programs are responsible not only for specifying the material to be presented in each frame, but also for deciding which frame should be presented next. In principle, this decision could take into account any information which the program may have gathered about the student; in practice, the decision is usually a function only of the student's last response. The specification of a branching program is a tedious business. Moreover it does not end there, for it is so difficult to set up a sensible sequence of frames for all possible series of responses that an equally laborious tuning process is also necessary.

It is natural to wonder whether some of this could be automated. In an attempt to develop optimum paths through the frames, Smallwood (1962) suggested a method whereby the program could improve its branching decisions by accumulating evidence about the paths of all students through the frames. For a student at a particular level of mastery the best frame to be presented next was taken to be the best frame for past students who had similar histories (that is, in some sense have executed similar paths through the branching program) to that level of mastery. But if the measure of similarity is narrow, then a large program must be run with a very, very large number of students for any changes in teaching strategy to occur. If the measure is broad, then the program will only be capable of very limited individualisation. It was, in any case, difficult to tell after the program had been run with students whether the teaching strategy had changed. These problems result from the manner in which knowledge about the student and the teaching situation is organised in the program. There is no basis for generalising the information obtained by experimenting with the branching decisions. Within this framework any attempt to individualise instruction greatly will result in a combinatorial explosion of student types and alternative paths:

If there are five instructional alternatives at each decision node and if there are two possible responses by the student for each instructional alternative, and if we desire to calculate the optimal instructional alternative based on those paths by the student that extend ten presentations into the future, then this will require the consideration of ten billion possible student trajectories for each decision. (Smallwood, 1970)

With generative systems the tutorial strategy is built upon a task difficulty model, as we described in Chapter 3. We showed how in the simple TESTADDITION procedure we could generate sums of an appropriate difficulty by adjusting s, the average size of digit. The general idea is to develop a set of independent task variables, with individual differences showing themselves in the particular values these variables assume. But there are problems with the method. First, we have to decide what we mean by an 'appropriate' difficulty: questions should not be trivially easy or impossibly hard. Secondly, it may not be easy to know how to adjust the values of the task variables (and hence the example difficulty): taking into account too many past examples may underestimate progress, but if too few are considered the differences between examples may be exaggerated, thus unsettling the student. And thirdly, there may be more than one feasible task difficulty model even for the simplest task, giving different estimates of example difficulty. (To illustrate: the task difficulty model given in Chapter 3 would say that $7+5$ is harder than $3+8$. But if our model assumed that a child set a pointer to the first digit position and then moved the pointer along a number of times given by the second digit t, then the probability of adding successfully would be m^t, and thus $3+8$ would be considered harder than $7+5$.)

In those systems in which the knowledge to be learned is stored explicitly rather than embedded in a set of natural language statements which the system cannot analyse further, there is at least some scope for devising flexible tutorial strategies to present this knowledge. SCHOLAR, the first such system, had a particularly simple tutorial strategy. The teacher using SCHOLAR was expected to specify an agenda of topics to be discussed. Whenever a topic was too general, SCHOLAR generated a subtopic on an essentially random basis. For example, the teacher might specify the topic of 'South America', and SCHOLAR would select a subtopic, e.g. 'Brazil', and then perhaps a sub-subtopic, e.g. 'topography of Brazil'. The random element leads, as we have seen, to somewhat disconnected discussions lacking the systematic development of ideas characteristic of a good tutorial, and is necessary because SCHOLAR's semantic network contains little information about desirable orders of presentation of topics.

SCHOLAR's deficiencies as a tutor spurred its designers into some experimental investigation of just what constitutes a 'good tutorial' (Collins, Warnock and Passafiume, 1975). Tape recordings were made of human tutorials in an attempt to elucidate when and why a good tutor changes topic, elaborates a point, gives a counter-example, asks a question, etc. Collins (1976) then attempted to formulate the Socratic tutorial method as a set of strategies expressed as twenty-three production rules.[14] The Socratic method is, of course, an ancient one, but has always been assumed to rely largely on intuition. (The original dialogues are not, in fact, rich in tutorial technique: Socrates makes most of the suggestions, with the student merely responding yes or no.) Collins' brave attempt to get a grip on the method is, as he admits, incomplete and imprecise. It is, however, a beginning and one exploratory computer tutor has been based upon it (Stevens, Collins and Goldin, 1979).

Echoes of SCHOLAR's agenda can be heard in Clancey's description of a 'lesson plan' for GUIDON. A lesson plan is a plan of topics to be sure are discussed, created by the tutor for each case. In later versions of GUIDON a lesson plan will be generated before each case session (Clancey, 1979b). We have decided, however, to avoid the future tense until we reach Chapter 7.

One of the most common techniques for establishing tutorial strategies in the knowledge-based teaching systems described in this chapter is to set up a network which relates skills in terms of their complexities and hence indicates the prerequisite structure of the material to be learned. For example, Gilkey and Koffman (1974) present the tree shown in Figure 4.9 as a specification of the inter-relationships of the concepts to be learned in a course on high-school algebra. The program maintains a student model which determines the level from which the next concept to be taught is selected. A modified form of this network was also used in Koffman and Blount's MALT system, described earlier.[15]

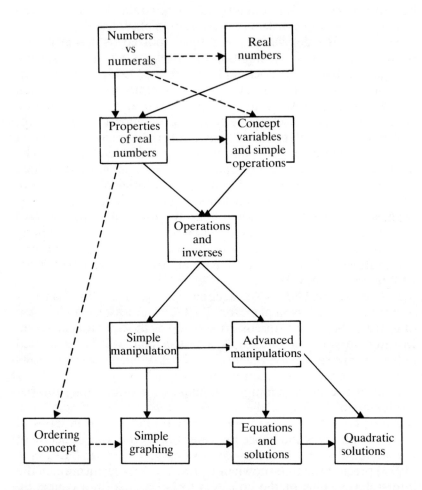

Figure 4.9 *A concept tree for first-year algebra* (from Gilkey and Koffman, 1974)

Many readers will no doubt be reminded of the 'learning hierarchies' of Gagné (1977). These also emphasised the importance of task analysis, the analysis of a learning task in terms of an ordered set of required capabilities. In contrast to programmed learning, there is, both in learning hierarchies and networks such as that shown in Figure 4.9, no attempt to prescribe each and every instructional action, some initiative being left with the teacher or teaching program. But, on the other hand, the similarity with Piaget's stages of intellectual development is superficial for Piaget is concerned with more general abilities than the specific skills isolated in task analysis. Gagné emphasised that he was concerned with the pre-design, rather than the extemporaneous design, of instruction, arguing simply that teachers can rarely do the latter satisfactorily. But he was also careful to emphasise that the interpretation of learning hierarchies could be adjusted to individual differences and that the same limitations on extemporaneous design may not apply to a computer program.

At all events, we must recognise that a tutorial strategy is an implementation of a 'theory of instruction', as educational psychologists would call it. With the possible exception of theories derived from mathematical models of learning (which as we have seen are of limited scope), psychologists' theories of instruction lack the precision needed for incorporation in a computer program.[16] They tend to emphasise pre-designed instruction, whereas it is in the potential for making moment-to-moment decisions that much of the promise of computer-based tutors lies.

Given that we do not have well-developed theories to prescribe the most effective methods to achieve some educational objective, most designers of computer-assisted learning systems make do with whatever ideas and intuitions they have. But there are alternatives. One could argue that theories of instruction are not only weak but unnecessary: that we can and should respect the student's freedom to assume responsibility for his own learning. Also, an optimist might believe that a program could be written which while not provided with a theory of instruction has the capacity for discovering one.

To consider the latter first, there is clearly some force in the argument that teaching programs should, as human teachers might be believed to do, improve their teaching on the basis of their experience. Present teaching programs may learn something about an individual student but in general they learn nothing about teaching. Smallwood's modification to branching programs, mentioned earlier, could be seen in this light. Kimball's symbolic integration tutor also incorporated a simple self-improving capability: whenever a student solved a problem in a fewer number of steps than in the archived solution then the student's solution replaced the archived one. In this way, the program's ability to carry out integration improves, and hence its hints to a student may change. (When this was first tried Kimball was surprised to find his archived solutions being rapidly replaced by particularly concise student solutions. These turned out to be fortuitous guesses! He then had to try to modify his program to trap such spurious solutions, which is not easy. How do *you* react to 'by inspection' solutions to difficult problems?)

O'Shea (1979) describes a more ambitious system which was provided with general and specific hypotheses about alternative ways of teaching, and which was programmed to carry out experiments to test these hypotheses and amend the teaching strategy accordingly. The basic system attempts to teach, using the discovery method, how to solve quadratic equations. The teaching strategy centres on giving the student carefully chosen examples which increase the likelihood of his discovering a particular rule. The strategy itself is expressed as a production system, the main virtue of which here being that it is a form amenable to automatic manipulation, i.e. the program itself may change the teaching strategy. In order to be able to evaluate any such changes, overall objectives must be specified: in this case, this was done in terms of the goals of increasing average post-test scores and number of students successfully completing the session and decreasing student time and computer time.

The next and most difficult step in the design of O'Shea's system is in setting up a method whereby appropriate changes can be made, since random changes are unlikely to be productive. The teacher/designer is required to specify a set of 'assertions' or guidelines, which may range from the specific, e.g. 'lowering the limit on the number of guesses allowed per example may lead to a decrease in student time', to the general, e.g. 'shortening sessions may decrease post-test scores'. The system then uses these assertions in a backward reasoning process similar to that of the MYCIN system to determine a change to make to the tutorial strategy.

The system carried out various experiments which led to improvements in all four of the goals mentioned above. But these results must be approached with caution: the number of students involved was small, the statistical evaluation could be improved, and the method itself has not overcome the standard limitations of learning programs, such as the hill-climbing problem and the frame problem.[17] Obviously, the potential for self-improvement depends on the initial set of production rules and assertions. The method is best looked upon as providing an economic expression of a partially ordered agenda of experiments for tuning an existing tutorial strategy.

Now to return to the other alternative mentioned above: that of obviating the need for a viable theory of instruction by encouraging learner control, that is, by making the learner responsible for making instructional decisions. The argument is that the learner himself is the best judge of appropriate instructional actions and that the extra responsibility should help increase his motivation. As such, the argument is not specific to computer-assisted learning. We shall, however, confine ourselves to a consideration only of the provision and effectiveness of learner control within computer-assisted learning.

In Chapter 3 we described how mathematical models of learning could be used by a program to derive a strategy for teaching a vocabulary. Atkinson (1976) reports an experiment which compares the effectiveness of this strategy with a self-selection strategy in which the student decides for himself how best to sequence the material, i.e. which words are to be presented to him. It was found that the self-selection strategy was 53 per cent better than a strategy in which words are presented at random, but that the decision-theoretic strategy was 108 per cent better. Atkinson concludes that 'the learner is not a particularly effective decision-maker in guiding the learning process'.

Similarly, Steinberg (1977), in a review of studies of learner control in computer-assisted learning, found inconclusive but suggestive evidence that learner control did increase motivation but might also decrease learning efficiency.[18]

But the term learner control has been used to refer to a number of different instructional conditions. Merrill (1980) postulates that there are four levels over which the learner can exercise deliberate control: content selection, display selection, conscious cognition and meta-cognition. Content selection refers to a decision about what segment, lesson or unit to study next. (The Atkinson experiment is really concerned only with content selection.) Display selection refers to a decision about what type of presentation to study next. On the TICCIT system (see Chapter 3), these two forms of learner control are implemented in a mundane manner – by letting the student point to a screen to select a lesson from the curriculum and push a button to ask for a harder or easier problem. According to Merrill (one of the designers of TICCIT), 'TICCIT maximises opportunities for content control'. But, as we saw in Chapter 3, the TICCIT system, which is advertised as a learner control system, presented unconvincing evidence, to say the least, that learner control is effective.

Consequently, Merrill proposes the third and fourth levels of learner control. Conscious cognition refers to the way a student processes the information presented by a given display (e.g. rehearsal, repetition, exemplifying). Meta-cognition refers to the 'how to study' model which the student uses to guide his interaction with the instructional system being used. Merrill is optimistic about the role of these two levels, going so far as to explain how he would give the student control over them in a more sophisticated TICCIT system, using, inevitably, the magical 'help' and 'advice' buttons. In the end, however, he disposes of the matter in this way: 'the challenge is not learner control versus no learner control but how to help students optimize the use of the learner control already available to them'. Our main conclusion must be that learner control presents no easy solution to our problems with tutorial strategies.

Communication

The student is not directly concerned with the issues discussed up to now in this chapter, these being matters for the implementer not the user of a computer-assisted learning system. He is however concerned with how the tutor communicates with him. While the provision of a convenient means of communication usually demands some support from the competence, student modelling and strategy components, there are also some problems specific to that of communication.

It is tautological that the communication should be in a natural language, where 'natural' means that the language is well-suited for discussing whatever topic it is. The student should not be distracted from the subject at hand by having to search for ways to express himself. For most of the topics dealt with by the programs we have discussed the natural language is of course English (for English-speaking people).[19] The difficulties in developing programs to understand and generate English have been investigated in artificial intelligence for some twenty years, and although impressive demonstration programs do exist there is little prospect of computer-assisted learning system designers being able simply to 'plug-in' such a program able to engage in unrestricted dialogue in English.

However, there is cause for some optimism since work in artificial intelligence has shown that provided the subject under discussion is severely restricted and the program has a detailed knowledge of this subject (conditions likely to be satisfied by good teaching programs in the near future) then special-purpose understanding systems can be effective. Also, tutorial dialogues are not 'unrestricted', but tend to have some overall direction which should help to resolve ambiguities and reduce misunderstandings.

It is this overall direction of tutorial dialogues which gives the high degree of predictability in student inputs which makes key word matching techniques surprisingly effective. Typically (and especially with author language systems), anticipated, i.e. key words in the response are pre-specified and looked for under various matching options. For example, in the dialogue shown in

161

Figure 3.2 the second question is probably considered to be correctly answered by any student input containing the key word 'Arrhenius' (or any reasonable approximation thereto). Carbonell (1970) also relied on key word matching techniques, as can be guessed from Figure 3.11. Most student inputs are one-word responses to questions: inputs which look like freely-formed sentences are accepted by matching them with partially-specified sentence templates, such as 'What — area of — '. The dashes indicate parts of the sentence which are ignored or which are used to derive a response to the student's input, e.g. 'is the' and 'Brazil', respectively, in the sentence 'What is the area of Brazil?'

Key word analysis schemes can be very useful in predictable situations but may easily lead to foolish conversations. For example, an early version of CALCHEM was programmed to accept in answer to a particular question any input containing the phrase 'equilibrium constant', or just its conventional symbol 'k'. The student's answer of 'don't know' was thus happily confirmed as correct. In addition, the arbitrariness of key word schemes makes them cumbersome to develop and they are unable to determine the structure of sentences, as is necessary to understand some sentences encountered in freer dialogues.[20] For example,

'What is the output voltage?'

might present no problems to a key word analyser, but

'What is the voltage between the anode of D6 and the collector of the voltage limiting transistor?'

is another matter.

Figure 4.10 gives part of a dialogue with the SOPHIE system (Brown, Burton and Bell, 1975) and shows that fairly free dialogues can be sustained by a computer tutor. Concentrating first on the linguistic capabilities of this system, we may point out some difficulties which may not be apparent to the reader. Among these are difficulties associated with the phenomena of paraphrase, ellipsis and ambiguity. The meaning of a given sentence can often be expressed in many ways: the designer of a natural language system has to decide how many of these are to be allowed (i.e. understood) by the system, and to provide means for the system to understand them. He must compromise between the necessity to accept enough sentences that the natural flow of communication is

Figure 4.10   *A dialogue with the SOPHIE system* (from Brown, Burton and Bell, 1975)

[A circuit schematic is displayed and the control settings indicated]
.
.

.
What is the output?
The output voltage is 11.7 volts.
What is it in a working instrument?
In a working circuit the output voltage is 19.9 volts.
That value is incorrect.
What is the voltage between R8 and Q1?
The voltage at N1 is 47.6 volts.
What is the bse emitter voltage of the voltage limiting transitor?
=base
=transistor
The base emitter voltage of Q5 is −0.037 millivolts.
What about for the current limiting transistor?
The base emitter voltage of Q6 is 0.349 volts.
What should it be?
In a working circuit the base emitter voltage of Q6 is 0.593 volts.
Replace Q6
I am going to ask you some questions about how Q6 is faulted.
Are any junctions shorted?
I don't know
Are any terminals open?
Yes
Which terminals are open?
The base
Q6 is not faulted in that manner. Q6 not replaced.
Is it possible that Q6 has an open base?
Is the complete fault mode eb/ec/bc =op/ok/op what you intended?
Sure
When the settings were: cc=1.0, cr=high, load=20, vc=1.0, vr=high.
That fault conflicts with the following measurements.

You observed that the output voltage was 11.7 volts.
If Q6 had fault mode eb/ec/bc = op/ok/op it would be 23.9 volts.
In a working circuit it is 19.9 volts.
Also:
That fault conflicts with the following measurement.
You observed that the base emitter voltage of Q6 was 0.349 volts.
If Q6 had fault mode eb/ec/bc = op/ok/op it would be 0.712 volts.
In a working circuit it is 0.593 volts.
That fault does not explain any of the symptoms you observed but
it is consistent with the base emitter voltage of Q5 and the voltage
at N1.
.

.

.

What could be wrong?
Here are some faults which explain the measurements you
observed:
The beta of Q3 is low
The beta of Q4 is low
or R22 has the wrong resistance.
.

.

.

Is the emitter current of Q4 correct?
The emitter current of Q4 is −61 milliamps.
In a working circuit the emitter current of Q4 is −49 milliamps.
That value seems to be incorrect.
Could R22 be low?
Is it okay if I use 25 ohms for the resistance of R22?
Yes
That fault agrees with all of the measurements you have made.
What is the resistance of R22?
The measured resistance of R22 is 25 ohms.
Replace R22
R22 replaced.
Now you should take measurements to see if there is anything else
wrong.
Now what is the output?

The output voltage is 19.9 volts.

.

.

.

Is anything else wrong?
No

---

not impaired and the need to keep the language understanding program from becoming excessively complicated. Ellipsis occurs when a word or words are left out and implied, and it occurs much more frequently than we are aware, especially when the student is engrossed in a problem. A program needs to be able to deduce the missing words to understand the sentences. Consider, for example, from Figure 4.10:

> 'What is the base emitter voltage of the voltage limiting transistor?'
> [The point in the circuit which is the 'voltage limiting transistor' needs to be worked out.]
> 'What about for the current limiting transistor?'
> ['Base emitter voltage' is implied – by the context, as is often the case, not the sentence itself.]
> 'What should it be?'
> ['It' refers to 'the base emitter voltage of the current limiting transistor', and 'should' implies a reference to the working circuit and not the given one.]

There is no general solution to the problem of ellipsis, although as Figure 4.10 shows techniques can be developed for special cases. Ambiguities are also more common than we realise, or, more precisely, our understanding of English and the context (which is what we have to try to endow our program with) enables us to resolve most potential ambiguities. For example, in the first sentence above 'voltage' is used first as a noun and then as (part of) an adjective: a program needs to decide which is which. Since many ambiguities are caused by ellipsis we cannot expect general solutions to this problem either.

A natural language system should be designed to take account of the fact that it will not be able to understand all the sentences that could be presented to it. So, for example, when misinterpretations are possible, SOPHIE responds with a full sentence (e.g. to 'What should it be?') to inform the student of its interpretation, which if it is incorrect may be annoying, but should not be confusing. Similarly, spelling mistakes and abbreviations should be allowed, but identified to reduce the risk of confusion. When no interpretation can be found for a student input, the system should help the student re-phrase it. Techniques for doing this are not well-developed and indeed in some cases are difficult to imagine. For example, how in general could SOPHIE respond to major but unanticipated misconceptions as in 'Make the output voltage 30 volts' (controls but not measurements can be changed)?

To be of any practical use, a natural language system needs to be efficient in two senses: it should be quick to implement and, when implemented, should respond to student inputs without undue delay. The implementers of SOPHIE realised that since they were not aiming for a general understanding program they would be wise to avoid traditional syntactic categories such as 'noun phrase', 'predicate', etc. and to use instead refined 'semantic categories' such as 'node', 'measurement', etc. between which powerful constraints exist. For example, a voltage measurement is either between two nodes, across a component, or across some output terminals. So, since a measurement is usually expressed by giving a quantity to be measured followed by a preposition and then a specification of where to measure, the SOPHIE system has a 'rule of grammar' along the lines of:

measurement = *quantity preposition part*

where *quantity* and *part* are defined by further rules of grammar and *preposition* refers to a list of words in a dictionary. Similarly, a student input is defined by

statement = *request* or *set* or *modify*

meaning that any statement is either a request for information, a command to change the control settings or a command to modify the circuit model.

For each of the categories in the SOPHIE grammar, such as *measurement*, *quantity*, *request*, etc., there is a procedure which determines whether a given sequence of words begins with an example of that category. So the procedure to recognise a *statement*

166

will first call the procedure to recognise a *request*, and then if this is not successful the procedure to recognise a *set* and again if necessary the procedure to recognise a *modify*. Whenever a rule of grammar is successful some structural description of the recognised phrase is created. For example, the *measurement* procedure creates a structure defining a call to a procedure which returns a measurement given inputs specifying what is to be measured and where.

This 'semantic grammar' helps tackle some of the problems discussed above. When the *measurement* rule is recognising the phrase 'the voltage at — ', by the time the word 'at' is reached the rule predicts the nature of the following word or phrase quite precisely. As a result, some potential ambiguities are avoided, and in the case of phrases such as 'the voltage at it' the set of possible referents is restricted. A refinement of the semantic grammar enables it to recapture one of the virtues of key word matching techniques, that of being able to ignore hopefully irrelevant parts of an input sentence. For example, in 'What is the voltage across resistor R8?' the word 'resistor' is redundant because it is implied by 'R8' (although in other sentences 'resistor' cannot be ignored). So each rule of grammar optionally specifies how many words may be skipped over. A close examination of the rules themselves[21] shows that they also accept phrases which are in fact meaningless, such as 'the power dissipation of node 4'. In a grammar-based system like SOPHIE there is a choice as to whether such phrases should be rejected syntactically, i.e. by the grammar alone, or semantically, i.e. in this case by the procedure which attempts to do the measurement. The latter is preferable because, apart from simplifying the grammar, it provides a means of explaining why a phrase has not been understood and hence perhaps help the student over some misconception.

To sum up, the SOPHIE system undeniably demonstrates that techniques for processing natural language are sufficiently developed to be usable in computer tutors. The language component of SOPHIE is robust (handling 'nearly all sentences generated by users who have had a few minutes of exposure to the system'), efficient (understanding a typical statement in a fraction of a second), and of some generality (since the notion of semantic grammar has been applied to areas other than electronics).

Before leaving the SOPHIE system we shall digress from the topic of this section to see how SOPHIE, perhaps the most advanced computer tutor in regular use, reflects the previous discussions in this chapter. SOPHIE aims to develop a student's ability at electronic trouble-shooting, an area of expertise involving skills which we poorly understand, but which underlie many intelligent activities. As we would expect from our previous comments, SOPHIE is built upon an expert 'performance program', a general-purpose circuit simulation package. And again, as we would expect, the simulator is executed under the control of a sophisticated monitor so that it can do more than merely take measurements. It can be used, for example, to

(a) answer questions, not only about the given circuit but about a hypothetically modified one, e.g. 'If C2 is shorted, is the output voltage zero?', requiring the simulator to be invoked with a modified circuit model;

(b) evaluate student hypotheses, e.g. 'Is it possible that R9 is open?' The circuit model is modified to satisfy the hypothesis and all the student's measurements are repeated within this model: if the actual measurements agree with these hypothetical values the hypothesis is consistent;

(c) generate hypotheses in response to a student request for help. The system first produces a list of possible faults consistent with the output voltage and then prunes this list by eliminating all faults which when introduced into the circuit model contradict measurements that the student has made.

In its typical use SOPHIE provides what its authors like to call a 'reactive environment'. SOPHIE inserts a fault into a given (simulated) instrument, and it is the student's task to isolate the fault by requesting measurements under any desired instrument setting. It is assumed that the student has already been taught the necessary electronics. For this reason, student modelling in SOPHIE, as in most systems, is relatively straightforward, consisting mainly of a record of the measurements that the student has made and, to some extent, inferences which can be drawn from them. The SOPHIE system has no direct knowledge of what it is

168

trying to teach, i.e. trouble-shooting-skills, and consequently maintains no representation of the student's particular abilities SOPHIE is unable therefore to comment directly on these skills.

To return to the subject of communication, the SOPHIE dialogue of Figure 4.10, unrestrained though it is, lacks something of the character of a true tutorial dialogue. As the description of SOPHIE as a reactive environment implies, it is a system which aims only to respond to the student's inputs. It never takes the initiative, as indeed neither did the 'mixed-initiative' SCHOLAR system. As Figure 3.11 showed, the mixed-initiative character of SCHOLAR dialogues was based on the shallow strategy of allowing the student and the program to take turns (on the student's request) at asking questions about simple facts. SCHOLAR does not support a prolonged, purposeful dialogue gradually unravelling some shared problem.

More recently, Clancey (1979b) has redirected attention to dialogue management issues, i.e. issues that centre on the problem of carrying on a coherent dialogue with a student, issues such as:

How does a tutor select a presentation technique?

How does he ensure dialogue connectedness?

How does he maintain and share dialogue context?

How can he provide for and cope with student initiative?

Human dialogues exhibit some regularity in the form of patterns that encompass several turns of initiative. There are places where questions make sense, where explanations are expected, and so on. The problem is one of structuring a sequence of remarks into a 'discourse pattern', rather than replying on a single-question/single-answer basis as most computer tutors do. Clancey has tried to identify these patterns for case method dialogues, which GUIDON tries to support. Each such discourse pattern is represented by a procedure made up of one or more steps whose applicability is determined by so-called t-rules, expressed as production rules.[23] These procedures attempt to ensure smooth transitions between discourse situations, to make dialogues sensitive to a student's knowledge (by, for example, not belabouring topics he is thought to know), and to take advantage of situations as they arise for 'opportunistic tutoring' (by, for example, quizzing the student about a rule related to the one just discussed). Other components of the tutoring system, the performance and student modelling components, limit what dialogue management can achieve. For example, the GUIDON program cannot discuss a student's line of reasoning since, as we described previously, it does not attempt to understand it. As with most other programs, errors are corrected immediately. Also, MYCIN's methodical depth-first solution tends to lead to step-by-step discussions without conveying a unified sense of purpose.

Some thirty discourse procedures are defined by Clancey and, although he is careful to say that he is interested only in exemplifying strategies and not in advocating them, these procedures are worryingly complex. However, there may be some hope as Clancey concludes, somewhat enigmatically, that 'the most effective pruning of topics in the current version of the program is a result of the student's initiative. Perhaps it is not necessary or desirable for a program to attempt to manage the dialogue too severely; deciding what would be discussed is naturally a shared task.'

Summary

The desire to build an intelligent computer tutor will not be easily satisfied. It certainly will not be by following the principles behind most existing teaching programs. The fundamental difficulties lie in the fields of educational psychology, for we do not know enough about how students learn, and of artificial intelligence, for we must try to build computer programs able to use their expertise, to model students and to plan teaching strategies.

The snippets of student-computer dialogues shown in this chapter compare well with those obtainable from the carefully engineered branching programs written in an author language. But nothing can be done to improve the latter, while there are many intriguing possibilities for the intelligent computer tutors. For the impressiveness of the dialogues obtainable with systems like SOPHIE and GUIDON should not conceal the fact that at this stage of the game it is how the programs work that really matters.

Almost all the programs described in this chapter were written as part of research projects to investigate the problems and potential of advanced computer tutors. None of the programs is commercially available. Their importance lies not in the contribution they can make to computer-assisted learning now, but in the perspective they give us on tutorial programs that can be bought now and that might be buyable in the future. As research efforts, the programs have highlighted the following issues:

To what extent do we need to understand a student's reasoning processes to be able to help the student to modify them?
How can we induce a student's misconceptions from what he says and does?
How can human expertise be transferred to a student?
What is the nature of a tutorial dialogue?
How does a good tutorial take account of a student's interests and aptitudes?

These sorts of questions may serve to direct attention towards the study of complex behaviours more typical of learning situations than the conventional laboratory-type experiments.

The actual implementation of intelligent computer tutors remains problematic. By present-day standards, programs like SOPHIE and GUIDON are very large ones and therefore not easily made generally available. But this is only transiently so – to anticipate Chapter 7, computational power will soon be such a common resource that teaching programs running on the present breed of classroom microcomputers will seem puny. No, the main implementation problem lies, and will continue to lie, in writing the programs in the first place. GUIDON, for example, is the result of a PhD project based on the MYCIN work, itself a PhD project and influenced by experience on the design of expert systems which has been accumulated over twenty years. It is difficult to imagine the ordinary teacher being able to develop such programs. As a result, certainly in the short term, intelligent computer tutors will be built around existing performance programs like MYCIN, and will be designed to demonstrate and to allow experimentation with tutorial strategies.

Our discussion of computer tutors echoes the 'expository teaching versus discovery learning' controversy in educational philosophy. It is fairly straightforward to implement tutors to expound the facts in response to each and every student error but, not unreasonably, students do not take kindly to such programs. The aim, as yet unrealised, must be to give only the suggestions, hints and corrections that a skilful human tutor would give. Some indeed take exception to the whole 'teacher knows best' philosophy behind computer tutors, preferring instead approaches emphasising discovery learning environments described in the next chapter.

Notes

1. First by Siklossy (1970) and subsequently by most of the writers mentioned in this chapter.
2. We can outline how this may be done in Logo. First we can store simple facts as 'triples', i.e. as lists of three items:
    [CAPITAL BUENOS-AIRES ARGENTINA]
    [IN ARGENTINA SOUTH-AMERICA].
Then we can have a variable DATABASE which is a list of these triples. A procedure PRESENTQ can now be written which takes a triple as its input and which gives the result 'TRUE if that triple can be found in the DATABASE, 'FALSE if not. The next step is to modify PRESENTQ so that it works with 'patterns', i.e. triples containing variables as well as strings, e.g.
    [CAPITAL ?X ARGENTINA].
(We would need a different Logo interpreter because these variables require special treatment. The prefix ? is used here to signify such 'pattern variables'.) This pattern is said to 'match' the triple
    [CAPITAL BUENOS-AIRES ARGENTINA]
if the variable X has the value BUENOS-AIRES or if X has no value. In the latter case, the matching process will cause X to be given the value BUENOS-AIRES. PRESENTQ should return 'TRUE if its pattern input matches a triple in the DATABASE. Thus
    W: PRESENTQ [CAPITAL ?X ARGENTINA]
will, assuming DATABASE contains the two triples given above, return 'FALSE if X has a value other than BUENOS-AIRES, 'TRUE otherwise.
    This procedure (in our extended Logo)
    W: BUILD 'FIRSTISINSECONDQ
    FIRSTISINSECONDQ ?X ?Z
        1 IF PRESENTQ [IN ?X ?Z] THEN RESULT 'TRUE
        2 IF PRESENTQ [CAPITAL ?X ?Y] THEN
          IF PRESENTQ [IN ?Y ?Z] THEN RESULT 'TRUE
        3 RESULT 'FALSE
when called as in
    W: FIRSTISINSECONDQ BUENOS-AIRES SOUTH-AMERICA

will first search the DATABASE for
   [IN BUENOS-AIRES SOUTH-AMERICA]
and, if this is unsuccessful, will apply the rule of inference 'if x is the capital of y
and y is in z then x is in z' to return 'TRUE or 'FALSE as appropriate.
   Not all properties can be inherited in this way. Consider a more general
version of the above procedure:
   W: BUILD 'XISPZQ
   XISPZQ ?P ?X ?Z
      1 IF PRESENTQ [?P ?X ?Z] THEN RESULT 'TRUE
      2 IF PRESENTQ [CAPITAL ?X ?Y] THEN
         IF PRESENTQ [?P ?Y ?Z] THEN RESULT 'TRUE
      3 RESULT 'FALSE
This does not correspond to commonsense for some P. For example,
   W: XISPZQ BIGGER-THAN LONDON SCOTLAND
would return 'TRUE (signifying that 'London is bigger than Scotland') if the
DATABASE contained
   [CAPITAL LONDON ENGLAND]
   [BIGGER-THAN ENGLAND SCOTLAND]
We cannot therefore expect it to be easy to provide semantic networks, or any
other representation, with advanced inferential capabilities but it is clearly
possible in simple cases. The advantages that accrue, in economising on the
amount of information that needs to be stored and in providing the means to
answer a wider range of unanticipated questions, ensure that continuing efforts
will be made in this direction. (As we have said, the SCHOLAR database is not
in fact organised as a simple unordered list of triples but as a network. This is
basically so that the PRESENTQ procedure can find relevant triples without
having to search through all of them.)
3. The work of Quillian (1969) led to a spate of psycholinguistic research,
   described by Collins and Quillian (1969), Frijda (1972) and Anderson and
   Bower (1973).
4. Sleeman (1975) writes that the 'experts whom we interviewed appeared to
   perform very complex analogies [which] are often difficult to explain to others'.
   Knowledge acquisition, as it is now called, is seen to be an important part of the
   work of a knowledge engineer, i.e. someone engaged in building an expert
   system in consultation with a human expert (Feigenbaum, 1980).
5. For example, Goldberg (1974) for tutoring elementary mathematical logic;
   Grignetti, Hausmann and Gould (1975), how to use an editor (i.e. a program
   for changing the text of other programs); Smith and Blaine (1976), university
   mathematics; and programs discussed later in this chapter.
6. See Feigenbaum (1980) and n. 4, Chapter 2.
7. Figure 4.4 is only a small part of a typical GUIDON tutorial session. Clancey
   (1979b) includes a 43-page typescript of a four-hour session.
8. For example, Ojemann and Wilkinson (1939) and Thompson and Hunnicutt
   (1944).
9. The technique of learning by coefficient optimisation has a long tradition in

artificial intelligence. Samuel (1959) used it in a classic program which learnt to play draughts. The limitations of the technique are discussed by Minsky and Papert (1972).

10. The term 'overlay model' was first used by Carr and Goldstein (1977).

11. See Young (1980). Klahr and Wallace (1976) and Young (1976) used production systems to represent Piagetian theories of cognitive development. Newell and Simon (1972), in their seminal work on human problem solving, confessed 'to a strong premonition that the actual organization of human programs resembles the production system organization'.

12. Related work is described by Brown and Burton (1978). They used 'procedural networks' to represent knowledge underlying basic arithmetic skills and attempted to develop a program which could automatically construct a diagnostic model of a student from his correct and incorrect answers. Analysis of thousands of students' work has provided an extensive catalogue of systematic errors for subtraction. Present research aims to explain the generation of these bugs. The key assumption is that a student who reaches an impasse when following an incorrect procedure will invent a 'repair' in order to be able to continue to solve the problem (Brown and VanLehn, 1980).

13. Ruth's program used the program-proving method of symbolic execution, in which generalised assertions about the values of variables are calculated through the program. He also used a mathematical programming method to determine the equivalence of predicates and algebraic simplification to determine the equivalence of expressions. His experiment involved analysing programs to find the zeros of a given function using the binary search method or Newton's method.

14. An example of such a rule is: 'If the student gives as an explanation a factor that is not sufficient, give him a counter-example, i.e. one with the right value for the factor but which gives a different result.' For example, if a student gives water as the reason they grow rice in China, ask him if they grow rice in Ireland.

15. Similar techniques are represented by the 'curricula' of the BIP system of Barr, Beard and Atkinson (1976) (see Chapter 5) and the 'syllabi' of Goldstein (1979).

16. The difference between a theory of learning and a theory of instruction has been elaborated by Bruner (1966). The former is descriptive – it attempts to provide a theoretical or empirical description of the learning process; the latter is prescriptive – it attempts to prescribe the most effective methods to achieve some educational objective. Theories of instruction are concerned therefore with the specification of objectives and costs, and a desire for precision tends to make these rather simplistic, being expressed, for example, in terms of the student's ability to give correct answers to specific questions, and ignoring the wider aspects such as a society's culture and sense of values. Bruner's own theory is relatively wide-ranging. His emphasis on the structure of knowledge (rather than factual details), the constructive role of feedback and the predisposition of the student to learn is in sympathy with the views of Piaget. Ausubel (1968) has applied the same principle – that new ideas are learned only if they

can be subsumed under more general cognitive structures – to expository teaching to derive the idea of 'advance organisers'. These are special introductory statements intended to facilitate the learning of meaningful prose material by activating relevant parts of the student's cognitive structure and to provide a framework into which the new ideas can be incorporated. These theories can be re-expressed in artificial intelligence terms, but they are rather vague and give only working guidelines to the educational practitioner. They are not detailed enough to tell us exactly how teaching programs should be written.

17. The hill-climbing problem occurs with any system which attempts to reach some optimum or 'peak' by successive small improvements or 'steps': if it reaches the top of a ridge it cannot take the big leap necessary to get off onto the higher summit some distance away. The frame problem occurs when a system makes certain conclusions in one situation but then changes the situation and is unable to say whether the conclusions still hold.

18. Other studies of learner control in computer-assisted learning include Grubb (1968), Judd, Bunderson and Bessant (1970), Beard, Lorton, Searle and Atkinson (1973) and Hansen (1974).

19. While it is accepted that human communication relies upon the interpretation of visual and aural clues, it is wishful thinking to imagine a computer program being able to work with more than the words of typed input or the phonemes of spoken input (in the near future, anyway).

20. An amusing example appears in Taylor (1969), describing an application of the key word matching technique to teach elementary theoretical physics. In the dialogue given (presumably the most impressive obtained) all student inputs of more than two words are either ignored or have to be rephrased.

21. Brown, Burton and Bell (1974) give the following as the grammar of 'measurement':

> *measurement* = output *meas-quant* of *transformer*
> or *transformer meas-quant*
> or *meas-quant* between *node* and *node*
> or *meas-quant* of *part-spec*
> or *meas-quant* between output terminals
> or *meas-quant* of *junction*
> or *meas-quant* of *node*
> or *meas-quant* from *junction*
> or *junction-type meas-quant* of *transistor-spec*
> or *transistor-term-type meas-quant* of *transistor-spec*.

22. SOPHIE has since been rewritten to include a new inference scheme which 'mimics methods used by human electronics experts and therefore provides a better basis for tutorial assistance' (Brown, Burton and deKleer, 1982). The scheme uses general laws of electronics and a collection of schema based on the functional decomposition of the circuit.

175

23. One such t-rule is as follows:
    t-rule 15.02
      If:
      1) The factor is not the goal currently being discussed
      2) There are rules having a bearing on this goal that have succeeded
      3) There are rules having a bearing on this goal that have failed
      4) Ask: wants-details
      Then:
      1) Discuss the goal with the student in a goal-directed mode (Proc 001)
      2) Say that the dialogue is returning to discussion of the goal currently being discussed.

This is a relatively clean production rule (note however that it is not of course expressed in this form, i.e. English, to the GUIDON system but in a special production system language): many of the other t-rules break the production system 'code of ethics', using loops, GOs and other programming constructions.

5. COMPUTER AS TOOL

'My mother doesn't like computers. She thinks they're boring.'
'Are they boring?'
'Not when I'm doing it.'

(from the report of the Logo project
in the Brookline public schools,
Papert *et al.* (1979)).

The proponents of the application of artificial intelligence research
to education divide into a reformist faction and a revolutionary
faction. The reformists look for a gradual improvement in the
quality of education by constructing intelligent computer tutors of
the type discussed in the previous chapter. They are interested in
the problems of using computers in conventional educational contexts, but at the same time utter polemics against those who produce 'stupid' computer-assisted learning. They use artificial intelligence work as a benchmark against which to assess computer-
assisted learning.

The revolutionaries believe that the computational means of
education should be put directly in the hands of the students. They
start from the same major premise as the reformists, namely, that
programming languages can provide excellent ways of expressing
both declarative and procedural knowledge and both teaching and
learning processes. They then continue to argue that the student
himself should use computer programming languages as a means of
expressing and developing his own understanding. Once students
are able to do this, they then become liberated from the tyranny of
a mass educational system with its national syllabuses and examina-
tions, and its unadaptive teachers demanding that groups of thirty
or forty children together in a classroom exhibit the outward forms

of learning. The most elegant expression of this revolutionary philosophy can be found in Papert (1980).

In this chapter we shall consider in detail some implementations of the revolutionary rhetoric. The revolutionary position has been discussed briefly in the context of problem-solving in Chapter 3. The main claim is that the learner can express his own problem-solving strategy as a computer program and then 'stand back' and watch himself, as embodied in the computer program, solve problems. Having stood back he can then reflect on his way of doing things and remove faulty methods and improve components of his strategy. In general, then, there is an emphasis on the process (rather than the product) of problem-solving, and an aversion to the 'right or wrong' model of learning prevalent in schools.

The problem-solving techniques appropriate to programming, such as planning, debugging and problem decomposition using procedures, are generally useful ones which, once learnt in the context of programming, may change the way all other learning takes place. Moreover, these techniques are exercised almost independently of the particular programming project involved.

Revolutionaries follow Piaget in seeing learners as builders of their own intellectual structures. Programming languages and the computer culture generally are merely new, but powerful, materials with which to build. Adopting the 'learning without being taught' paradigm, exemplified by the way children learn to speak, revolutionaries foresee a time when the computer culture will be so pervasive that the learning environment outside classrooms will be so modified that most if not all learning will take place without organised teaching.

Before looking at existing demonstrations let us consider the obvious objections to this approach to education:

1. Computers are too expensive to be available for programming by individual students;
2. Programming languages are too hard for young students to learn;
3. Programming languages do not provide good ways of expressing problem-solving strategies;
4. Uncoordinated activity by individual students will be impossible to assess by educational institutions.

The first objection is losing credibility month by month. Papert's old claim that 'if every child had a computer, computers would be cheap enough for every child to have a computer' (Papert, 1973) is now quickly coming true. The persistence of the second view, that programming is a complex skill, is remarkable. There are a number of examples, some of which will be detailed later in this chapter, of young, average ability children learning to use programming languages. The third objection is an important one. Programming languages do vary significantly with respect to what can easily be expressed in them, and we shall argue that one weakness of the revolutionaries' argument has been their failure to specify clearly those domains for which the language they are championing is particularly suitable. The last objection is grand. An educational innovator ought to worry if the existing institutions did *not* start bleating about their impending loss of control over their learners. So in this chapter we shall concentrate on two questions when considering computers as tools for learning. First, is the computer tool learnable? Secondly, to what range of learning activities can the tool be applied?

Learning programming

The aim of this section is to consider what can be done to enable students to learn how to program. We are concerned with general programming concepts rather than a particular programming language (although it will be necessary to comment on how the latter may obstruct the former).

In Chapter 4 we described two computer tutors for programming (Ruth, 1976; Koffman and Blount, 1975), neither of which is in regular use. However, a similar system, called BIP, provides a fully self-contained course in BASIC programming for undergraduates at Stanford University (Barr, Beard and Atkinson, 1976). The BIP system includes:

1. A BASIC interpreter much extended in comparison with standard BASIC systems to give, for example, additional help with syntax errors (this interpreter is written in SAIL, the

Stanford artificial intelligence language);
2. A set of problem-solving aids to give hints, traces and flow diagrams and to check solutions (intended to give tutorial assistance without a thorough analysis of programs);
3. A curriculum of about 100 problems with varying levels of difficulty;
4. A student model which is expressed in terms of the acquisition of fundamental skills, which enables individualised problem selection;
5. A reference manual on BASIC syntax.

An example dialogue with BIP is shown in Figure 5.1.

Figure 5.1 *A dialogue with BIP* (from Barr, Beard and Atkinson, 1976)

[The student has been asked to write a program that computes and prints the number of gifts sent on the twelfth day of Christmas.]
Hint
This program requires a loop. Each execution of the loop involves accumulating the value of the index into a total.
Hint
Finding a total or sum almost always means two things:
1. Setting a variable equal to zero outside a loop.
2. Accumulating values into that variable within the loop. In words, total equals old total plus another value.
Sub
[To ask for a subtask]
Begin task :s:forloop
Write a program with a little – for..next – loop.
The work of the loop is just to print the value of the loop's index (the variable that keeps track of the number of times the loop has been executed).
When you run the program, it should look like it is counting from 1 to 10.
10 Let I = 1

20 Print "The index is; I
Syntax error: unmatched quote marks – found near "The index is
Line not accepted (type ? for help)
?
' "The index is' has an odd number of quote marks.
Remember that all strings must have a quote at the beginning and
end.

.

.

[After some time the student manages to type the following pro-
gram]
10 For I = 1 to 9
20 Print I
99 End
Run
Error Doctor diagnosis: 'for' statement without matching 'next'.
Look at line number: 10
[BIP checks the structure of complete programs before they are
run, so that such errors do not appear as less informative execution
time errors.]

.

.

30 Next I

.

.

Your program doesn't seem to solve the problem.
[Because it does not give the same output as a model solution]
Demo
[The student asks for a demonstration of the required output,
corrects his program, runs it and is told that it 'looks ok'. He is then
shown a model solution and led through a 'post-task interview'.]

.

.

.

Returning from a subtask.
You are in task Xmas.

.

.

.

While such an approach does recognise that programming is better learned through experience than through direct teaching, we should be uneasy about it for two reasons. First, BIP's multiplicity of roles, as tutor, interpreter, editor and commentator, can lead to difficulties for the novice who must keep in mind with which of these notional machines he is dealing. Secondly, the BASIC language itself is inappropriate.

Quality in programming language design is one of the central concerns of computer science and a detailed survey is not possible here. However, computer programming language theorists are unanimous that BASIC has serious flaws. BASIC was designed in 1964 to enable arts undergraduates to write simple programs. It happened to be the easiest language to provide on microcomputers when they arrived in about 1975. To microcomputer enthusiasts, BASIC thus became synonymous with programming and, as Papert (1980) describes, by a social process of myth construction became ideal for various activities such as teaching children programming and developing large-scale application programs for which it was never intended.

Du Boulay, O'Shea and Monk (1981) identify 'simplicity' and 'visibility' as two important characteristics of programming languages for novices. The language should be syntactically simple, that is the rules defining the language should be uniform, with few special cases to remember, and without potential ambiguities (as in BASIC's use of the = symbol to do a variety of different jobs including assigning values to variables and testing for equality). The language should provide constructions to aid the expression of problem-solving strategies. BASIC's lack of such constructs encourages contortions which soon render a program incomprehensible, and the language has an impoverished mechanism for

182

defining procedures, upon which the problem decomposition strategy relies.

The Logo language can be regarded as the interactive teaching version of the artificial intelligence programming language LISP in much the same way as BASIC is the interactive teaching version of the scientific language Fortran. Like LISP, Logo requires programmers to create procedures to carry out tasks or solve problems. These procedures are defined in terms of procedures provided in Logo or already created by the programmer. Once defined, a procedure is used as a 'building block' just like the initial procedures of Logo. This makes Logo a natural way of expressing procedural knowledge and programming style follows the problem decomposition strategy. An appropriate linguistic metaphor is to compare Logo programming to teaching the computer the meaning of new words.

A second aspect of simplicity is what du Boulay *et al.* call 'logical simplicity', which implies that problems of interest to the novice can be tackled by simple programs. In Logo, this is achieved by the 'turtle geometry', through which spectacular effects can be achieved with the minimum of effort. The beginner learning Logo has a straightforward meaning that he can attach to each individual procedure, namely, a picture. But more important than this the learner can also 'act out' the execution of his Logo program because he can associate each FORWARD or RIGHT in his program with an action he can physically carry out while playing turtle. It is not necessary to look over a child's shoulder to determine whether he is programming in BASIC or Logo – it is enough to look at his back. The Logo programmer will be moving his shoulders left and right as he thinks through the execution of his program. Of course, it is possible to write BASIC programs to produce drawings, but this will usually demand knowledge of the Cartesian coordinate system.[1] However, more importantly, such programs cannot be used in the same flexible way as subcomponents of new programs that Logo procedures can.

So, Logo is a more powerful language than BASIC in that complex, abstract constructs can be expressed more parsimoniously and elegantly. It is generally assumed that the more powerful a programming language is, the harder it is to learn. In fact there is no evidence for this, and our own view is that the crucial factor that affects ease of learning is the visibility of the language, that is, the extent to which a novice can 'see the works' of the language. One of the difficulties of teaching a novice how to program is to describe, at the right level of detail, the machine he is learning to control. Novices are usually ignorant about what the machine can be instructed to do, and about how it manages to do it. Basing one's teaching on the idea of a notional machine is an effective strategy for tackling this difficulty. The notional machine is an idealised, conceptual computer whose properties are implied by the constructs of the programming language. The notional machine should be simple, that is, it should consist of a small number of parts that interact in ways that can be easily understood, possibly by analogy to other mechanisms with which the novice is more familiar. Visibility is concerned with methods for viewing selected parts and processes of this notional machine in action. To illustrate this idea we shall now describe some methods that have been used to help students learn Logo.

The button box introduced in Chapter 1 implies a particularly simple notional machine upon which can be built an understanding of the complete Logo system. The elimination of the possibility of making spelling or syntax errors means that (almost) any sequence of button presses will produce some sort of drawing, increasing the effect/frustration ratio for young children. Perlman (1976) describes a 'slot machine' which has been used successfully with children as young as four. The slot machine (see Figure 5.2) consists of several coloured boxes with slots. Each box represents a procedure, and programs are constructed by placing cards in the slots. The cards are marked with visible symbols (to be read by the child) for particular commands, and carry punched holes to be read by the machine. A coloured card represents a call of the procedure of that colour. Pressing the button on a box causes the commands on the cards in that box to be executed in order, for example pressing the blue button in the slot machine shown will draw a square and toot. Again, placing cards randomly will produce some drawing and in fact the ease of so doing is 'almost a drawback', according to Perlman, for children will not thereby be forced to

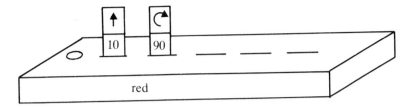

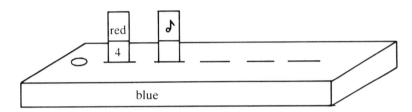

Figure 5.2   *Perlman's slot machine*

acquire concepts like sub-procedures. It is important therefore to move the novice on to a fuller Logo system once he has mastered the computing concepts which the button box or slot machine introduces.

As Mayer (1981) describes, one technique for helping novices understand new technical information is to provide a 'concrete model', a framework that can be used for incorporating new information. In mathematics, for example, manipulatives, such as coins or blocks, are used in order to make computational procedures more concrete (Resnick and Ford, 1981). The button box and slot machines are similar manipulatives. For teaching Logo to children, Howe, O'Shea and Plane (1980) introduced a 'notional machine', a simplified description of the language's operation within the computer. Its purpose was to provide a descriptive model as a context for introducing programming concepts, for interpreting the machine's responses, and for establishing a small vocabulary for teaching about programs.

Logo programming was then taught by means of a self-paced set of worksheets which introduced computational ideas, problem-solving tactics and debugging skills (du Boulay and O'Shea, 1976). These worksheets made much use of analogy, for example a procedure 'is like a worker who knows how to do a particular job and will execute that job when commanded to by having his name called'.

The use of such educationally conventional worksheets by the Edinburgh Logo project is somewhat at odds with the philosophy held by the MIT Logo workers of encouraging learning by discovery. The MIT Brookline project (Papert *et al.*, 1979) adopted a less structured approach. First, it was emphasised that there is more to programming than learning a particular language: children have to learn to feel comfortable with a computer, to absorb the 'computer culture', if you like; to learn the subject matter of turtle geometry in the case of Logo; to learn problem-solving and debugging skills. Secondly, each child's work was different, so as the classes continued, the teacher guided the children by suggesting projects based on their interests and abilities. Children were encouraged to borrow each other's procedures and to discuss their work. No attempt was made to ensure that all children covered the same material. There is no question that the MIT approach is superior to the Edinburgh teaching method if an appropriate ratio of skilled teachers to learners can be achieved. However, given the economic constraints on teacher provision in state schools in most countries, it is necessary to adopt worksheets or some other form of systematic support for learners if Logo is to be successfully used in the classroom.

The most impressive current use of Logo with young pupils is that to be found in the Lamplighter school in Dallas, Texas. This lavishly equipped private school has some 400 pupils and about 100 microcomputers manufactured by Texas Instruments. The version of Logo implemented on these microcomputers has colour and 'sprites' which can be used for animation and simple cartoons. Sprites can be thought of as turtles which move at a fixed speed and in a fixed direction (both of which can be altered) and carry on their backs a Logo drawing. The typical use that a 7-year-old makes of this Logo system is to create drawings of complicated vehicles or spaceships and then cause them to be moved by sprites across the screen. Talking to the young programmers one is impressed by their ease with the computer keyboard and the way they exchange technical information, for example, 'Tell sprite 32 to go forward 5 and a system bug will make the background change colour'. One is also struck by the typical Lamplighter scene of a 6-year-old teaching a pair of 5-year-olds how to use the space bar on the keyboard, or alternatively how to 'crash the system' using control characters. This scene of course reveals the communication of specific technical magic. In fact the authors have often been disappointed (in Boston, Dallas, Palo Alto and Edinburgh, for example) when discussing computer programs with pupils to find jargon prevailing over the expression of general problem-solving skills.

However there is no doubt that the large majority of Lamplighter pupils enjoy using Logo. Even more impressive is the fact that the teachers at Lamplighter have succeeded in creating Logo programs which can be used by very young(3-5-year-old) children. These programs involve using the computer keyboard as if it were the button box described above. One program lets the pupils construct coloured pictures piece by piece, another allows the pupils to alter the speeds of any one of a collection of coloured trucks that are moving across the screen. The child who uses these programs receives practice in keyboard skills and reading. At the same time he becomes familiar with the use of simple Logo programs. It will be interesting to see the Logo programs that future Lamplighter pupils create, and to hear how they are described. At present the ease of use of the computing medium demonstrated by the pupils is pleasing, but it is difficult to remain interested in the many different configurations and types of battleships which may be made to sail across the computer screen. The Lamplighter experiment does demonstrate that an important change takes place when the ratio of pupils to computers approaches one to one, and that the rudiments of Logo are easily learnable (and teachable) by very young pupils.

Learning mathematics via Logo

Programming is not (yet) a self-sufficient academic subject, and advocates of teaching programming have often justified their cause by emphasising the contribution programming might make to understanding other subjects, especially mathematics. Logo itself was first presented as 'a conceptual framework for teaching mathematics' (Feurzeig *et al.*, 1969). Mathematics is either very difficult, or else the educational system makes it appear so, judging by the high proportion of adults who remain mathematically illiterate. Before giving general reasons for hoping that Logo and other languages might help overcome the problem let us look at a vignette of Logo being used in the classroom.

Two pupils with one year's Logo experience are attempting to write a program that generates the series 1, 2, 3, 5, 8, 13, 21, 34, . . .(the fibonacci series). They search through the Logo programs they have stored in previous weeks but none of these seems useful. They ask some other pupils using other Logo computers in the classroom for help. One of their friends offers them a program he has written that takes a single number, doubles it, doubles that, etc. and continues forever. They take this and adapt it so that instead of taking one number it takes two. But the behaviour of the program does not change and it just keeps doubling the first number. After half an hour's experimentation there is great excitement. They have successfully modified their friend's Logo program so that it seems to work. They try it out with various starting pairs of numbers and call their friend across. They create a wallchart for the classroom that explains the way their new program works (Figure 5.3). They are determined to use their own name 'asterix' for the program. They resist the teacher's idea that they use the name 'Fibseries' that is suggested by the Logo worksheet they have been using. They clearly think that he is silly to believe that his name for their program would be better than theirs for helping them to remember what their program does.

Now let us offer some general comments about Logo as a learning environment:

1. There is no sense in which the Logo programming language can

be said to instruct. It does what pupils tell it to and when, for example a program intended to draw a house and named House fails to draw a house it does not tell the pupils they have made a mistake because it has no view about their intentions. This allows the learner to attach the values he wants to the results of running his programs and he is able to both enjoy and learn from his mistakes.

2. In some ways Logo is just a well-designed piece of classroom apparatus in that the pupil can easily see the result of his programming experiment.

3. Since the pupil can use the computer to remember the programs he has created they become his personal intellectual property to be re-used or given to friends. Pupils tend to work co-operatively on the design and testing of programs.

4. Logo is especially well-designed to give the learner visual experiences related to mathematical ideas. The clumsy term 'visual experience' rather than 'drawing' emphasises something

```
w:TO ASTERIX :NUM1 :NUM2
d:1 PRINT SUM :NUM1 :NUM2
d:2 ASTERIX SUM :NUM1 :NUM2 :NUM1
d:END
asterix defined
ASTERIX 2 1
3
5
8
13
21
34
55
etc.
```

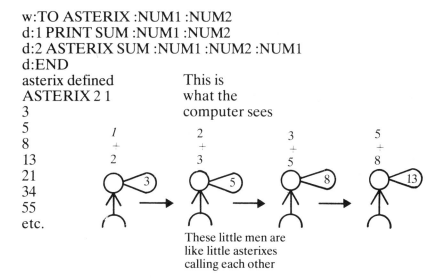

This is
what the
computer sees

These little men are
like little asterixes
calling each other

Figure 5.3   *The Asterix procedure* (written in a Logo dialect different from the one we have used)

difficult to convey in writing. When a Logo program draws a house it does it step by step so that the learner can relate these to the components of the program. In general, Logo programs generate sequences of drawings rather like cartoons.

5. Watching a program tackle a problem can be a powerful source of insight for a pupil when the program is a statement of how *he* solves that problem.

6. Programming can provide metaphors for mathematical concepts, for example, the Asterix program can be used as a metaphor for the concept of a function with arguments.

Figure 5.4   *A worksheet on adding positive and negative numbers*

To get the procedures you will need to use in this note type the following:

W: LIBRARY "FRAN "ALLNUML

You will also need to connect to a drawing device.

In this note we shall represent numbers by using half circles. A right-hand half circle ⊃ will stand for a positive unit and a left-hand half circle ⊂ for a negative unit.

So 4 will be represented by: ⊃⊃⊃⊃

and −3 will be represented by: ⊂⊂⊂

To draw a picture which represents addition we use the procedure ADDALL.

This needs two inputs, the two numbers we want to add.

EXERCISE 1: Use ADDALL to add two positive numbers.

Type in:

W: ADDALL 3 4

You will see that the answer is given as seven right-hand half circles which represent the positive number 7.

$3 + 4 = 7$

EXERCISE 2: Now use ADDALL to add two negative numbers.

W: ADDALL −3 −4

$(-3) + (-4) = -$

So adding two positive or two negative numbers is straightforward. When we want to add a positive to a negative number we shall need to use another symbol O. This represents the addition of a positive unit ⊃ and a negative unit ⊂. It also represents nought as this is the result we get when we add +1 and −1.

EXERCISE 3: Type in:
    W: ADDALL 1 −1
    1 + (−1) = —
    W:ADDALL −3 3
    (−3) + 3 = —

So each time we can match up a positive unit with a negative unit in our addition picture they 'cancel out' giving nought as the result. The symbol O means the same as nothing drawn on the picture.

EXERCISE 4: Type in:
    W: ADDALL 4 −3

You will see that three of the positive units combine with the three negative units to form three noughts. This leaves one positive unit.
So   4 + (−3) = 1

EXERCISE 5: Type in the following and fill in the answers.
    W: ADDALL −5 2
    (−5) + 2 = —
    W: ADDALL 7 −5
    7 + (−5) = —
    W: ADDALL −3 6
    (−3) + 6 = —

EXERCISE 6: Use the procedure ADDALL to help you find the answers to the following:
    1. (−4) +(−5) = —
    2. 6 + (−7) = —
    3. (−8) + 3 = —
    4. 5 + (−6) = —
    5. (−2) + 7 = —

PROBLEM
    Could we have used the symbol ⊂ to represent a positive unit and ⊃ to represent a negative unit?   YES/NO

What aspects of mathematics can Logo programming help the learner understand? The Edinburgh Logo project developed sets of worksheets (similar to the programming worksheets) for the mathematical topics presenting particular difficulty for a class of

11-12-year-olds. Some deal with particular topics, such as co-ordinate systems, equations and ratios; others deal with more general concepts, such as variables or the distributive law: an example is shown in Figure 5.4 above. Many of the worksheets require use of pre-written Logo procedures which can generate simple visual demonstrations of the concepts 'in action'.

Our description of these worksheets may suggest that the Edinburgh Logo sessions are rather more regimented than is in fact the case. Scope and encouragement is given to more open-ended experimentation. For example, pupils working through the worksheet shown quickly turn it into a game where they devise 'hard' arithmetic for the computer to carry out and then predict what they will see drawn. Without noticing they start predicting the result of the arithmetic rather than the drawing they will see. Another example is that of the boy whose house turned out to be the envelope shown in Figure 5.5. After correcting the house bug, he resurrected the envelope procedure and used it in a procedure to draw the Maltese cross shown.

The evaluation of the Edinburgh project concluded that Logo programming can contribute to the overall learning of school geometry and some specific concepts in school algebra (Howe, O'Shea and Plane, 1980). But Logo work may contribute more to under-

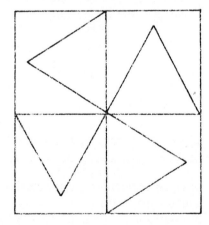

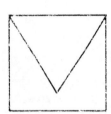

Figure 5.5   *The Maltese cross*

192

standing fundamental mathematical concepts which are not in-cluded in present syllabuses. The turtle trap in Chapter 3 intro-duced the idea of a *state*, a description of relevant aspects of a changing situation, fundamental to many sciences. The input to a procedure (for example, our shell procedure in Chapter 1) cor-responds to the concept of a *variable*, the idea of using a symbol to name an unknown entity, and illustrates how effects can be con-trolled by a *control variable*. Turtle geometry is a 'differential geometry', that is, movements are relative to where the turtle is now (as in the circle procedure of Note 1). It thus captures the essence of the *differential equation*, the basis of much applied mathematics and physics. The turtle trap program, and others to be discussed in the next section, illustrate the concept of *feedback*, how mechanisms can adapt their behaviour in response to external stimuli. And, as we have seen, programming may help the develop-ment of problem-solving skills, such as the 'divide and conquer' technique and the idea of debugging.

To return to school mathematics, it is also clear that some of it does not marry well with Logo. Much schoolwork involves the recall of particular algorithms, e.g. long division, rather than creative problem-solving. Many of these algorithms depend on physical layout on the paper: writing a program that will do the layout is very difficult and not relevant to an improved under-standing of the algorithm. Another example of the way program-ming may obstruct understanding is given by du Boulay (1981). Students studying the topic of fractions began by trying to repre-sent fractions as pie-charts but they had such difficulty constructing the drawings that they never got to grips with fractions themselves. Even when given procedures to do the drawings, the task of interpreting the drawings proved too hard. This demonstrates that the choice of representation needs to be made with great care. There are undoubtedly some kinds of knowledge the representa-tion of which in Logo would be extremely clumsy. The procedural bias of Logo does not lend itself to the creation and manipulation of passive structures expressing declarative knowledge, such as data-bases or mathematical facts. For example, a pupil may know that the prime factors of 15 are 5 and 3. This fact can be used during a variety of arithmetical tasks. But in the pupil's Logo procedures it will be necessary to compute (and probably be prepared to recompute) these factors. The Logo procedure that decomposes all numbers into prime factors is non-trivial and requires repeated division by successive prime numbers. But the pupil may well know the prime factors of most of the numbers he routinely encounters. So Logo does not match well with one aspect of many children's mathematical skill. We may conclude that the Logo language has already provided evidence of the contribution of programming to mathematical learning but that it is not the 'ultimate' educational programming language. In fact we should expect that just as every so often there is some new advance in mathematical notation making different mathematical ideas easier to express (and teach or learn), so, perhaps every decade, we shall see some new advance in programming language design.

Learning other subjects via programming

The aim of this section is to show how the computational perspective can enrich traditional curricula other than mathematics. In particular, we shall describe a sampling of projects in biology, writing, music and history.

How does an animal find food? Obviously, it uses its senses, but can we be more precise? Exactly what information does the animal use, and how is it used? Abelson and his colleagues (Abelson and Goldenberg, 1977; Abelson and di Sessa, 1981) have used Logo programming to provide insights into these questions.

First, let us consider the sense of touch. How can our turtle be programmed to follow a wall? In Chapter 3 we gave a procedure for doing this:

```
CRAWLROUND
    1 IF LEFT TOUCHINGQ THEN RIGHT 1 ELSE LEFT 1
    2 FORWARD 1
    3 CRAWLROUND
```

If the turtle feels a wall to its left it veers away a little, otherwise it turns back a little to avoid wandering too far from the wall. This procedure works for any shape of wall. The feedback that the turtle receives via its sensors enables it continually to correct its path as it moves along.

The sense of smell is more subtle. A turtle could be programmed in different ways to find food 'by sense of smell'. One possibility is to assume that smell gives no information about direction or distance but that at each move the turtle can detect whether the smell is getting stronger or weaker. Then the turtle could keep going forward while the smell is getting stronger, otherwise it turns:

```
SMELL
    1 IF NEARERQ THEN RESULT 'STRONGER
    ELSE RESULT 'WEAKER

FINDBYSMELL 'TURN
    1 FORWARD 1
    2 IF EQUALQ SMELL 'WEAKER
    THEN RIGHT :TURN
```

Figure 5.6 shows how the path varies for different turn angles: a more realistic simulation would also include some random motion. A student could now compare these paths (and any from other 'smell' procedures) with those followed by actual (sightless) animals.

If we ignore colour, texture and shape, the main difference between sight and smell is that the former is directional. It is easy to get the turtle to face a point and go forward. A variation is to have

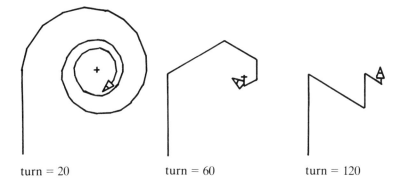

turn = 20   turn = 60   turn = 120

Figure 5.6 *Paths generated by FINDBYSMELL* (from Abelson and di Sessa, 1981)

195

the turtle keep a fixed bearing on the point:

```
FINDBYSIGHT 'POINT 'ANGLE
    1 FACE :POINT
    2 LEFT :ANGLE
    3 FORWARD 1
    4 FINDBYSIGHT :POINT :ANGLE
```

This causes the turtle to spiral about the point (like a moth trapped by a light[2]). Other embellishments are to model predator-prey situations (i.e. to allow the point to move), to model two-eyed vision, and to take account of the intensity of the light received (Abelson and di Sessa, 1981).

That all this would be fun hardly needs saying, but there is a serious backcloth. The student is learning what it means to investigate a phenomenon by making a model of it. He is not using a pre-programmed simulation package: the models, the Logo procedures, are developed by him and can be used to carry out meaningful scientific investigations. This kind of material has been used with high school and undergraduate students at the Massachusetts Institute of Technology.

Turning now to the subject of the English language, we are reminded by Donaldson (1978) that a child 'is not much given to thinking about his thinking or his language. Yet if he is to bring thinking and language under deliberate control he has to become more aware of them.' We have seen that computational ideas might illuminate thinking – might they also illuminate language? Sharples (1981) describes a series of programs for use with children aged about eleven, including a random word generator (which demonstrates that sentences are more than a random sequence of words), a context-free generative system (which clarifies the role of parts of speech but produces sentences which, though well-formed, are often meaningless), and a word game in which the pupil had to try to use words unknown by the program. These programs could be executed 'by hand', which reinforces the idea that language use is a process: the computer's role is merely to improve efficiency and to capture the imagination. The programs were written in Logo, but subsequently rewritten in POP-2, a more powerful language for artificial intelligence research. The pupils did not write the programs, but used them.

196

The programming metaphor comes into its own when we consider creative writing. The stages of planning, draft writing and revising (or debugging) are the same for writing and programming. The teaching of writing has undergone something of a revolution in recent years, with much less emphasis on the mechanics of spelling, punctuation and traditional parsing. Rubin (1980) and Sharples (1981) both describe programs which help students exercise the higher-level skills in writing (see Figure 5.7). Rubin's 'storymaker' presents the student with a part of a story and offers a number of possible continuations. For each choice of continuation a new set of possible continuations is presented. As with the button box, this releases the students from problems of typing and punctuation to higher-level problems – in this case, to questions about the flow of the narrative. Variations on the basic storymaker are to ask for a story to meet a particular description, e.g. a sad story; to ask

a) Part of a story tree. The child generates a story by choosing one branch at each node.

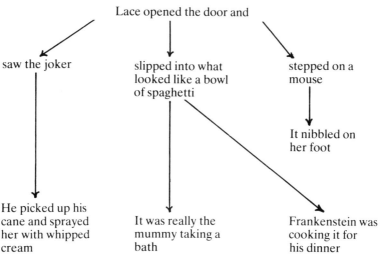

b) Part of a story.

Lace opened the door and slipped into what looked like a bowl of spaghetti. Frankenstein was cooking it for his dinner.

Figure 5.7 *Storymaker*

197

children to create a sensible ordering or structure of given parts of a storymaker; to ask children to create the parts of a storymaker as well.

We may conclude that the role of Logo programming has vanished. Certainly, Logo itself has vanished in this work, but given Logo's limitations this is no surprise. However, the students *are* programming: they are involved in making deliberate decisions in the process of story production. Just as the Logo environment provides a resource for exploring mathematical ideas especially, so the work described above provides a resource, admittedly less well-developed, for exploring linguistic ideas.

The inspirational role of programming can also be seen in attempts to provide resources to support learning in music. There are many applications of computers to music teaching, including programmed learning and microcomputer-based sound generation[3] but we shall concentrate on those which attempt to enable students to experience higher-level skills such as composition, by-passing the lower-level ones, such as playing an instrument, writing notes, etc. There are now several 'music editor' systems which make it easy for a student to enter notes, hear them, change them, and thus compose.

Bamberger (1974, 1979) describes an early attempt to clarify the nature of musical knowledge. Working within the Logo laboratory, she tried to help students

learn to bring to the surface those 'invisible' ideas inherent in what they can *do* – like clapping a rhythm or singing a tune. In this way they learn to bridge the gap between intuitive knowledge and powerful representations of this knowledge which will lead them to new knowledge.

The computer's role is to enable students to explore their own intuitive knowledge. Bamberger describes a simple game in which the student is given a small set of 'tune blocks', i.e. brief motifs, and asked to arrange them to make up a pleasing tune. The student specifies the tune by typing the block numbers and the computer generates the music. (This game is thus analogous to the storymaker game, a motif corresponding to a part of a story.) The students adopted different strategies and produced melodies which were met with astonishment by the rest of the students, causing

198

each to reflect on his own composing style. Bamberger goes on to develop higher-level representations of music which, by expanding the student's perception, lead the student to more complex compositions and a greater awareness of the nature of musical invention.

The common theme of these three projects (and of other discussions of 'non-academic' learning, e.g. juggling (Papert, 1980) and skiing (Fischer, 1981)) is the adoption of a programming metaphor, and the recognition of the importance of high-level representations of knowledge to provide resources which enable students to explore skills which would be otherwise difficult to get to grips with.

Logo, as we described in the previous section, is not ideal for expressing declarative knowledge. One outcome of the procedural-declarative controversy (mentioned in Chapter 2) has been the development of 'logic programming', in particular the language PROLOG (Clocksin and Mellish, 1981), which is essentially a notation for predicate logic. In PROLOG, the programmer may state facts, e.g.

> Henry-VIII father-of Mary

and rules of inference, e.g.

> x parent-of y if x father-of y

He may then ask questions:

> Which (x x parent-of Mary)
> Answer is Henry-VIII
> No (more) answers

A rule of inference thus doubles as a description of what it means, in this case to be a parent, and as an instruction as to how to answer questions about parenthood. It is relatively easy in PROLOG to set up databases of facts and rules for interrogation by a student. In one sense, the student is using PROLOG as an information retrieval query language; in another sense, he is writing programs in a 'non-procedural' programming language. The merits of teaching logic to children using PROLOG and its application to history teaching are being investigated in a project based at Imperial College, London (Ennals, 1982). For example, a census has been transcribed into PROLOG (cf the Micro-QUERY project mentioned in Chapter 3):

(Belvedere House) person ((Henry Holland) Head M 47
Male
(Linen Manufacturer and Merchant) (Dorking Surrey))
to be interrogated by questions like:
   Which ((x y) x sex F and x age z and 40 less z and x job y).
The extent to which students actually have questions they want
answered and are able to express in PROLOG remains to be
determined.

The Smalltalk philosophy

If programming is to be a potent force in education we should be as
clear as we can about just what programming is. It is deceptively
easy to write short programs in almost any language: writing large
programs and designing good languages, however, demands considerable skill and knowledge. Any programming language is a
system for communicating with a computer, and again it is easy to
allow the properties of present (or older) computers to influence
our conceptions of the nature of programming. Some fifteen years
ago (well before the first commercially-available microcomputers),
the Learning Research Group at Xerox Palo Alto Research Center
began dreaming about 'a personal dynamic medium the size of a
notebook (the Dynabook) which could be owned by everyone and
could have the power to handle virtually all of its owner's infor-
mation-related needs' (Kay and Goldberg, 1977). The Dynabook
would, of course, be active, that is, able to respond to questions; it
would have enough capacity to store anything the user would like
to remember; it would have high-quality visual and audio output;
and it would have sufficient power to respond instantly. The
Dynabook did not and does not exist. However, a series of 'interim
Dynabooks' have allowed Xerox to investigate the possibilities of
such a medium.
   The hardware details are less important than the vision, which
has inspired the design of a series of software systems with the
generic name of Smalltalk. Smalltalk should be 'simpler and more
powerful than (say) Logo and better than the best state-of-the-art

"grown-up" programming languages for serious system design' (Learning Research Group, 1976). The Smalltalk language is based upon the single metaphor of communicating objects. Every element in the system is represented as an 'object', and every object communicates with other objects by 'sending messages'. We shall sketch a simple example to give the flavour of Smalltalk – for details of the language see Goldberg, Robson and Ingalls (1982).

Imagine that you wanted to write a simulation of a game of billiards. In Logo and most other languages you would probably attempt to write procedures describing how balls move over the table and bounce off other balls and cushions. Each procedure would be called by giving inputs specifying coordinates, velocity, etc. That is, a distinction is drawn between inputs, representing the information to be manipulated, and procedures, representing how to manipulate information. This is a distinction which the Smalltalk designers believe to be not only unnecessary but unsound. Instead, in Smalltalk there is only one type of entity, the 'object', which is both a package of information and a description of its manipulation. So our billiards simulation might proceed by defining an object 'billiard ball' by defining its state (which would include location, velocity, acceleration, colour, weight, etc.), and 'methods' by which its state could be changed (i.e. by moving for say 0.1 seconds without collision, and bouncing off a ball or cushion). Each method naturally has to be defined: for example, moving might involve first, compute the likely location in 0.1 seconds; second, ask all balls and cushions if they are in this position; third, if no then move there; four, if yes then bounce. This bounce is a 'message' sent to the object 'ball' specifying the manipulation to be carried out. The object receiving a message decides what to do with it. A method is therefore like a procedure, except that it cannot directly call another method, it can only send a message. Of course, as we explained in Chapter 1, Smalltalk does not enable the programmer to do anything he could not, in principle, do in Logo or any other language: the issue is whether the single unifying concept of communicating objects is more natural for programmers.

How does one draw a square in Smalltalk? First, we must explain that each object belongs to a class, for example, 'billiard ball' might belong to 'ball' and '2' to 'number'. Each object inherits the properties of its class, and of course a class is an object too. In Smalltalk, 'turtle' is a predefined class. So

fred ←Turtle new

makes fred an example of a turtle. Then

fred go: 50

would send fred forward 50. In these messages we specify the receiver of the message, then the selector of the manipulation to be performed, followed by any arguments.

do 4 (fred go: 50 turn: 90)

will draw a square of size 50. Members of the turtle class already understand the message 'go:'. The class can be taught to understand the message 'square:'.

Turtle
square: size
do 4 (self go: size turn: 90)

Now if we type

fred square: 100

then fred can use the above method for drawing squares known to all members of the class Turtle. Any new language, especially one based on novel concepts, looks odd, and any written description of Smalltalk cannot capture its immediacy and interactive nature. However, we hope that we have indicated that, while Smalltalk shares with Logo an emphasis on the visual and an orientation towards children users (at least historically), Smalltalk's philosophy of objects communicating by sending messages, with classes of objects inheriting properties, leads to a different style of programming.

One of the key considerations in the design of Smalltalk is the ability to simulate complex systems,[4] for 'simulation is the central notion of the Dynabook' and 'every message is, in one sense or another, a simulation of some idea' (Kay and Goldberg, 1977). Smalltalk is designed to enable a programmer to describe both the individual parts of such systems as well as their combinations. Smalltalk is best suited to an exploratory style of programming, since it is easy to create, test and change prototypes. This is achieved partly through the design of the language itself, but more by the programming environment. It is probably obvious that by contemporary standards Smalltalk demands considerable computing resources. Smalltalk can be run in 'as little as 80K bytes of main memory' but 'you should have at least 256K bytes' (Tesler, 1981) to enable all program development aids to exist in memory simultaneously.[5] Smalltalk is designed to be used on a personal computer with a high-resolution display (that is, one capable of producing detailed graphics), a keyboard and a pointing device such as a 'mouse', which is a small mechanical box with wheels to move a cursor around the screen, for example, to select an item from a 'menu'. There are tales of users continuing to use Smalltalk for weeks with a defunct keyboard!

The designers of both Logo and Smalltalk originally explored the possibility that school-age pupils could acquire extensive programming skills. The intended audience for Smalltalk has matured with the language: in about 1970, the designers, encouraged by the Logo work, 'became interested in focussing on children as our "user community" ' (Kay and Goldberg, 1977); by 1976, we have 'Smalltalk: a communications medium for children of all ages' (Learning Research Group, 1976); but in 1981 it is necessary 'to disabuse readers of the idea that the Smalltalk-80 system is a language for children'; instead it 'focusses more on software development for the professional' (Goldberg and Ross, 1981). However, the concepts of objects and message-sending might aid problem-solving by both adults and children, and initial forays into the classroom are described by Goldberg and Kay (1977), Goldberg (1977) and Goldberg (1979). These investigations were intended to assist the refinement of the Smalltalk system, to help develop methods for teaching the language, and to provide insights into how the eventual Dynabook could be used profitably in education. The main pedagogical technique was to present students with model object definitions and to require students to use, improve and combine these objects. For example, one activity involved using a 'box' class, which could be drawn, erased, shrunk, expanded, rotated and moved, to 'play leap frog' and make designs on the display. The evaluation concluded that 'children (twelve years and older) can learn to write Smalltalk class definitions and to embed instances of the classes in complex environments. . . they can build tools that demonstrate an integration of problem-solving skills'

(Goldberg and Kay, 1977). However, the classroom experiment involved sympathetic tutoring of 'mentally gifted minors' some of whom had already had programming experience. As Goldberg and Ross (1981) concede, Smalltalk has only 'potential for educational use'. This potential will be fulfilled, they believe, by providing 'kits' (i.e. sets of components and tools to manipulate them) for developing flexible educational activities. In the next two sections we shall look at some examples of such kits. This provision of kits is a more sophisticated response to the difficulties of teaching programming than that adopted by Logo workers. As described above, the latter have either produced highly structured worksheets or implemented new packages (e.g. Sharples, 1981) which hide the underlying Logo programs.

The role of graphics

The programs described in the previous chapter were predominantly oriented to dialogues with words. In this chapter, however, where we have been concerned with tools designed to stimulate thought, we have increasingly recognised the role of imagery in thinking. People can much more rapidly absorb visual information than verbal information, and since both the technology of computer graphics and techniques for manipulating representations of visual information are improving rapidly, the role of graphics in computer-assisted learning is bound to increase.

The production of graphical output is relatively straightforward. One technique is to associate each point on the screen with a specific bit in store, and to map each bit (0 or 1) into light or dark illumination of the corresponding point on the screen. The Smalltalk display is so produced, usually with 606×808 points, giving very fine detail. Visual images in Smalltalk are objects and therefore can be manipulated, providing the possibility of animation, as we shall see.

Graphical input from the user is more problematic. In Smalltalk, the mouse can be made to simulate a pen or paintbrush, and movements of the mouse can be tracked. Thus, the user can not only point to parts of a display, but input 'freehand drawings'. With the provision of commands to manipulate graphics, a picture becomes a fully-fledged manipulable object.

In Smalltalk, the display of text is an expression of personal taste. Many character founts, including sans serif, serif, cursive, ITA, Sanskrit and fingerspelling (Learning Research Group, 1976), are stored as arrays of black and white dots. The user can select a fount by pointing, and change text by using a simple 'menu' of commands: he can, if he wishes, create his own characters. For example, a noun might be embellished by a visual representation of the object referred to. A teacher of early reading might use such a device to help children understand the correspondences between words and objects.

With the Paintpot program (Kay, 1977), the user is provided with a set of brushes and colours. He can use the mouse to select a brush and colour, and then move the mouse to 'paint' on the screen. He can edit the drawing in the normal Smalltalk fashion. He can create his own brushes, even two-dimensional ones – to give the effect of 'painting wallpaper'. As an artistic medium the computer has some advantages over standard media: paintings can be easily changed (e.g. erased, recoloured), they can be kept and duplicated, we can use special 'brushes' and we can animate our drawings relatively easily.

If an image is repeatedly and rapidly drawn, erased and displaced slightly an impression of movement is created. If the image changes slightly with each displacement we have animation. Animation is useful to display simulations (such as our billiard balls). It is possible for children to create movies in which parts of the screen can be overlapped and separately changed (as described by Goldberg, 1979) and professional animators and designers have experimented with the Smalltalk system (Bowman and Flegal, 1981). The visual aspect of Smalltalk is very important. In the first place it provides a much more powerful medium than Logo for providing pleasing graphics and animations which illustrate the knowledge or processes expressed by the user in Smalltalk. Secondly, Smalltalk breaks new ground in providing visually mediated ways of creating and changing computational objects.

205

Learning via Smalltalk

It is the thesis of this chapter that programming languages provide students with tools for self-expression and the exploration of thinking. With an eye on the future, the Smalltalk designers have tried to provide as complete a set of tools as they can conceive. As we have seen, considerable computer resources are needed to support Smalltalk but it is presumed that advanced tools will enable a more effective educational job to be done.

Take, for example, the subject of music which we discussed briefly earlier in this chapter. In Smalltalk students can create music much like they can create animations:

animation, music and programming can be thought of as different sensory views of dynamic processes . . . music is the design and control of images (pitch and duration changes) which can be painted different colours (timbre choices); it has synchronization and coordination, and a very close relationship between audio and spatial visualization. (Kay and Goldberg 1977).

Consequently, students do not need any new concepts to write music in Smalltalk: they do, however, need to know how to use the special 'music kit' which is provided to enable them, for example, to display music as a conventional score or in any other representation, to input music using the mouse or keyboard, and to edit music in various flexible ways. As before, the intention is to allow students to learn skills of composition without necessarily having to learn the lower-level skills which are normally taught first. In addition, the concrete demonstration that there are strong similarities between scientific, artistic and musical skills may be beneficial.

Of all the various modes of computer-assisted learning described in Chapter 3, simulation is the one to which Smalltalk is best suited. However, before looking at a Smalltalk simulation which has been experimented with in an educational context, we might recall that the Dynabook was envisaged as being able to handle all one's information related needs. If and when such a device exists, it will profoundly change decision-making processes: just as the calculator has eliminated arithmetic guesswork, so the Dynabook should provide reliable answers to any question requiring the retrieval and analysis of information. At the present, however, little has been done to develop information retrieval systems in Small-talk. Weyer and Kay (1977) describes an experimental Findit system, but this seems not to have been pursued.

As regards simulation, Gould and Finzer (1981) describe a system called TRIP which animates certain algebra word problems. It is intended for students who can solve algebraic equations but who have difficulty forming the equations from the problem statement. Figures 5.8 and 5.9 give an illustration of an initial and final screen configuration for a session with TRIP. It is not easy to capture the dynamic nature of the interaction which transforms this screen display, but in outline the process is as follows: The student is required first to draw a picture to represent the given problem – he does this by using the mouse to move the depicted icons about the screen. He must then estimate a solution to the problem: an animated simulation then proceeds on the screen. The student may repeat this stage to converge on a solution. A record of each guess and its consequences is kept in a 'guess table' (as shown), from which the student is required to induce an algebraic equation to describe the problem.

TRIP is written in Smalltalk, which necessarily makes it a large, complex system, but TRIP itself was written in about four months. To compare TRIP with systems described in previous chapters, we may note that:

1. It is, to some extent, a generative system in that new problems can be created by editing the template for trainwreck (and other) problems – the new problem would inherit the properties of all collision problems. (At the moment, this editing is not done automatically, but by a teacher.)
2. Individualisation is possible by adjusting parameters to suit the ability of the student, but again this is not done automatically.
3. TRIP cannot derive solutions to its own problems; the equation must be specified by the teacher. TRIP judges the student's picture by checking that it satisfies a set of about fifty constraints (such as for collision problems the two travellers must be facing each other).
4. While TRIP's checking and help facilities do explain what is wrong and what is to be done next, there is no intelligent tutoring

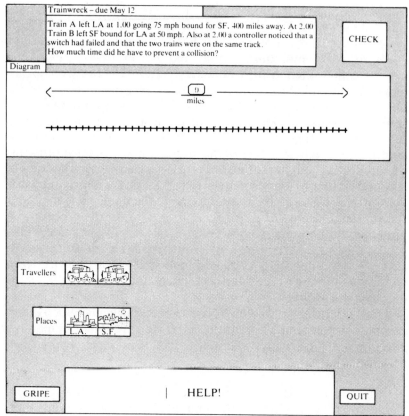

Figure 5.8   *An initial screen configuration for TRIP* (from Gould and Finzer 1981).

as described in Chapter 4: TRIP has no understanding of the subject matter, or of the student's knowledge.

· TRIP aims to exercise 'the intuitional rather than the analytical aspects of problem solving'. Is there any evidence that it works? Gould and Finzer did carry out a small-scale evaluation with four matched pairs of students, and managed to show that TRIP helped students draw pictures of problems but not that drawing these pictures improved problem-solving performance. One technical difficulty was noted: students sometimes did not know where to

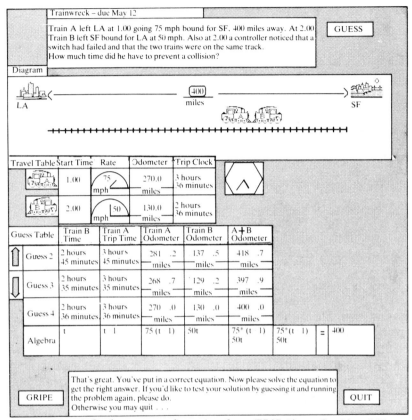

Figure 5.9 *A final screen configuration from TRIP* (from Gould and Finzer, 1981).

look during an animated sequence. Gould and Finzer conclude by listing a series of possible improvements, with the addition of which 'TRIP might make a good testing instrument for educational research'. With all these conditionals, the educational case for Smalltalk remains not proven. However the expressive power and aid to visualisation offered by Smalltalk makes it the existing programming system with the greatest educational *potential*. Before the potential can be achieved ways of making Smalltalk accessible to learners and teachers will have to be found.

Further examples

The educational uses of Smalltalk are based upon a more sophisticated concept of simulation than is usually understood by the term. Students are not merely trying out different values for fixed parameters, but are developing or modifying the actual model itself. By providing more advanced tools, language designers hope to give students computational props to aid their thinking at a higher level about what is simulated. The development of these advanced tools is a continuing research effort, but two systems already implemented as extensions of Smalltalk and Logo indicate what is possible.

The first, Thinglab (Borning, 1979), provides an environment for specifying complex situations. The simulation is programmed by describing constraints, that is, relationships that must exist between parts of the system (we met the idea of constraints when discussing TRIP). Thinglab ensures that when one part of the system is changed other parts are updated to re-satisfy the constraints: thus, a student may easily experiment with the model. A simple example is illustrated in Figure 5.10. Here, the modeller has created pictures representing the constraints that exist between Centigrade and Fahrenheit temperatures. Changing one temperature will automatically change the other. Other examples described in Goldberg (1979) include visual representations of mathematical theorems and of physics problems.

Details of the programming language aspects of Thinglab are given in Borning (1981). As a language, Thinglab reinforces many of the themes of artificial intelligence research. Constraints are devices for managing complexity.[6] Constraints are specified independently of one another – hence new constraints can be added without regard to the constraints that already exist (the virtues of such modularity were discussed with reference to production systems in Chapter 2). The programmer is responsible for specifying the constraints but not how they are to be satisfied (that is Thinglab's responsibility). He therefore thinks in terms of goals to be achieved rather than the details of how to achieve them. The development of programming languages in artificial intelligence has similarly been concerned with devising means to express knowledge to enable a system to solve problems. The Thinglab design also recognises the necessity for multiple representations or views of knowledge in solving problems (in Figure 5.10 the temperature is represented as a number and on a thermometer, as a simple example). Visualisation is an effective aid to problem-solving: consider the use of drawings to prove theorems in geometry and notations such as Venn diagrams for problems in set theory.

The Thinglab environment is intended to enable a student to explore his intuitions about relationships holding between elements of a problem. He may use existing models, as in conventional simulations, but in the flexible, graphic mode supported by Smalltalk. Alternatively, he may define a problem in Thinglab by specifying constraints and constructing graphics which should be a fruitful way to clarify understanding.

Finally, in this chapter let us return to our Logo turtle. This turtle was very simply defined in terms of its state (i.e. its position and heading) and operations for changing its state (i.e. forward motion and turning on the spot). It has, however, proved powerful enough to provide insights into certain mathematical ideas. We shall now consider how different kinds of turtle might provide an alternative path to understanding other ideas.

Papert (1980) describes how a series of refined turtles provide a computational tool for thinking about Newton's Laws of Motion. To children, these laws are counter-intuitive. The traditional route to understanding them is the long, formal one leading to the differential calculus. Papert's idea is to refine our geometry turtle into a 'Newtonian turtle' by progressive changes to the definition of its state and operators. First, we add a velocity component to the state, then acceleration, and finally mass (and, to introduce Newton's third law, the idea of linked turtles). The learner may experiment with these intermediate turtles to develop an intuitive understanding of their laws of motion. Each step builds upon earlier ones, the learner assimilating new knowledge by actively constructing his own learning. Thus, such computer-based environments provide unprecedented Piagetian learning paths into Newtonian physics.

This approach is taken further by Abelson and di Sessa (1981). First, they imagine the turtle to be walking on a curved surface

211

rather than a flat one. The 'turtle trip theorem' (which states that the total turning along any closed path is an integer multiple of 360 degrees), which is the basis for a turtle-based investigation of Euclidean geometry, does not hold for curved surfaces. By considering why this is so by, for example, redefining what it means for a line to be 'straight' (for a turtle, a line is straight if it takes equal-sized strides with its right and left legs), and by providing turtle interpretations of various ideas in modern mathematics, Abelson and di Sessa manage to provide a framework for understanding Einstein's general Law of Relativity. It would be foolish to pretend that the path is an easy one (even for one of the present authors with a degree in theoretical physics!), but there is no denying that it is an alternative to the usual undergraduate course and one conspicuously devoid of the apparatus of formal mathematics. Both the Logo language and the turtle survive as expository devices until the end of Abelson and di Sessa's book, but even without them it is clear from the numerous references to program-

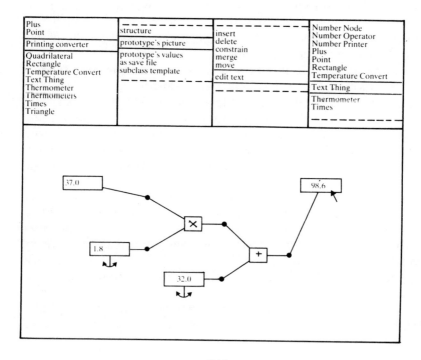

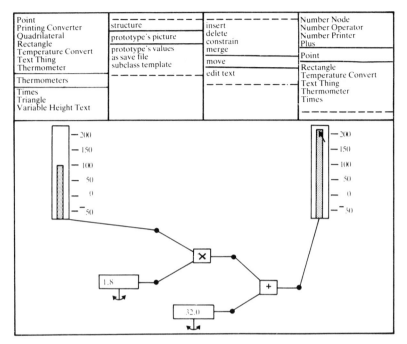

Figure 5.10   *Temperature converter in Thinglab* (from Borning, 1981).

ming concepts (e.g. 'we debugged the curvature interpretation of gravity by . . . ') that the conceptual framework is built upon the computational metaphor.

Summary

Piaget's theory suggests that children progress from a stage of 'concrete thinking' (entered at about age six) to one of 'formal thinking' (at about age twelve). It is Papert's belief that this ordering is not in fact universal: his conjecture is that 'the computer can concretize (and personalize) the formal'. We have seen examples of computer-based environments which enable learners to build their intellectual structures spontaneously and autonomously, without being taught in the conventional, artificial and inefficient classroom.

The educational role of programming languages is to enable learners to express things which in the pre-computer culture have been hard to work with and understand. Languages differ considerably in the ease with which they permit ideas to be expressed. The design of languages for novices and for advanced programmers is a continuing research effort. A programming language should be both powerful (in that worthwhile effects can be achieved with a minimum of effort) and learnable, which implies a simple conceptual basis and the provision of learning tools. More powerful languages are not necessarily harder to learn. At present, however, these more powerful languages do demand exorbitant computer resources, although this will no doubt change. In the meantime 'special-purpose languages' are being developed for microcomputers to enable learners to understand specific topics, such as music. This might well prove a sensible longer-term development than attempting to design a single all-purpose language for, after all, different subjects have developed their own specialised 'natural' languages.

Notes

1. The need to know about coordinates effectively bars young children from using BASIC to draw, but Abelson and di Sessa (1981) give reasons why turtle geometry may be appropriate for older learners as well. In summary, these are:
   (a) Turtle geometry emphasises intrinsic properties of geometric figures, i.e. ones which are independent of a frame of reference. For example, the Logo procedure
   CIRCLE
     1 FORWARD 1
     2 RIGHT 1
     3 CIRCLE
   makes it clear that, for a circle, the curve is everywhere the same, which is not at all evident from the Cartesian representation $x^2 + y^2 = r^2$.
   (b) Turtle geometry is more 'local', and does not require references to far away points, such as the centre of a circle or the axes.
   (c) Descriptions in terms of procedures rather than equations gives access to mechanisms, such as repetition, hard to capture in the traditional formalism.
2. It is believed that night-flying insects follow such a procedure keeping the moon at a fixed bearing: this enables them to fly in a straight line.

3. For example, Foltz and Gross (1980), Kuhn and Lorton (1981), Hofstetter (1979), and Placek (1980).
4. The fundamental ideas of Smalltalk are not unique to that language. Limited versions of objects, messages and classes existed in Simula (Dahl and Nygaard, 1966), a language for discrete event simulation. The concept of an object is also found in some languages for artificial intelligence research (Hewitt, 1976; Bobrow and Winograd, 1977).
5. Smalltalk-80 runs on Xerox Alto, Dolphin and Dorado computers (Krasner, 1981). A subset, Tiny Talk, is available for 64K byte microcomputers (McCall and Tesler, 1980). Smalltalk-80 is being implemented on a variety of non-Xerox computers.
6. Steele and Sussman (1978) have developed a constraint language to apply artificial intelligence techniques to computer-aided design.

6. MAKING THE COMPUTER EFFECTIVE IN THE CLASSROOM

This chapter describes the problems which arise when computer-based innovations are introduced into the educational system, and discusses the work that has been done to attempt to overcome these problems. As we have seen, the computer is capable of assisting the learning process in a variety of roles. So far, these roles have been minor, supporting ones. It is easy to imagine that in the next act (or indeed the next chapter) the computer will steal the scene. But in the meantime we would be wise to learn what we can from the experience of others.

We shall first describe some reasons for the failure of computer-assisted learning projects. The perspective adopted in this book may enable us to understand, and perhaps overcome, these failures. Then we shall look at the various ways in which the use of computers in education may be organised, for (notwithstanding the title of this chapter) the computer does not have to be placed in the conventional classroom alongside all the other unused gadgets. Finally, we shall recognise that, in accordance with our emphasis on the individual's contribution to learning, the computer may not be uniformly beneficial, but that its distinctive properties may be particularly suited to certain classes of students.

Problems

There seem to be basically four sources of difficulty:
    the reaction of the people involved;
    the poorly-designed materials;

technical matters, such as cost and reliability;
evaluation, that is, in actually deciding whether what has been
done was worth doing.

Inertia and resistance

The teaching profession is constitutionally conservative, and for
good reason: it has fallen for educational quackery in the past and is
reluctant to do so again. But the resistance to computer technology
is particularly marked (Johnson, Anderson, Hansen and Klassen,
1981) because:

1. Teachers do not want their jobs usurped, and since most
   programs do aim to mimic human teaching activities this is an
   understandable fear.
2. Teachers do not appreciate the new role proposed for them.
   They 'will remain necessary to fulfil the essential emotional
   needs of students . . . [and] so fulfil essential societal needs
   of custody and socialization . . . the role of the teacher will be
   modified to include being a resource person and learning
   manager' (Morgan, 1977).
3. Teachers have little time or incentive to keep up to date with
   developments in computing and feel unable, therefore, to
   make proper use of them.
4. Teachers do not want their normal routines disrupted by, for
   example, the need to be responsible for the security and
   scheduling of the use of computer resources.

These are generalisations, and there are exceptions. In Chapter
3 we mentioned the TICCIT and PLATO evaluations, which in-
cluded a survey of teachers' reactions to the systems. PLATO's
take it or leave it philosophy seemed more popular, since the
teachers' autonomy was perceived not to be threatened. In a survey
of the teachers involved taken at the beginning of the TICCIT and
PLATO experiments, it was clear that the teachers were most
concerned about the possible effects on two things: their own
autonomy, and their own interaction with students (Alderman and
Mahler, 1977). Interestingly, this survey also showed just how
sceptical the faculty were about the whole business – for almost
every question about the future of computer-assisted learning the

most common response was 'not sure'. This in itself may help to explain the results of the TICCIT and PLATO experiments and other computer-assisted learning experiments if it is generally true, for it has been shown that differences in student performance can be attributed in part to their teachers' attitudes to the media involved (Dodge, Brogan, Brodgen and Lewis, 1974).

In fact, House (1974) identifies the need for an entrepreneur, an advocate working within the system, as the crucial requirement for the success of any educational innovation. Innovations are described as 'acts of faith' requiring considerable personal commitment often with no tangible incentive. A lively case-study gives a fascinating insight into the political background of the 'PLATO saga', the appeal of which apparently 'approached religious fervour' and 'exercised enormous control over the lives of hundreds'. The adoption of a past tense throughout – as in 'PLATO looked as if it could become one of the most widely distributed educational reforms of all time' – makes it clear that House believed, well before the end of the NSF project, that the PLATO innovation would not be generally welcomed, irrespective of any academic or technical merits.

Poor materials
Most commercially-available computer-assisted learning material is of poor quality. As we described in Chapter 3, much of it is based upon impoverished theories of learning, and reflects little programming skill. Sadly, this situation has been perpetuated by the advent of microcomputers for their small memories mean that only small teaching programs can be run on them. We can only hope that such approaches do not become institutionalised, as they say, and do not lead to a lasting disaffection with computer-assisted learning in the teaching profession.

In a survey intended to examine teachers' evaluations of existing computer-assisted learning programs for microcomputers, Hartley and Bostrom (1982) encouraged some 100 teachers to consider using any of 91 programs (not a large number, reflecting the paucity of material of any kind) in their classroom teaching. Only fifteen programs were taken up, the rest being rejected as being irrelevant, inflexible, inaccurate or difficult to use. Most of these fifteen were simulations written in BASIC, and they were used mainly to consolidate previously taught principles.

Teachers confronted with such material may be inclined to try to write better. This is not a promising avenue to follow. The lack of precise design principles, concerning, for example, screen layout,[1] conversational conventions and different modes of use, does not imply that arbitrary decisions will do. It means that educational software should be particularly skilfully designed to cater for a range of users and applications. 'The single most critical issue in computer-assisted instruction today is the development and sharing of quality CAI materials' (Chambers and Sprecher, 1980); in reality, it always has been.

As regards the sharing of quality material (if and when it exists), then this is a technical problem and therefore more amenable to solution. While no satisfactory equivalent of the publishing industry for printed material has yet evolved, directories, registries and clearing houses are mushrooming.[2] Some textbook publishers now market computer-assisted learning material, or are considering doing so, using floppy discs, videodiscs or perhaps eventually telesoftware (see Chapter 7).

A further problem for computer-assisted learning material is that of documentation, for although the need for good documentation of computer programs in general is well-recognised in the data processing community, techniques for providing such documentation are still not entirely agreed upon. In addition, for computer-assisted learning programs, the problem is compounded by the fact that documentation is needed for different classes of users, in particular students, teachers and programmers, who require quite different kinds of information about what a program does. For a good discussion of the problem, in terms of what is to be documented and how the documentation is to be produced, see Kearsley and Hunka (1979).

Reliability and cost

The average teacher would prefer to avoid technicalities, and if he does not get satisfactory answers to his first two questions 'How well does it work?' and 'How much does it cost?' then he feels safe in doing so. Up till now, computer-assisted learning has been unable to jump both hurdles.

The reliability of any educational device is a major determinant of its acceptability in the classroom. Enthusiasm evaporates with the first disaster, for apart from the waste of time and the embarrassment, the teacher realises his impotence to rectify matters. The unreliability of computer-assisted learning systems derives from two sources: hardware malfunctions and program errors. A teacher is at least familiar with machines that do not work, but he may well be at a loss with programs that behave unexpectedly. It is very easy for a programmer to overlook possibilities with the result, for example, that an unexpected student input produces nonsensical output.

As we saw in Chapter 3, the hardware reliability of the PLATO system, the most sophisticated commercially available, was considered acceptable by the evaluators, although a sizeable proportion of students were less impressed. The new microcomputers are very reliable, but then so are new mainframes since they are built on similar logic. The difficulty with large multi-access systems like PLATO has often been with communications, with a reliance on ordinary telephone lines and a lack of agreed standards. A classroom full of microcomputers is not incapacitated by an isolated failure, but the price paid of course is in much reduced processing power and accessible information. The advent of cheap, reliable networks may however overcome the present disadvantages of stand-alone computers (see Chapter 7).

The cost question is very complex. The advocates of computer-assisted learning have been obliged to defend themselves on the battlefield of cost, with little success. First, we need to see things in perspective: education costs are mainly in the areas of salaries, buildings and administration, with expenditure on equipment being only a tiny investment, but one vulnerable to economic stringency. Secondly, the costing of any educational innovation is largely a subjective matter (Fielden, 1978). Also, the cost of computer-assisted learning depends upon the particular kind of computer-assisted learning involved and on the computing resources used to provide it. However, it seems to have been generally conceded that computer-assisted learning has been, and will remain in the near future, an add-on cost, and not a replacement

221

cost. Braun (1977) concludes that 'our only hope is to make the add-on cost so small that the cost-benefit ratio tips dramatically in favour of the computer'. The monthly charge to use PLATO is £900 (1982 prices), and is clearly not an attractive proposition to the typical school headmaster who, with government encouragement, can buy a microcomputer for the same amount or less. Indeed, microcomputers are now cheap enough to be buyable by departmental heads without more senior authority. This has led some enthusiasts to see a new dawn for computer-assisted learning, one created by the microprocessor revolution (Sugarman, 1978; Frenzel, 1980). Unfortunately, this overlooks the fact, long recognised, that 'the critical cost factors are those associated with instructional materials' (Levien, 1972). Personal computers make no direct contribution to lowering this cost, although they may help to create a market to reduce the amortised cost of courseware production.

Evaluation

Computer-assisted learning has faced peculiar difficulties in the attempt to provide evidence of its contribution to the learning process. The traditional method, the one most likely to convince sceptics and decision-makers, uses pre-test and post-test scores for a computer-assisted learning group of students and a control group. This methodology is encouraged by the fact that the computer is well-suited for collecting and analysing such statistics, and indeed for amassing all kinds of details about the students' use of programs, the particular route followed through a branching program, the time taken on each part of the program, and so on. The result is usually inconclusive. As we saw in Chapter 3, the PLATO evaluation found no significant impact on student achievement and TICCIT's positive result was complicated by high drop-out rates. Jamison, Suppes and Wells (1974) concluded that computer-assisted learning was effective at the elementary school level but that 'at the secondary school and college levels, a conservative conclusion is that computer-assisted instruction is about as effective as traditional instruction'. Kulik, Kulik and Cohen (1980) present a comprehensive meta-analysis (i.e. a statistical analysis of a large collection of results from individual studies) of 59 evaluations of computer-based college training. They conclude that the computer

1. provided small but significant contributions to student achievement;
2. produced positive, but again small, effects on the attitudes of students toward instruction and the subject matter;
3. reduced substantially the time needed for instruction.

These encouraging results are however less impressive than those for some other applications of instructional technology, such as the Keller plan. But there are so many uncontrollable variables in such evaluations that it is not surprising that the statistics tell us little (and the problem is not confined to computer-assisted learning). Also the need for a control group makes the method inappropriate for some of the more interesting kinds of computer-assisted learning. Much computer-assisted learning is not merely reworking older instructional methods, but is concerned with adding new skills or knowledge to instruction. We need to assess the value of the additional objectives to the student. Other means of evaluation are therefore required, for example, to assess the influence of a longer-term experience of a computer-rich setting on a child's natural learning. In this spirit, Lawler (1981) presents a study of his six-year-old daughter's progress during six months' experience of the Logo environment. Such studies verge on the anecdotal, being concerned with the particular changes observed with an individual child or student. But this is only to be expected. We have rejected the view of learning as a gradual, 'statistical' process and are bound to reject statistical evaluations; we have emphasised the view of learning as an individually-based activity and are bound to look at individuals for evidence.

The attitude of the revolutionaries (see Chapter 5) to evaluation is to advocate taking over a group of students, working with them for as long as necessary to test the innovation, and to expect results so qualitatively different as to make statistics redundant. One attempt along these lines involved using Logo and turtle graphics in an elementary school in Brookline, Massachusetts over an extended period of time (Papert, Watt, di Sessa and Weir, 1979). The students were not presented with a 'standard Logo curriculum', but a teacher introduced new Logo ideas on an individual basis and in a way which could be integrated in their individual projects. Consequently, much of the final report consists of individual profiles, which it is difficult to analyse, with summative remarks such as 'all students were to some extent engaged by Logo activities'.

There is a need to develop rigorous methods for detecting changes in individual understanding and attitude and ways of presenting the evidence convincingly. Consider the following experiment, intended to test the hypothesis that programming in Logo improved a child's ability to formulate verbal descriptions (Howe and O'Shea, 1978). A pair of children sit one on either side of a screen. In front of one of the children is a target shape made out of regular, flat, wooden, diamond- and triangle-shaped pieces (Figure 6.1). The other child has a heap of pieces. The children are asked to have a conversation until both are sure that the child with

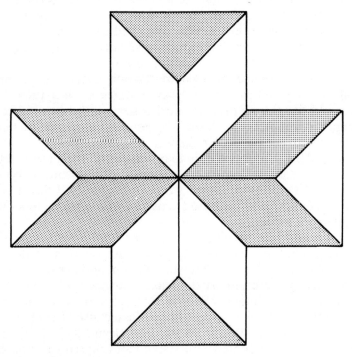

Figure 6.1   *The target shape*

the heap has constructed a shape identical to the target shape.

Here are three different examples of the kinds of instructions given for the construction of the above figure:

(i) 'Make a black and white cross.'
(ii) 'Put a black diamond next to a black diamond. Put a white diamond next to it. Put another white diamond next to it . . .'
(iii) 'Put two black diamonds together to make an arrow head. Make another black arrow head. Put them tip to tip like an egg timer. Fit the points of a white arrow head into each side of the egg timer. Now you should have an eight petalled flower. Now put white triangles into the ends of the black arrow heads, and black triangles into the ends of the white ones. It should look like a cross.'

The instructions given in examples (i) and (ii) are quite inadequate. In the first example, the description is under-specified, and in the second one the description is highly ambiguous. In contrast, the third example reveals a deep understanding of the task to be carried out by the child receiving instructions.

The evaluation (Howe, O'Shea and Plane, 1980) did in fact show that teachers considered that children who had taken part in Logo-based activities 'could argue sensibly about mathematical issues' and 'could explain mathematical difficulties clearly', but rated control group children poorly on these abilities. In addition, there was evidence of an improvement in mathematical understanding and in attitudes to the subject. Of course, those improvements might not be due to the programming activity but to other, uncontrolled factors, for example, increased attention from a teacher. The next step is to evaluate the contribution of the programming activity when integrated with classroom mathematics teaching.

Modes

Among the computer's possible roles in education are many which simulate conventional teaching activities. The conservative might

	Conventional classroom	Project group	Resource centre/ science museum	Distance learning
Is a teacher present?	yes	no	no	no
No. of students involved	c.30	c.4	many (but not all on the same activity)	many
Is the activity assessed?	yes	yes	no	yes
How long does activity last?	c.40 mins	weeks	variable	variable
Is activity timetabled?	yes	maybe	no	yes
Are teaching materials costly?	no	no	maybe	yes

Table 6.2 *The four modes*

be inclined to believe, therefore, that the computer will be used mainly to buttress the existing educational system. However, as long ago as 1970, a report to the US President, no less, emphasised that formal education was insufficiently responsive, and advocated using computer technology to catalyse educational reform (Commission on Instructional Technology, 1970).

In this section we shall briefly consider the advantages and disadvantages of using the computer to support learning activities in each of four different modes: conventional classroom, project group, resource centre (or science museum) and distance learning. At the risk of being superficial, we present Table 6.2 to summarise the differences between the four modes.

Conventional classrooms

The political ambition to 'put a micro in every school' assumes that this is the best place to put one. Certainly, the numbers of computers in schools are rising rapidly: Chambers and Bork (1980) estimated that the percentage of US school districts using computers for instruction had increased from 13 per cent in 1970 to 74 per cent in 1980, and the French Ministry of Education is well on the way to meeting its objective of installing 10,000 microcomputers in secondary schools by 1985 (Hebenstreit, 1980). But computer-assisted learning remains a very scarce resource in schools. For example, the French plan gives a theoretical average of less than 10 minutes' individual use of a computer for each secondary student per week in 1985. Consequently, for most schoolchildren the main experience of a computer takes the form of a class demonstration rather than an individual interaction of the kind we have mainly considered in this book. The merits of the computer as a demonstrator derive mainly from its flexibility and its ability to interact with a user, usually the teacher directing a class discussion.[3]

However, there are considerable administrative complexities to be overcome for these sessions to be successful. These range from the mechanical – getting the computer in a working condition (a non-trivial obstacle for the typical harassed teacher); through the organisational – getting the computer and the students in the right place at the right time; to the educational – ensuring that students can read and absorb the material displayed on a screen by a program probably not designed for this mode of use. In addition, the image of a teacher controlling a computer in front of a class reinforces the barrier between teacher and student which many would like to dismantle. Papert (1980) concludes that his educational revolution will not take place within the social context of conventional schools.

Experience, however, is accumulating on using computers in

normal schools. The Brookline Logo project, mentioned earlier, is one example. But at the elementary level the main emphasis is still on drills and games (Jones, 1980). The Stanford drills (mentioned in Chapter 3) to supplement instruction in the basic skills of reading and mathematics are taken by more than 150,000 students a year, many of whom are disadvantaged or handicapped (Suppes, 1979). In secondary schools, most computer-assisted learning programs are BASIC drills and simulations, the idea of which has filtered down from universities where the 'laboratory mode' is more appropriate. The school district of Philadelphia has used the computer in instruction since 1966 and, in addition to drills, tutorials, simulations and information retrieval systems, supports a 'parent partnership' programme under which individualised worksheets are generated for 35,000 children to be used with help from parents.

There is more variety in computer-assisted learning at university level. The predominant modes are problem-solving, information retrieval and simulation, with the occasional tutorial and rare drill. The longest established, entirely computer-based course is the introductory logic course at Stanford, which has catered for up to 300 students a year since 1972 (Suppes, 1979). Bork (1980) describes one of the more advanced projects using computer-assisted learning in an undergraduate course. A computer-based course is offered as an alternative to a 'standard' course on introductory mechanics. The alternative course is characterised by the following features:

1. it assumes students will write programs (as well as use provided material);
2. each student has to pass a series of computer-generated (not pre-stored) tests which in addition to evaluating student responses can provide detailed assistance to students in difficulty;
3. some tutorial programs attempt to develop student intuition (although this has 'not proved easy');
4. a course management system maintains student records, enabling teachers to identify problems either with the material or with students, such as procrastination.

Project groups

Most of the other modes of computer use to support learning involve learner-centred activities rather than the teacher-centred ones of the typical classroom. They represent also a swing towards discovery or inquiry learning and away from expository teaching. The discovery method is ineffective in achieving limited objectives, for it generally takes a student much longer to discover something than to understand it when told. The merits of discovery learning lie, rather, in (it is claimed) the student attaining a deeper understanding of what is learned and in his attaining higher-level objectives, such as experience of planning scientific experiments. Since discoveries, by their nature, are unlikely to occur simultaneously to all members of a heterogeneous class discovery learning tends to imply working individually or in small groups. One advantage of the latter is that it encourages co-operation, rather than competition, between students. An activity which occupies the group for several days or weeks (a project) gives the members of the group some idea of what open-ended research is like.

An example of the use of computer-based projects is described by Abelson and di Sessa (1976). Fourteen high-ability secondary students spent six weeks on a Logo-based curriculum for mathematics and science.[4] The students attended informal lectures, did computer-based exercises, and participated in one of three mini-research projects. One project, for example, designed a system for modelling stress in complex structures such as bridges. Throughout the six weeks the students had unlimited access to computer facilities. Abelson and di Sessa classify the computer's contribution to the success of the course under four headings:

1. as research tool, not only within the projects but also when students spontaneously extended the given exercises;
2. as understanding exerciser and evaluator, for the students' confidence seemed to be boosted more by the computer's response to their work than by any supervisor's comment;
3. as a design medium for self-expression;
4. as a 'toy', indicating the degree to which the computer functioned as a natural part of the environment.

Successful computer-based project work is very educationally desirable. The students learn to pose, refine and solve problems and they learn how to learn from each other. But the designer of learning materials (text books, notes or software) to support project work faces a harder task than the teacher who works with more educationally constraining tasks. To create project materials successfully it is necessary first of all to identify projects that are neither trivial nor impossible but soluble by, say, a group of average ability 14-year-olds in, say, one month. Secondly, the computer software must be such that the project group receives intelligible feedback in response to their work. At present, achievable project topics for the various programming languages are few, highly prized and passed from one university research group to the next. Other examples of successful project work include Sharples' poetry project, discussed in Chapter 5, which occupied a group of pupils for two or three hours a week for almost a whole school term, and some of the Edinburgh Logo mathematics worksheets which can be regarded as the basis of one- or two-week projects. However whether project work is designed for an hour or a year it entails a very substantial instructional design activity.

Resource centres and science museums
Class-based activities may encourage the student to visit public resources such as libraries and museums. Unlike schools, libraries and museums may be visited by a member of the general public *by choice*. One reason why he may be inclined so to choose is that such centres are now redefining their traditional role so that they are no longer merely repositories and showcases, but places in which interesting, informative activities occur. Computers are well able to contribute to this more active role, and there is a need to make computers more accessible and understandable to the general public. In a resource centre, computer and other equipment is made available to be used as desired by anyone who wishes to use it; in a science museum, we might also expect to find organised computer-based activities, informal computer courses open to the public, and demonstrations of frontier technology.

The Lawrence Hall of Science at the University of California, Berkeley has more than 250,000 visitors a year many of whom will be participating in computer-based activities. The objectives of its computer education programme have been listed by Kahn (1977) as:

1. to educate children and adults about the milieu of computers in an enjoyable, intriguing, non-threatening learning environment;
2. to offer the public hands-on computing at low cost;
3. to develop an exportable educational programme of computer activities that will serve as a resource for schools and other learning centres and public educational institutions.

To this end, the Hall offers a range of classes for schoolchildren on topics such as 'creative play with the computer', exhibits and workshops which provide structured access to computers, and unstructured access whereby people may simply execute or write any program they wish. The modern science centre attempts to arouse people's curiosity about science and technology and, in particular, provides an opportunity to discover and explore the power of computing at a personal level.

The Hall is a very pleasant place to wander about in, and one observes a variety of activities ranging from compulsive computer game playing to the thoughtful development of computer programs that themselves play games. In either case the member of the public has paid for his computer time and chosen how to use it to meet his needs. For us, the main reason for judging the educational computing activities of the Hall a success is the observation that many of one year's young teachers of introductory classes were last year's attendees. In addition to recycling its visitor-students in the guise of teachers, museums may also recycle the software that is produced. A well-organised public museum may take the most interesting program or package produced by a visitor and turn it into the basis of a computing exhibit. Thus, in the successful open-access institution both the teaching methods and the computing learning materials may evolve to meet the visitor-students' needs and interests through interaction. This approach requires sufficient resources to monitor activities, identify educational quality and implement change. It also requires the complete absence of some rigid set of educational objectives or scheme of assessment of the conventional educational institutions like schools and colleges. Finally, of course, it requires the computer to serve primarily as an educational medium and not as a surrogate teacher.

231

Distance education

Distance education occurs when the student is physically distant from his teachers and institution (Kaye and Rumble, 1981). Correspondence courses have existed for many years, but it is only in the last decade that large numbers of students in the United Kingdom have taken university courses 'at a distance'. We are referring of course to the Open University which was established in 1969, and which has probably more experience than any other institution of the problems of distance education and the role the computer might play in solving them.

Open University teaching makes use of printed material sent through the post, supplemented by radio and television programmes and, for some courses, 'home experiment kits', such as calculators, microscopes, etc. Students study at home, at 'study centres' (i.e. areas which the Open University leases for periods, especially evenings, from other educational establishments) and at one-week residential 'summer schools'. Since computers can be linked into networks and information transferred between them, computers would seem well-suited to contribute to the organisation of such courses, apart from any possible direct role in the teaching process.

The present set-up consists of two computer systems at each of three sites, each system being capable of supporting thirty-two terminals (Bramer, 1980). Students gain access to these computers by dialling up from one of about 240 terminals distributed around the study centres. This computing service is used mainly to teach computer science courses and to provide computational support for other courses. A computer-managed learning system has been introduced and used by a few courses to enable a student to assess his own progress. The Open University has so far made very little use of computer-assisted learning. Some tutorial programs have been written and some adopted from the National Development Programme, e.g. CALCHEM (see Chapter 3), but in 1979 only 7 per cent of the total time spent by students at terminals was accounted for by tutorial programs: this works out at an average of 4 minutes of computer-assisted learning a year for each enrolled student. Some tutorials take a semi-automated form, in which the student works through a question-answer dialogue, but may 'phone a human tutor for advice if needed. This tutor monitors the work of a group of students, and can ask a student to make direct contact with him if he wishes to do so.

Using the computer for Open University courses presents many problems. The mixed bag of students includes many who are entirely unaccustomed to the operation of terminals, keyboards and related equipment, and to the necessary logging-on procedures. A first contact with these in isolation is likely to prove a daunting experience, however carefully the 'user's guide' is prepared. In addition, the student first has to get to the study centre. In order to be accommodated by host institutions and to reduce the cost of telephone charges, most terminals are available only in evenings. This leads to an uneven loading of the computer systems, and so to poor response times. Also, a general difficulty of Open University courses, their long life-cycle, is particularly acute for courses using computer technology. A typical course may take three years to prepare, be expected to run for eight years, and yet cannot be changed during its lifetime. Courses have to be designed on the basis of computing facilities that already exist, and once designed they make it difficult for the facilities to be updated.

It is salutary to see that, as far as computer-assisted learning is concerned, high technology has barely begun to influence the Open University, an institution with a relative passion for innovation. Of course, serious consideration is being given to improvements, such as home-based microcomputers as experiment kits, and the use of the Post Office viewdata system to transmit programs and other information, but these are still apparently 'some way in the future' (Bramer, 1980), and thus rightly belong in the next chapter.

Beneficiaries

Most computer-assisted learning research has been concerned with teaching conventional subjects to normal children and adults. In recent years, however, it has been recognised that the virtues of computer-assisted learning may be particularly suited to certain classes of students. The computer's infinite patience may help with difficult students. Children with communication problems may be stimulated by the computer's ability to give interesting responses to simple actions, such as pressing a button. For such children, the computer's own inability to use natural language freely may be less of a limitation. The regimentation of straightforward computer-assisted learning (drills and tutorials) may seem less objectionable to committed adults, as in, for example, military and industrial training. Also, of course, computer-assisted learning should be applied where there is most need: to children with handicaps or learning problems which cannot be catered for by normal schools; to adults to provide skills which society decides it is short of. This section will look at a few examples of work that has been done in these areas.

Special needs

Computer-assisted learning may be able to provide the extra guidance and remediation which an under-achieving child needs. For example, Sandals (1980) describes a project involving several schools in Canada to look at the use of the computer as an adjunctive teaching resource tool in elementary and secondary schools. The teaching programs are drills covering skills in mathematics and language, plus a number of educationally-oriented games. Typically, students referred to the remedial programme by a teacher are administered a diagnostic test to determine areas of weakness, which provide a guideline for planning individual programmes. Students then obtain extra practice in their areas of weakness by using the interactive terminals. They work independently with the aid of student proctors, older students who may themselves have been involved in the remedial programme in previous years. Sandals reports that

the mathematics program is having particular success due to the motivation it gives the students to practise their mathematical skills. Students are eager to work and often complain about not getting more time at the terminal. The self-pacing and immediate feedback are very appealing to these students. There are no judgements or discriminations when mistakes are made.

An example of the dramatic changes that can occur with an under-achieving child is described by Howe and O'Shea (1978).

The child had been diagnosed dyslexic and, despite specialist reme-dial teaching, his class work was poor and nobody, including him-self, expected him to understand anything. He had a well-defined role in class as a buffoon. The class, however, was engaged on a Logo programming exercise (as described in Chapter 5) and this boy soon discovered that he could write and understand Logo procedures to drive the turtle. Furthermore, he could explain these procedures to his classmates. His nickname changed to 'teach'; his self-confidence changed dramatically and was remarked on by his teachers and parents. For example, when the class was asked to describe the set of even numbers divisible by two and the set of odd numbers divisible by two, he answered in terms of set-generating procedures, namely, 'a set that doesn't finish' and 'a set that doesn't start', and justified his answer quite articulately in front of the other boys when challenged by the teacher.

Mentally and physically handicapped children may be unable to acquire language naturally and thereby have great difficulty in fulfilling their academic potential. Computer-assisted learning may offer an alternative to the traditional (oral and written) systems of learning.

We can see first that much can be done with the equipment itself to help the developmentally handicapped (Brebner and Hallworth, 1980). Some students, such as the cerebral-palsied, who are unable to use a standard keyboard can use an input device like a joystick to move a light over a transparent board. Light pens and touch-sensitive displays allow less handicapped students to answer ques-tions without the need to use a keyboard. For partially-sighted students, characters can be magnified for displaying on a screen. In addition, since programmes for the handicapped should be speci-fically aimed at the development of 'social survival skills', we can design special keyboards to simplify matters. For example, Brebner and Hallworth describe the use of keys representing 'early', 'on time' and 'late' in a program to teach the sense of time, and of keys representing the four food groups in a program teach-ing basic nutrition.

One project investigating computer-based education for the hearing-impaired has been supported by Control Data Corpora-tion, who market the PLATO system (Richardson, 1980). Most

PLATO material is largely print-based and backed by auditory prompts, which effectively blocks its use by the hearing-impaired. Richardson describes how these barriers have been lowered by modifying material and equipment and reports that 'attitudes toward PLATO have been very positive. Children voluntarily stay 30 or 60 minutes after school instead of going home to play.' Particularly noted is the fact that PLATO motivates deaf students to overcome their usual hesitance to generate written language. Richardson also comments that 'the gains in student achievement appear promising; however, the gains in student self-confidence in the process of acquiring the requisite skills to manipulate the terminal are equally promising when evaluated in the context of a handicapped child.'[5]

Weir and Emanuel (1976) describe an experience with a 7-year-old autistic child who explored controlling the Logo turtle over a period of six weeks. Autism is a syndrome characterised by a background of serious retardation (a disturbance of interpersonal relationships, profound abnormalities in language development), in which islets of normal or exceptional intellectual function or skill may appear. The approach to the autistic child sought to bring together two assumptions. First, that all behaviour is meaningful, relevant and valid for the person concerned, so, no matter how bizarre it is, we should look for the meaning of behaviour rather than its cause. Thus, if we adopt the artificial intelligence view that perception is in terms of internal models or schemata, the hypothesis is that autistic children do not communicate because they are unable to use their 'interpersonal' schemata to add information to what is given to the senses. The second assumption is Piaget's one that a child learns by actively exploring his environment – the 'learner as a model builder' paradigm, elaborated in Chapter 5. So it is only in circumstances where the child is the agent of his own learning that spontaneous communicative behaviour will begin to manifest itself.

The autistic child, David, was introduced to the Logo environment and a simple button box and had seven sessions playing with the turtle. Piaget's view that understanding ideas depends on the ability to relate them to already existing schemata and, in particular, that the sources of thought lie in body schemata (Chapter 2) is strikingly illustrated. For example, in the fourth session we find this description: 'David pushed *PENUP*, then *PENDOWN*. He then clutched the sides of his chair, poked the region of his belly button with his hand, said "up" and stood up; poked his belly button again, said "down" and then sat down.' And later, 'David imitated the light in the button going on and off each time he pushed it, by opening and closing his eyes in synchrony.' Also in the fourth session, David began a conversation about the words 'back' and 'forward', accompanied by much laughter and excitement. This behaviour contrasted with the 'passive pupil' role (no eye contact, no spontaneous activity) adopted whenever he perceived that he was being prevented from being the free agent of his own activity. By the seventh session, David was deliberately seeking eye contact before speaking and was wanting to engage in two-person games.

In summary, we see the onset of spontaneous language (based on descriptions of the turtle's behaviour) and the active seeking out of social interaction. Weir and Emanuel argue 'that this follows from the self-validating effect of understanding and being understood, i.e. sharing a sense of relevance, and that this in turn follows from the highly structured but creatively open-ended nature of the Logo environment.'[6]

More recently, Weir and her colleagues have used the Logo environment regularly for up to two years with a group of physically handicapped but mentally alert cerebral-palsied adolescents (Weir, 1981). The Logo activities provide information about spatial reasoning deficits which form the basis of remedial programmes and, in addition, the way that the Logo environment places control and initiative in the hands of the user helps to overcome the passive role imposed by physical handicaps. As Weir reports, 'the resulting dramatic improvement in sense of personal worth and the consequences for intellectual activity has led the school to implement its own computer centre using a recently implemented microcomputer Logo system'.

In-service trainees
It may be the case that the formal educational system's antagonism to technology will force computer-assisted learning into a role

outside the school and university. It seems likely that the more rapid obsolescence of job skills and the increased leisure time will create a demand for retraining services, perhaps at home. The computer would be well-suited to play a role here, but not yet. To our knowledge, the only large-scale, in-service training schemes using computer-assisted learning are those of military and defence departments, who make use of the PLATO systems. Details of this work are difficult to obtain, so let's look instead at two small investigations on the use of computer-assisted learning with mathematics teachers.

Many teachers of primary mathematics have little understanding or liking of the subject. Often they are unable to explain or justify arithmetic processes, even if they are able to perform them. If some programming experience increases the understanding of mathematics of children (as discussed in the previous chapter) then so it might of teachers of mathematics. Du Boulay (1978) describes an experiment in which a few student teachers weak in mathematics were asked to develop certain Logo procedures. One case-history describes the attempt of a teacher, weak in geometry, to draw a

'house': This took 'quite a lot of time and effort' and brought the comment that 'It's an awful lot of paper just to do that. I suppose you learn by . . . making mistakes and having to put it all together again . . . I think you do. It really makes you think about it.' Later she was able to give a clear description of how she would set about drawing the pattern shown in Figure 6.3. She went on to drawing more interesting patterns (spirals and tessellations) and to writing procedures concerned with basic algebraic and arithmetical concepts.

The experiment's conclusion was that writing Logo programs can promote understanding of the underlying mathematics and improve attitudes towards the subject. But some particular problems were noted: first, being singled out for remedial treatment was in itself likely to reinforce negative attitudes, at least initially; secondly, there was a preoccupation with drawings as products

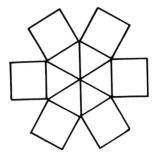

Figure 6.3   *A rotated house*

('. . . just to do that') rather than with planning and analysis; thirdly, the programming activity itself frequently distracted attention from the concepts involved; and fourthly, the computer system's response time was so poor that it made programming rather difficult.

Our second example suggests that the pedagogy of good computer-assisted learning may profitably be conveyed to teachers. In Chapter 4, we emphasised the role of student models in understanding a student's performance at some task. In particular, in arithmetic student errors result not from the erratic execution of a procedure, but from the competent execution of a wrong procedure. For example, one student produced

365	679	923	27,493	797
+547	+749	+481	+ 1,509	+48,632
819	111	114	28,991	48,199

68	734	543	758	2764
×46	×37	×206	×296	×53
24	792	141	144	2731

239

Figure 6.4 *Protocol of a team using BUGGY* (from Brown and Burton, 1978)

I have chosen a bug. Here is an example of the bug.

```
  17
+  5
─────
  13
```

Now you can give me problems to determine the bug.
[Here the team provides two numbers to be added]

```
  18        43
+  6       +79
─────      ─────
  15        23
```

Got the bug!
Please describe the bug.
Student adds the number to be carried into the last column worked in.
Here are some problems to test your theory about the bug.
[Here the team provides the 'buggy' sum]

```
  21
 +39
─────
  51
```

That's not the bug I have. Using my bug:

```
  21
 +39
─────
  15
```

Try giving me some more examples.

```
   51        99        68
+1707       +99       + 9
─────      ─────      ─────
   21        36        23
```

Got the bug!
Please describe the bug you think I have.
The student is adding all the digits together.
Here are some problems to test your theory about the bug.

33	1091	8	28	15
+99	+60	+34	+70	17
241	17	15	17	15

Very good. My description of the bug is:
The student always sums up all the digits with no regard to columns.

The bug in his addition procedure is to just write down the carry digit and forget the others. In multiplication, we have the same 'carry bug', plus a 'column bug'. If a teacher could diagnose such bugs he would be better able to remedy them.

Brown and Burton (1978) describe a game in which a program (BUGGY) simulated a 'buggy' student and student teachers had to discover the bug. Figure 6.4 gives a contrived example game. The revelation that errors that appear random are the manifestations of systematic bugs is a breakthrough for many student teachers, and all those involved in the BUGGY game felt they gained something valuable. A teacher unable to diagnose a bug can only go over the whole procedure, leaving the student puzzled why answers are marked wrong seemingly at random. Similarly, computer-assisted learning drills based upon mathematical models of learning (such as the Stanford drills, see Chapter 3) implicitly assume that errors occur at random and as a result such drills can do little more than suggest more practice.

The principal virtues of computer-assisted training for the working adult are that he may acquire new skills without leaving his employment, and that he may make his mistakes during learning in private. Much has been written about the potentially dehumanising effects of learning with machines. In contrast to this, consider the alienating experiences to which an adult 'dragged back to school' may be subjected. The computer can offer training with immediate feedback in private. But of course all our usual comments about the difficulty of designing good quality computer-assisted learning apply with equal force to training. Many industrial skills are not sufficiently well understood to be expressed with the clarity and rigour demanded by a computer program.

241

Summary

This review is not intended to be exhaustive, but to give a sampling of attempts to introduce the computer to the educational system. We are led to two conclusions: that despite the advent of micro-computers and encouragement from the educational establishment, the actual implementation of computers in schools and colleges is still proceeding painfully slowly and that the computer holds special promise for helping certain classes of students. Within the conventional system it is clear that, apart from a multitude of practical difficulties, it is not possible for the designers of acceptable drills and simulations (for example) to bypass the problems of knowledge and understanding. Good programs must know what the student is learning and understand his mistakes. In any case, individualising instruction, one of the main objectives of computer-assisted learning, would crash the gears of the present educational system. It is always easier to view computer technology primarily in a role of patching-up or supporting the existing system. Using the computer to create a wide range of interactive learning environments very different from the conventional classroom could, however, initiate a re-thinking of the goals of the educational system itself.

Notes

1. See Jenkin (1982) for an interesting survey of the 'relatively unexciting issue' of screen design.
2. For example, MUSE (Freepost, Bromsgrove, Worcs), AUCBE (Endymion Road, Hatfield, Herts) and CEDAR (Imperial College Computer Centre, Exhibition Road, London) in the UK, and CONDUIT (PO Box 388, Iowa City, Iowa) and MECC (2520 Broadway Drive, St Paul, Minnesota) in the US.
3. Fraser (1981) considers the design of programs for group presentation in classrooms.
4. Other computer-assisted learning work involving gifted children is described by Gallagher (1980) and Kolstad and Lidtke (1981). It is clear that programmes for gifted pre-college students need to be designed with care: on one programme using PLATO some students spent 95 per cent of the terminal time playing games.

5. Watson (1978) reviews the uses of a computer with deaf learners. Two well-known projects are described in Fletcher and Suppes (1976), using the Stanford drills mentioned in Chapter 3, and Dugdale and Vogel (1978), using PLATO.

7. THE NEXT DECADE

Computer-assisted learning is not short of visionaries. But then the crusade is scarcely worth embarking on without some convictions about the cause to be furthered. In this book, we have been careful up to now to describe only what exists and what has been done, but what we have chosen to describe has been determined by our own vision of the future of computer-assisted learning. In this chapter we shall consider possible developments in the next decade, aiming not to make faultless predictions, but to give an appreciation of the range of options, their advantages, problems and costs, upon which sensible plans may be based.

The future of computer-assisted learning depends on developments in technology, education and society. The impact of technology is perhaps easiest to foresee for, assuming that it continues to be true that no matter how hard it is pushed a newly discovered device or process cannot be developed into a marketable product in less than ten years (both Logo and PROLOG were conceived more than ten years ago, and are just now appearing in schools with some manufacturer support), it is largely a matter of extrapolating on what we have today. As regards changes in society we are no more qualified than most to make predictions about these, but a few comments about this background seem necessary.

Background

In about 1920 the increasing spread of telephones prompted the prediction that by 1970 all women would be employed as telephone operators. Whether serious or not, this shows that forecasts can be rendered not merely wrong, but offensive by changes in social attitudes. Such changes are hard to foresee. The public reaction to computers is still a mixture of awe, anxiety and puzzlement, especially if the subject of intelligent computers is raised. In 1950, the computer pioneer, Alan Turing, predicted that by 2000 the general understanding of what it means to 'think' would have subtly changed in that it would no longer be odd to refer to 'thinking machines' (Turing, 1950). There are signs that this is happening. The computer-brain analogy seems to be becoming culturally acceptable as evidenced, for example, by advertisements which make use of it. Perhaps by 1992 we shall be sufficiently far along this road for it not to seem inherently objectionable to a parent (as, on the whole, it does today) that his child be taught by a computer and not by a man or woman.

In general, we must assume that we shall continue to move into the post-industrial society, as described by Bell (1974), without any major hiccups in the western democratic system. The main characteristics of this society, for our purposes are: a shorter working life; less manufacturing industry, and more service and information industry; an increase in the rate of accumulation of scientific knowledge; and an increase in the reliance on technology. Political confusion and indecision is likely to make this transition unnecessarily painful and lengthy. In the area, for example, of unemployment it is hard to see how the politicians' tendency to patch up the present system will ever lead to the necessary changes in attitudes.

In education specifically, political influence is, we hope, likely to be less significant: changes will develop a momentum of their own. There are, however, several issues brewing which do require political rather than technical solutions. Among these are: the privacy question – who has access to educational records soon to be in computer databases? How will access to educational programs be equitably distributed? Will, and if so how will, the content of teaching programs be certified and controlled? How will the authors of programs be rewarded and protected? Governments will not develop consensus answers by 1992, but working guidelines will develop, as they have in the data processing industry.

We feel fairly safe in predicting that in 1992 there will be fewer students reaching university entry age; the birth rate figures tell us

246

so. However, this may well be one of those predictions which grows out-of-date rather than wrong. The idea that universities are for an 18-21-year-old élite is already under attack. The proportion of older students in higher education will increase, especially if governments provide incentives, as perhaps they will. It will, however, be beyond the political wit to organise by 1992 the 'life-long education' that has been advocated, i.e. the planned continual retraining of the work force and updating of its skills and knowledge. Developments here will continue to be patchy, relying on uncoordinated initiatives.

The declining school rolls will make the 1980s a decade in which it will not be sensible to try to sell computers in schools as labour-saving devices. Most large-scale, computer-assisted learning projects of the past have set out to teach what was already being taught but more effectively and at lower cost. They have failed; but even success would not have made them acceptable to most teachers. Teachers will be more impressed by demonstrations that computers contribute something different and important to education – new and more enjoyable ways for the learner to gain insights into existing subject matters and the skills necessary to use computers productively and creatively.

As we discussed in the previous chapter, there is considerable resistance to technology. The ability of educational institutions to assimilate new technology is a greater problem in the short term than is the development of the technology itself. There are a few reasons that this resistance may diminish. The increased computer literacy of the new generation of teachers and educational planners should help to reduce the intrinsic offence at the style of a new technology. Also, the more widespread use of computers in society may make their presence in classrooms seem inevitable. In universities, the cost of computing has already overtaken the cost of libraries, and while computers are mainly used for administration and research at the moment, their contribution to teaching is bound to increase.

We should, however, be wary of suggestions that technological progress is inevitable. Society will form its own view of what constitutes progress. Disillusionment with the apparent dehumanisation of society would seriously inhibit technological intrusions in education. The effect of technology on society is often discussed (e.g. Forester, 1980), but the effect of society on technology is harder to foresee.

Technology

Information technology is already at a stage where it can change education significantly. It has not yet done so for the reasons we have described. This may change by 1992, but so will information technology. The purpose of this section is to try to anticipate the computer capabilities available in 1992, and then to consider their probable impact on education.

Microcomputing

As everyone knows, we are the victims of a microprocessor revolution. We must first appreciate where this revolution stands now, then consider whether developments will continue, and so see where we are likely to be in 1992.

Figure 7.1 is a multi-purpose graph which summarises the important facts about the development of chip technology. The vertical axis can be used to represent various chip parameters by adopting different values for a and b, e.g. for the number of transistors on a chip set a to about 20, b to about 30. The actual figures are not too important, but the exponential growth is.[1] Thus, for example, since 1965 the number of transistors that could be put on a single chip has been doubling every fourteen months or so.

The effect of this on the microcomputers available to educators has been equally dramatic, as discussed by Aiken and Braun (1980). The Altair 8800, perhaps the first such microcomputer, was introduced in 1975 at a cost of £1000-1500. The first personal computers (i.e. ones designed for non-sophisticated users), the Pet and Tandy, were introduced in 1977, and were soon followed by others, with colour graphics, music generation capability, and so on. These cost about £600 or less in 1982.

Now, any prediction about the role of microcomputers in education in 1992 must be based on assumptions about whether these trends will continue. Licklider (1979) points out that the elements

The next decade

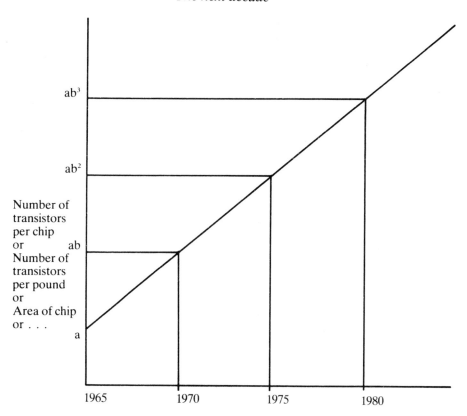

Figure 7.1   *Developments in chip technology*

on a chip cannot be made any smaller by processes similar to etching and engraving with visible light: any further advances will require moving to shorter wavelengths, that is, to X-ray and electron beam techniques. This is already happening and no major problems are anticipated. A realistic estimate would seem to be that the rate of progress will be reduced to a doubling of complexity every other year. The possibility that the incentive for maintaining this rate of progress will diminish can be discounted, since the main motivating factors will remain: to increase reliability, decrease cost, and produce computers capable of more sophisticated applications.

So, if we assume the 'doubling every two years' rule, in one

249

decade we will have computer hardware that is thirty-two times as cost-effective as present hardware. The 1992 version of the 32,000 byte Pet might contain 1 million bytes of main memory. Of course this is a simplification for there are considerations other than just main memory. None the less, it is clear that the 1992 personal computer will be, by present standards, a very powerful machine. It may even perhaps be thought too powerful, in which case the same amount of money could be used to provide more, but less powerful, computers. Either way, computer power should not be a scarce resource. Licklider (1979) distinguishes three kinds of microcomputer potentially important to education:

1. The minimal hobby computer, without backing store, the price of which is considered unlikely to drop much below £100. This might be suitable for learning about hardware/software itself, and for simple drills and games but not much more.
2. The minimal computer with minimal backing store, with its price stabilising at about £250. This would support Logo-like environments and straightforward simulations, tutorials and information retrieval packages, provided little data were required to be stored.
3. The small computer, with millions of bytes of backing store, costing perhaps £500 in 1992 and able to support any of the programs and environments we have described.

To this must be added a fourth category, the mainframe and minicomputer, for these will continue to be favoured by larger-scale educational institutions, and technological developments affect computing at all levels not just the smaller end. For example, processor, main memory and disc costs of mainframes have been decreasing at about the same rate as for microcomputers and improvements in reliability apply also to mainframes. In terms of value for money, mainframes may well retain their advantages – for example, at present the cost per bit of a floppy disc is about fifty times that of a mainframe disc.

Microcomputer technology may still in 1992 be thought incompatible with existing educational systems. Even so, microcomputers are bound to play a part in education. Nilles (1980), considering the future of personal computers (i.e. general-purpose computers affordable by an individual), states that 'no major technological breakthroughs are necessary at this stage before a fairly substantial market can be developed' and goes on to predict that 'by 1990 there could be more than 40 million personal computers in use' (in America). Home learning programs will be developed for such a market. The first programs are already available, but are of course rather simple-minded, being aimed for the present breed of microcomputers. How educational institutions will react to significant amounts of formal learning taking place elsewhere remains to be seen (but benign indifference seems the most likely reaction).

The microprocessor revolution also influences some of the problems identified in the previous chapter. With the cost of manufacture of a chip staying constant at about £2, the costs of processor logic and memory will be negligible by 1992. The same will not necessarily be true of the costs of peripherals, communications and programming (as discussed later). Large-scale integration certainly leads to improved reliability: 1000 byte memory chips are as reliable as the single circuits of ten years ago. But again this is only hardware reliability – programming errors will remain. The pious hope is that programmers, relieved of the need to worry about the efficiency of computer usage, will concentrate more on reliability.

Microcomputer developments are luring educational technologists back to an emphasis on devices rather than concepts. The history of computer-assisted learning shows that better equipment does not necessarily imply better learning. We should not expect too much from the microcomputer in education, or indeed attribute too much to it. Evans (1979), for example, discussing the impact of the micro in education, illustrated with the PLATO system, the design and philosophy of which owed nothing to microcomputers.

Peripherals
Large-scale integration not only gives us cheap computer power, but makes it possible to incorporate the microprocessors in peripherals, thus opening up new possibilities here as well. These microprocessors can be programmed to perform functions that previously required special circuitry, so reducing cost and perhaps

improving performance. So the terminal, which in the time-sharing systems of the 1970s merely transmitted messages to a mainframe computer for processing, is already able to operate in a stand-alone mode to perform routine jobs, such as handling the log-in procedure, detecting and correcting simple errors, keeping statistics, and so on. Such intelligent terminals, as they are called, therefore function rather like resourceful receptionists. It is not clear at all how far and how fast this dispersal of computer power will go. Perhaps by 1992 it will be standard to have terminals capable of running programs which today require medium-power computers. The terminals could be linked to a larger computer, which could be called upon to run large programs, or to provide requested data.

The microprocessor of visual display terminals will handle colour, animation and curve drawings, and at little extra cost. Consequently, by 1992, the graphics terminal will be standard, the alphanumeric terminal obsolete. The cost of non-refresh displays used in earlier computer-assisted learning projects (e.g. PLATO's plasma panel and the storage tube display, used by some NDPCAL programs) seems to have stabilised at about £2000-5000, significantly more than the raster scan devices standard in present microcomputers. These devices seem likely therefore to remain the leading technology for the next few years. At all events, it is clear that the style of teaching programs will continue to move away from textual to visual presentations, especially as experience and experiment begin to show how to make best use of the new interactive dynamics of computer graphics. The most important source of such expertise and design experience is the Smalltalk project discussed in Chapter 5.

Raster scan graphics require a lot of memory which can be read quickly: Smalltalk's present 606×808 display would require about 60,000 bytes. For this and other reasons, the main memory capacity of microcomputers will continue to increase. As far as secondary memory is concerned, the mature disc and tape technologies may well be displaced in certain applications by optical disc memories. The basic mode of operation of an optical disc is much like that of a normal floppy disc, except that data are written on and read from the disc by laser beam. One side of such a disc can hold 10 billion bits of information (about five times the textual information in the *Encyclopedia Britannica*), which is equivalent to about 50,000 video frames or about 30 minutes of film. Any single frame can be retrieved in 2-3 seconds. Videodiscs may also include other digital data such as computer programs, slides, audio sequences, and so on. A single disc costs a few pounds (assuming that it is one of many made in quantity) with the playback device costing about £500, but rather more for the freeze and slow-motion facilities probably desired for education. The videodisc could therefore replace conventional videoplayers in education but is unlikely to become standard with microcomputers.

While videodisc technology is very appealing, there are a number of outstanding problems, including the competition by manufacturers supporting different and incompatible disc formats. In addition, the problem of reading digital data from videodiscs has not been entirely solved, and writing (even once) to a videodisc remains very problematic. However videodiscs with stored analogue coded TV frames are now available to the commercial market.

The videodisc has in fact been identified as 'the single development that is most likely to have a profound effect, both on educational products and on systems and organizations for delivery education' (Luehrmann, 1977). We do not think so, and it may be worth saying why. If we think of a frame as containing some teaching material – text or picture (rather than say the stills of a film) – then, since each frame has an address which can be specified by a user, a student has a way of controlling the material presented to him. Interactive applications require the addition of a microcomputer to control the videodisc player. Schneider (1977) proposes the following:

the simplest machine would accept multiple-choice answers and would branch to a specific frame, depending upon which answer was selected . . . a little more memory . . . would allow the videodisc system to support a slightly modified version of the learner – controlled computer-assisted instruction that is now being evaluated on the TICCIT system.

This is ominous: the videodisc encourages the freezing of chunks of teaching material and a reversal to modes of teaching which have not been found effective. So, although by 1992 the videodisc may have been adopted by the mass entertainment market, we doubt that its influence on the quality of education will be thought beneficial. Luehrmann and Schneider's remarks were made at a 1975 conference on 'Computer Technology in Education for 1985'.

The videodisc does provide a finesse to the problem of creating graphics and animation sequences for use in computer-assisted learning. Whether a designer is using PLATO or Smalltalk it is very difficult to create good graphics, let alone cartoon sequences. For the novice programmer (who may be an expert instructional designer) it is almost impossible using existing software tools. But, in principle, the videodisc is easy. All you have to do, in some sense, is point the camera and then label the frames. We expect that the likely educational use of videodisc technology will be under microcomputer control in industrial training. There already exist videodiscs for product familiarisation for sales staff in US motor and pharmaceutical firms. These videodiscs when played have an immediacy and familiarity (it's just like watching real television) and can be easily used for practice and self-administered quizzes: 'How many colours does the four-door model come in?' Of course you get to see all the different cars played back on the videodisc. Obvious non-industrial educational applications are subject areas like fine art and architecture that require students to become familiar with large bodies of visual material: 'Which of these four 1930s houses could not have been designed by Le Corbusier?' So while none of the problems of adapting to the learner or helping him to express processes is affected, there is the possibility of easily inputting and storing large amounts of visual information. But, by analogy, if printing photographs suddenly became cheaper we would not expect textbooks suddenly to improve in educational qualities. We would not, however, be surprised to encounter the odd, badly-designed book which despite being cheap was packed full of photographs.

A development eagerly awaited by some computer-assisted learning enthusiasts is that of speech input/output. Speech output by computer is already acceptable, if rather unnatural and squeaky. TUTOR, for example, provides a 'say' command to allow speech generation in various languages, including arithmetic! (Sherwood, 1978). Speech input is more problematical. It is not being developed for education alone, and some proposed applications (e.g. monitoring telephone conversations) ensure that the research is carried on in secrecy. Dixon (1977) predicted that 'by 1985 we should have practical systems capable of handling fairly large vocabularies [1000-5000 words] under essentially natural language conditions where the domain of discourse is known'. Trade rumours suggest that this may prove true. In 1992, then, we shall have speech input/output, but it is not clear that it will be considered worth the extra cost in education or what its role will be apart from the obvious one of facilitating the use of computers by blind students (speech output) and physically disabled students (speech input).

Distributed computing

The changed balance between processor logic and memory has rewritten the premises on which the design of computer systems should be based. In future, the total system will contain many distributed processors, and keeping them all busy will become less important. The time-sharing system, in which the time of a central large processor is shared among several 'dumb' terminals, will be obsolete. However, personal computer users will continue to pay a price for their independence: they will lack many of the programming tools and resources provided on mainframes and, almost by definition, they will be unable to communicate (via their micro, anyway) with other users and equipment. As a result, personal computer networks will be developed enabling users to share data and to connect to larger computers for the more powerful facilities they provide. Such networks could take one of several forms, such as the Cambridge Ring or Ethernet (Alty, 1982), but standardisation is emerging, and already commercial systems are available to enable educational institutions to link together sets of microcomputers and peripherals. Apart from distributed processing, other possibilities of interest to education arise: the linking of home to school, the ability to access large information files, electronic mail, and the enhancement of new media, such as cable television. (Cable television, incidentally, is another example of a technology whose promise has taken longer to fulfil than forecast.) Thus, networking will be common in 1992, but precise predictions are difficult, partly because there are several unresolved policy issues and partly because the technology itself leads to a blurring of definitions.

Where does this leave the large-scale computer network, like PLATO IV? Bitzer (1976, 1977) described plans for, by 1980-1, a million-terminal network, consisting of 250 processors all communicating with each other by telephone lines and, if necessary, satellites and costing $1 billion. This was presented as a technological inevitability: 'We start with one, we've got 1000 and that's the order of magnitude and where we are. Somewhere in the 1980s, we expect to be near a million terminals' (Bitzer, 1977). It has not happened. PLATO has been hoist with its own petard: technologically, high communication costs and the forbidding complexity of the system programming leave PLATO V stillborn, and PLATO IV comparatively expensive; educationally, lessons are considered time-consuming to produce and too standardised – it was precisely the twin problems of productivity and individualisation which PLATO was supposed to solve (House, 1974). Only highly financed institutions, such as large universities or industrial organisations, can afford PLATO IV. Control Data's response is to introduce Micro PLATO, a microcomputer-based version which can be linked to a mainframe PLATO system, and to emphasise the pedigree of its educational software, developed over two decades. Thus the lasting contribution of the original PLATO concept will prove to lie in the quality of its teaching programs, as discussed in Chapter 3.

Information systems

It is already the case that the cost of storing and transmitting information electronically is less than doing so by print technology. In 1992, therefore, a much higher proportion of the information needed by a student will be made more economically available to him by computer than by book. Videodisc-based libraries are likely to be common for relatively stable bodies of information (encyclopedias and other books of reference). To access large-volume information of a more temporary nature (news), microcomputers will be linked to centralised computer databases.

Viewdata systems (Martin and Butler, 1982) are the first examples of such databases aimed at the mass market. In such systems the ordinary television set is adapted to display pages of information retrieved over telecommunication lines to which the television set has been linked by microcircuitry.[2] The television adaptor rental, telephone charges and the actual viewdata charge should give a total cost low enough for the general public. Simple extensions can be anticipated, e.g. hard-copy printers for the business world. In education, viewdata systems will be used, of course, to retrieve information,[3] but perhaps a more constructive role will be sought. The user of viewdata systems presses buttons to work his way through a hierarchy of pages to reach the particular page of interest. If each page were one frame of a programmed learning text then we would be back again to multiple-choice questions and branching programs. Brahan and Godfrey (1982) are a little more optimistic about the prospects of marrying viewdata and computer-assisted learning.

As usual, we are encouraged to believe that a new technology, viewdata in this case, 'provides the greatest opportunity to stimulate learning since the introduction of the printed word' (Aston, 1981). In 1978, the British Post Office predicted there would be about 1 million viewdata receivers in 1982: in March 1982, there were only 13,933, only a small proportion of which belonged to private subscribers. 'In-house' viewdata systems are beginning to expand in the business world, but there is little sign that educationalists yet see viewdata as a solution to any of their problems.

Software technology

The astonishing developments in computer hardware technology since 1970 continuing to 1992 and perhaps beyond are overshadowed by the question of software technology. Boehm (1979) writes that the annual cost of software in the United States is about $20,000 million, which is about five times the cost of computer hardware. Hardware and software costs were about equal in 1965. The increasing importance of software, and the painful realisation that good programming is difficult, led to the coining of the term 'software engineering' in about 1970 to emphasise that as in conventional engineering we should be concerned with the cost-effective and reliable design, construction and maintenance of products. But, as Wegner (1979) describes, software is a logical rather than a physical product, reliability, for example, being determined by logical features such as fault-tolerance rather than by not 'wearing out'. He points out the following characteristics of software products:

> they generally support a greater variety of functions than conventional engineering products;
> they can be produced by any number of 'correct' implementation strategies and design guidelines are needed to choose between them;
> they should be constructed for evolution and easy repair;
> they can be very hard to assess or monitor while they are partially completed;
> they are discontinuous, i.e. small changes in the product may cause large changes in the functional capability.

These characteristics combine to create special problems in the management of software complexity. Software for computer-assisted learning is not immune to these problems: it may appear to be so if we judge only from the programs now flooding the educational market. These programs have often been written in the spare time of teachers with little training in programming. They may be the best available on microcomputers now, but they are often less carefully designed than say PLATO programs of ten years ago. Much better quality programs will be demanded well before 1992.

The new hardware technology is causing a more integrated approach to the design of computer architectures and programming languages, with potential benefits to programmer efficiency, but software problems arise essentially from human fallibility and it is difficult to foresee any major breakthrough in the short term. However, there are several reasons to expect continued improvements in programmer productivity. First, there will be better development tools, especially on the more powerful microcomputers. These may, for example, include graphics-based operating systems rather than the present text-based ones: one research organisation predicted in 1982 that 'it will be possible to run full Smalltalk on a $2,000 system in 1990' and hence that it 'will be the choice for all business systems and as many others as it can fit on'. Secondly, with the development of formal verification techniques (i.e. methods for showing that a program and its specification are consistent), we may expect the provision of certified software components. Large, one-off programs will be prohibitively expensive: instead, programs will be constructed from standard components. Thirdly, the value of high-level programming languages in writing quality programs will be increasingly recognised, even by computer-assisted learning programmers, who have tried to turn the necessity of BASIC into a virtue. Fourthly, the nature of programming itself is bound to change, for example, by the development of improved methods of automatic programming (the synthesis of programs from problem specifications) or by the development of program skeletons, like the production system framework, to be fleshed out with specific knowledge (as for the MYCIN program). Many of these ideas are considered further by Wasserman and Gutz (1982) in an interesting essay on the future of programming.

Instructional technology
The softer sciences are reclaiming the word 'technology' (derived, after all, from the Greek 'techne', meaning 'art'), hoping perhaps to share in the aura of dramatic progress. Instructional technology seeks to provide a set of principles for making sound instructional decisions. A significant advance in this field might have more influence on computer-assisted learning in 1992 than anything mentioned previously: unfortunately, it cannot be predicted and, unhappily, we don't see any signs of it.

None the less, we may expect a continual refinement of theories in developmental psychology and more concern for their implications for education. Computer-based environments will themselves help in this refinement and from psychologists we can expect more attempts along the lines of Case (1978) who, while accepting the fundamental aspects of Piaget's theory, emphasised the need for models describing the *process* of acquiring cognitive structures (not just the structure itself). His proposals, in terms of 'a series of intellectual strategies of increasing complexity', bear comparison to those of artificial intelligence researchers in knowledge representation.

Educational computing

With this background, we may try to make predictions about the role of computer-assisted learning in 1992. First, however, let's look at some previous forecasts.

In the United States, the Carnegie Commission on Higher Education (1972) said that 'by the year 2000 it now appears that a significant proportion of instruction in higher education on campus may be carried on through informational technology'. More specifically, technologists predicted that simple computer-assisted learning (computerised programmed learning and drill-and-practice) would be in routine use by 1979 and advanced computer-assisted learning (e.g. Socratic dialogues, tutorial exercises) would be by 1989. Faculty predictions added three years to these estimates. The Commission reported before the microcomputer developments had really started. It estimated that it would be 1995 before computer terminals were installed in 10 per cent of households, an estimate which led Rockart and Morton (1975) to write that 'there is no technical possibility of a radical revision of the organization of the campus toward individual home instruction' by 1990. The rapid expansion of the personal computer field, largely unforeseen in 1975, has invalidated this.

The United Kingdom's Council for Educational Technology reported in 1977 that computers 'will not revolutionise teaching and learning in the next ten years, and they remain obstinately expensive' (CET, 1977). This was written in the wake of the National Development Programme (see Chapter 3), whose final report scarcely acknowledged that its minicomputer – Fortran/BASIC approach was already out-of-date.

More boldly, Bork (1979) predicted that 'by the year 2000 the major way of learning at all levels, and in almost all subject areas, will be through the interactive use of computers'.

It's a little perplexing that those who were making predictions about educational computing ten years ago were either wildly over-optimistic or over-pessimistic. In fact, the awful truth is that over the last ten years the availability of mediocre, computer-assisted learning material has increased in a steady and boring way – the main effect of the microcomputer revolution being to decrease the average quality of computer software. The creation of the occasional program or system of high educational quality like some of those described in Chapters 4 and 5 seems to have had little effect. Obviously we are hoping and praying that particularly Smalltalk and Logo are germinating and will sprout, flourish and spread before 1992.

Computers in schools

The teaching profession as a whole resists innovation. Since, in addition, decisions about curricula are made by individual head-masters, and schools do not operate under the philosophy of the free market economy, it would seem reasonable to expect the growth of the use of computers in schools to depend on enthusiastic entrepreneurs rather than on direct government pressure (or en-couragement, if you prefer). And yet, in England and Wales, computers in schools means 'the MEP', the Microelectronics Education Programme. £12.5 million was allocated to this pro-gramme in 1979 to increase understanding of microelectronic tech-nology, by advising schools about computers, and by retraining teachers (DES, 1980). The programme began inauspiciously: a change of government brought a cut in the budget to £9 million and a delay of 18 months in appointing a director of the programme. When the programme finally started the two main aims were said to be: to alert children to the way in which the microchip will increas-ingly change office and factory work, and to use the computer to enrich the study of traditional subjects. Later, we find that the Microelectronics in Education Programme is intended to help 'teachers acquire the skills and educational material needed to enable the computer to be used as an aid to teaching and learning' (DoI, 1981). The 'in' that has crept into the programme's title is symptomatic of the profound confusion in the stated aims of the programme.

The MEP is hampered by an associated Micros in Schools Scheme funded by the Department of Industry. This is designed to put a microcomputer into every secondary school in the United Kingdom by the end of 1982 (more precisely, half a micro: the schools have to provide the other half). This scheme has the political virtue of being visible and quantifiable. It has been successful and is being extended to primary schools and schools for the handicapped. However, the Micros in Schools Scheme is not the MEP – the latter's aims, whatever they turn out to have been, are unlikely to be helped by an effective standardisation on two or three British microcomputers centred on BASIC and based on increasingly outdated technology. The Micros in Schools Scheme does not address the two problems which will determine the success or otherwise of the MEP: the shortage of teachers trained in the new technology and of good educational software. Hastily acquired equipment which cannot be used effectively may well be left idle, to become obsolete. The chauvinistic scheme makes it difficult for teachers to use any software developed for the American microcomputers, because of incompatibilities of computers and languages.

Other governments have adopted different policies. For example, France has a longer-established, more ambitious plan, made possible because of their more centralised system of education and, it seems, a greater awareness of what needs to be done. The plan has three prongs: tackling equipment, teacher training and educational software. First, 10,000 micros, distributed in groups of eight to support class activities, will be in secondary schools by 1985. Secondly, since 1971, 100 (now 200) teachers a year have attended a year-long university course, and many more have taken the course by correspondence. Thirdly, to help overcome the software 'bottleneck', a special language was defined in 1971 (although the premature standardisation on a language can itself cause problems) and the government is now offering £1,000 for acceptable one-hour 'courseware packages'.

So schools will have computers, but not necessarily very many. Ten thousand micros is only one per 200 students, and there may not be much political appeal in a 'More Micros in Schools Scheme' if it remains unclear how they are to be used. Computers will be in schools because of individual initiative or government encouragement and not because of any general agreement on the contribution they can make. Computers will, naturally, be used to support awareness courses for all children and computer studies courses for some, but as far as computer-assisted learning is concerned the focus will increasingly be on the quality of educational software. Most present, commercially-available teaching programs are in tune with a watered down version of the educational psychology and computer-assisted learning of the late 1950s. It will be sad and surprising if they are still around to waste the computer technology of 1992. Unfortunately, microprocessors pre-programmed with some simple computer-assisted learning program will be cheaper than general-purpose microcomputers with more advanced programs supplied or to be developed. Good tutorial programs will still be hard to develop in 1992 (as expanded on in the next section), and in any case seem unsuited to school children. It seems to us that, as far as schools are concerned, computers will be accepted in roles which do not attempt to mimic other teaching processes, that is, in providing computer games and computer programming environments.

The concept of a 'computer game' will have changed considerably by 1992. Most subjects on conventional curricula can, with imagination, be made into meaningful and enjoyable computer-based activities. They will be games to the extent that children *want* to play them. As described in Chapters 3 and 4, designing and implementing a good computer game demands unexpected skill, and it is perhaps doubtful that this will have developed sufficiently to overcome the present fixation on arcadia by 1992. We hope not, for as Plato (the Greek one, that is) said 'No compulsory learning can remain in the soul. . . . In teaching children, train them by a kind of game, and you will be able to see more clearly the natural bent of each' (*The Republic*, Book VII).

Most programming done by schoolchildren is of small, un-inspired efforts in BASIC. If this persists until 1992, it will be through inertia, not because of any merits of BASIC or because technology cannot support anything better. Logo, for example, has just become available on some microcomputers and soon will be on the British government-supported micros. The benefits of Logo-like environments will be well-established, and there will be pressure for a reorientation of the mathematics and science curricula to take account of the Logo philosophy. The emphasis on Logo may in turn prove shortsighted for, although at the moment it is almost the only alternative to BASIC for children, it is very likely that a range of languages and environments will be developed which recognise the differences in cognitive development of children of different ages.

Finally, as a reminder that the future of computer-assisted learning will remain vulnerable to the political gesture (and the MEP at about 0.02 per cent of the annual education budget is little more) we may quote a report from the Conservative Party's Bow Group: 'Two years and a million or so pounds to assemble quality packages which can be mass-produced on discs or transmitted over the air or down telephone lines, is a lot faster and cheaper than retraining several thousand teachers over a decade or so' (Virgo, 1981).

Computers outside schools

This emphasis on schools may turn out to be misplaced, but we fear not. For children, most formal education will still take place in schools in 1992. Informal learning, at home and elsewhere, will of course be influenced by developments in technology. The video-disc, for example, will be bought first for home entertainment, but significant contributions to learning at home will only come through skilfully designed games. Proposals to put computers in public places, such as shopping centres and airport lounges, to aid learning by the general public seem somewhat fanciful. The main educational role of personal computers in 1992 will be as it is now — to enable people to learn about computers and how they are used.

However, outside compulsory education changes are likely. Here, almost by definition, education must centre on the needs of the student, not on those of any institution he is compelled to attend. At the least, computer-assisted learning will add another alternative to those from which the student may choose. Some current institutions will resist the changes: for example, university computer science teachers soon objected to their territory being invaded: 'If we are not careful we shall have enthusiastic amateurs at home doing things for fun for which we have registered Ph.D. students to do in universities. This would be ridiculous, and we must not let it happen' (Glaser and Heath, 1978).

In fact, the conventional university in general looks particularly vulnerable to any technology-based revolution. For a start, there is widespread disaffection with the contribution that universities are making now, reinforced by government attacks which will in turn further lower the quality of education provided. Universities are arranged to suit academic staff rather than students, and given a choice the latter may well turn elsewhere. In particular, universities seem unable to meet the need for a wider range of continuing education. By 1992, some universities at least may have re-organised themselves to provide the 'open learning networks' envisaged by Gilbert (1980) and, in the United Kingdom, to challenge the developing monopoly of the Open University which, for example, taught 1600 teachers on special in-service courses in 1980 in addition to many thousands among the 70,000 students enrolled on the degree programme (Clarke, 1981).

Expert teaching systems

First, a thought experiment. Imagine that programs like SOPHIE and GUIDON (see Chapter 4) could be bought much as textbooks are today, and perhaps more cheaply, on cassettes or floppy discs. Imagine also that anyone interested in buying such programs has convenient access to a computer capable of running them. Would the programs sell? We believe so. There will be a market for educational programs, and quality programs will not necessarily cost much more than the mundane. Both the conditions mentioned will be satisfied by 1992.

Researchers in artificial intelligence have, after two decades trying to understand general problem-solving abilities, begun to turn their attention to building useful, high performance, 'expert systems'. Techniques for implementing expert systems are stabi-lising, and Feigenbaum (1980) is able to write in terms of man-weeks of effort needed. By 1992 therefore it may not require quite such a large-scale, expensive research project to implement systems like MYCIN. The Japanese 'fifth generation computer system' programme, announced in late 1981, draws primarily on artificial intelligence techniques and particularly on the technology of expert systems. This programme aims to produce a radically new family of computers for the 1990s, with interim products through the 1980s, and the plan emphasises, in addition to expert systems, new computer architectures, very large-scale integration, func-tional programming and distributed processing. While western

computer scientists have expressed some doubts about the programme, it will undoubtedly help to determine areas of research to
be supported. If there is to be a rapid expansion of expert system
technology then there will be increased demand for 'expert teaching systems'. But as Clancey's GUIDON project showed, expert
teaching systems may not prove so tractable. Whereas the skills for
present expert systems (e.g. bacterial diagnosis, spectra investigation) can be extracted from one of the few acknowledged human
experts in the field, where do we get the acknowledged human
experts in the field of teaching?

As described in Chapter 4, there are still many largely unsolved
problems in developing advanced computer tutors. Among them
are:

1. How to represent relevant knowledge of the subject.
   Are suggested mechanisms likely to prove adequate?
   How can the advantages of each be made best use of?
2. How to relate these representations to the necessarily imper-
   fect representations that the student has.
   Not enough thought has been given to representing inexpert
   reasoning.
3. How to apply these representational techniques to support
   gaming and programming activities.
4. How to provide an acceptable 'man-machine interface', using
   natural language and visual displays.

As with most problems in artificial intelligence, the best to be
hoped for is that gradual progress will continue (or perhaps that
some problems will be identified as insurmountable). We agree
therefore with the conclusion of Howe (1980): 'Given these kinds
of pedagogical problems, and financial considerations, and the
teacher's traditional dislike of machines in the classroom, we can
confidently anticipate that expert systems in the shape of computerised tutors will play a minor role in education for many years
to come.' A few tutorial programs will be generally available in
1992, but there will be little incentive to develop more. The type of
application where there is an incentive is in areas where failures in
training result in great cost. For example, if errors in operating
nuclear power plants could be reduced by training with an expert

teaching system (like SOPHIE but incorporating a simulation of a power plant) then such a system might well be developed.

Research on computer tutors should continue, however, not so much for practical reasons but because it should lead to a deeper understanding of tutoring by human tutors. It is often the case that the attempt to automate an activity forces a better understanding of the activity itself.

Educational philosophy

It is usual to think of the future of computer-assisted learning in rather concrete terms – how classrooms will be organised, how much equipment will cost, how various kinds of programs will be written, and so on. In the long term, however, the main contribution of computer-assisted learning will probably prove to be its contribution to fundamental changes in educational philosophy. Whether these changes will be manifest in 1992 is hard to say for it depends on how quickly society understands and encourages them.

An analogy is with the practice of medicine. The application of science and technology has not only made medicine more effective, but has transformed our appreciation of our physical selves. Perhaps we are beginning to develop a science of 'bugs of understanding' which may similarly transform our appreciation of our mental selves. No doubt the analogy soon breaks down, but we have seen in this book several examples which ought to make us think more deeply about the process of learning. To mention a few:

the realisation that apparently random errors are often symptoms of systematic non-standard processes, which once identified may be more directly corrected;
the importance of the debugging process while writing computer programs and the consequent appreciation that bugs should be actively sought;
the possibility of providing precise descriptions of informal tutorial techniques such as the Socratic method;
the realisation that good teaching is a problem-solving activity and that expert teaching systems may be developed along the lines of expert systems for other specialist skills.

These ideas are derived from the field of artificial intelligence,

267

which incomplete and incorrect as it undoubtedly is in many respects, already provides new perspectives on the learning process – see, for example, Schank's application of artificial intelligence to the teaching of reading and understanding (Schank, 1982). Computer science is not just about computer machinery. It is also about ways of describing processes – understanding, thinking, reasoning, recognising, learning. Education could well do with more precise descriptions of these activities.

We have seen that improvements in computer technology, and consequently in the cost-effectiveness of computer-assisted learning, have not led to significant changes in educational practice. Still today the emphasis is on equipment. In this book we have not predicted any definite outcome but we have discussed some examples which demonstrate that the new technology can be used to support work of high educational quality. But we have seen also that it is easier to write programs that trot out simple facts, than to write programs that discuss concepts sensibly; it is easier to let children try to learn BASIC, than to develop learning environments which facilitate intellectual discoveries; it is easier to write programs which treat students uniformly, than to write programs which try to take account of an individual student's interests, errors and aptitudes. In the long run, it will be in all our interests to try to do what is hardest.

Notes

1. This rate of development was predicted by Moore (1965), although its implications did not begin to become apparent to many for some ten years.
2. Videotex is the generic term for systems which retrieve and display text information on modified televisions: viewdata (e.g. the British Telecom Prestel) is one method. An alternative method is teletext (e.g. BBC's Ceefax), in which pages are broadcast on otherwise unused television lines. Since teletext is a one-way system, with limited capacity for information and relatively long retrieval times, it is less suitable for computer-assisted learning.
3. Educational software is one kind of information which may well be transmitted via viewdata or teletext ('telesoftware'). Telesoftware is already cheaper, quicker and more reliable than the most common method at present, floppy discs through the post. However, a tariff scheme will have to be devised to overcome the fact that any transmitted programs, being publicly accessible, are likely to be worthless.

268

GLOSSARY

access time _the time it takes to find a piece of data.

adaptive program – a program which makes itself more suited to the user of it.

algorithm – a precise description of how to solve some specific problem.

artificial intelligence – the science of getting computers to do things which, if done by humans, would be said to be intelligent.

author – the writer of a program to teach.

author language – a programming language designed to be used by an author.

autonomy – the freedom to be a law unto oneself (Greek *autos*, self; *nomos*, law).

branching program – a teaching program organised as a set of frames.

bug – an error in a computer program.

calculator – an electronic device for performing simple arithmetic.

chip – a small piece of silicon onto which have been etched many circuit elements.

compiler – a program which converts programs written in some language into a form which can be executed on some computer.

courseware – the set of programs and associated materials for a computer-assisted learning course.

database – a collection of facts, usually organised in some systematic way.

debugging – the activity of finding and removing bugs in programs.

dialogue – the sequence of messages between the user and the computer.

discovery method – a method of teaching in which the main content of what is to be learned is not given but must be discovered by the learner (contrasted with 'reception methods').

drill – a series of questions of the same sort for a student to practise on.

educational technology – the endeavour to use relevant knowledge in some systematic way to solve problems of learning and teaching.

evaluation – the attempt to determine the extent to which educational objectives have been attained.

expert system – a program which tries to solve problems using specialist knowledge.

execute – carry out (as in execute a program).

feedback – in general, a technique whereby part of the output of a system is redirected to the input; in education, the information provided to a learner about what he has done.

frame – in teaching programs, one step consisting of some text to be presented to the student and a specification of how the next frame is to be determined by the student's response to the text; in artificial intelligence, a data structure intended to describe some stereotyped situation.

game – an activity that is not compulsory.

generative program – a teaching program which produces questions, text, etc. from partial specifications while it is running.

graphics – drawings.

graphics terminal – a terminal for displaying drawings.

heuristic – a piece of information that might be useful in solving a problem (often contrasted with 'algorithm').

high-level language – a programming language which permits a programmer to write programs without knowing the details of a particular computer's built-in instructions (as opposed to a 'low-level language').

individualised instruction – instruction which is geared to the individual student's competence and aptitude (rather than those of a hypothetical average student in a group).

integrated circuit – a small piece of plastic which contains a chip and has metal leads extending from it for connections to other components.

intelligent (terminal, etc.) – containing its own processor.

interactive system – a computer system which responds to the user quickly (as opposed to a batch-processing system which does not).

interface – a shared boundary, between two pieces of equipment, between two programs, or between a user and a computer.

interpreter – a program which allows a computer to execute a program text directly.

keyword matching – the comparison of words specified by the author with those contained in a student's response.

learner control – the means by which the learner determines (or helps to determine) learning activities.

linear program – a teaching program organised as a set of frames, each of which always goes on to the same next frame.

mainframe – a computer which offers the full range of facilities (often opposed to mini- and microcomputer).

memory – a device for storing programs and data.

microcomputer – a computer based on a microprocessor.

microprocessor – an integrated circuit that executes instructions.

minicomputer – a computer similar to a mainframe but smaller.

monitor – a television set used with a personal computer, or a program that allows a user to operate a computer, or a program that watches over a student's activities.

multiple-choice question – a question to be answered by selecting one from a set of given possible answers.

network – a group of computers which can communicate with one another, or, in artificial intelligence, a data structure in which items are linked together.

objectives – the aims or goals of instruction.

package – an educational program plus teaching materials.

processor – that part of a computer which controls the other components, manipulates the information and performs the calculations.

production rule – a rule in which a condition is associated with an action to be carried out if the condition holds.

programmed instruction – a method of teaching based on linear programs, and now branching programs.

PROM – programmable read-only memory, i.e. memory in which programs can be stored but which thereafter, to the normal user, is read-only memory.

271

RAM − random-access memory, in which programs and data can be stored and changed.

reinforcement − in behaviourist theories of learning, the presentation of a reward after the desired response has been made.

remote access − use of a computer by means of a terminal distant from the processor.

resolution − referring to graphics, the higher the resolution the finer the lines which can be drawn.

resource centre − a centre which provides educational technology support for schools.

response time − the time between a question being asked (e.g. by a student at a terminal) and a reply being received.

ROM − read-only memory, the contents of which a user can retrieve but cannot change.

routine − a piece of program for performing some generally useful task (also *subroutine, procedure*).

semantic − to do with meaning.

simulation − a program which mimics part of a real-life system and which can be used by a student to learn about this system.

statement − in programming, a single instruction in a program.

string − a sequence of letters, digits or other symbols.

student model − that part of a teaching program which provides it with information about the student using it.

syntax − grammatical structure.

teaching machine − a device for presenting programmed instruction.

telesoftware − the transmission of software by viewdata systems.

teletype − an electromechanical printing device at which strings may be typed in to the computer or out by the computer (becoming obsolete, see 'terminal').

terminal − a device consisting of a keyboard and printer and/or screen (at least) by means of which a dialogue may be carried on.

time-sharing − a computer system which can be used simultaneously by several users at different terminals.

VDU − visual display unit, a terminal with a television screen for displaying messages from the user and the computer.

word − a unit of memory, usually the smallest amount which can be read from or written to by a single instruction.

word processor − a computer system designed for editing text.

ACRONYMOGRAPHY

The computer-assisted learning fraternity is blessed with a multitude of acronyms to bewilder the novitiate. Some are listed below, but beware! the addresses, or even the associations themselves, may be transitory.

AAAI: American Association for Artificial Intelligence
A society to further the dissemination of information on artificial intelligence in the US. c/o B.G. Buchanan, Computer Science Department, Stanford University, Stanford, Calif, 94305, USA

ACAL: Association for Computer-Assisted Learning
Educational Computing Section, Chelsea College, University of London, Pulton Place, London, SW6 5PR.

ACM: Association for Computer Machinery
The American association of computer scientists.
1133 Avenue of the Americas, New York, NY 10036, USA

ADCIS: Association for the Development of Computer-Based Instructional Systems
Computer Center, Western Washington University, Billingham, WA 98225, USA

AEDS: Association for Educational Data Systems
1201 Sixteenth St NW, Washington, DC 20036, USA

AISB: Artificial Intelligence and Simulation of Behaviour
A society which acts as a focal point for news of artificial intelligence research in Europe. c/o R.M. Young, Applied Psychology Unit, Cambridge University.

AUCBE: Advisory Unit for Computer Based Education
Endymion Road, Hatfield, Herts, AL10 5AU

BBN: Bolt Beranek and Newman
A firm active in computer-assisted learning research.

50 Moulton Street, Cambridge, MA 02138, USA
BCS: British Computer Society
13 Mansfield Street, London, W1M 0BP
CEDAR: Computers in Education as a Resource
An information and advisory service. Imperial College Computer
Centre, Exhibition Road, London, SW7 2BX.
CERL: Computer-Based Education Research Laboratory
Where PLATO was developed. University of Illinois, Urbana, IL
61801, USA
CET: Council for Education Technology
3 Devonshire Street, London, W1N 2BA
CONDUIT: Computers in Oregon State University
North Carolina Educational Computing Service,
Dartmouth College and the Universities of Iowa and Texas.
A centre which reviews and distributes educational software.
CONDUIT Central, PO Box 388, Iowa City, Iowa 52440, USA
ERIC: Educational Resources Information Center
Designed to provide access to the findings of educational research.
National Institute of Education, Washington DC 20208, USA
GAPE: Geographical Association Package Exchange
Department of Geography, University of Technology, Lough-
borough, LE11 3TU
HUMRRO: Human Resources Research Organization
Includes several computer-assisted learning projects.
300 North Washington Street, Alexandria, VA 22314, USA
ICCE: International Council for Computers in Education
An organisation for people interested in pre-college computer-
assisted learning. Department of Computer and Information
Science, University of Oregon, Eugene, OR 97403, USA
ITMA: Investigations on Teaching with Microcomputers as an Aid
College of St Mark and St John, Derriford Road, Plymouth,
Devon, PL6 8BH
MAPE: Microcomputers and Primary Education
A group which aims 'to promote and develop the awareness and
effective use of microelectronics as an integral part of the philo-
sophy and practice of primary education'. c/o Derrick Daines,
Carsic Junior School, St Mary's Road, Sutton-in-Ashfield, Notts.
MECC: Minnesota Educational Computing Consortium
Coordinates computer services in Minnesota and distributes

educational software. 2520 Broadway Drive, St Paul, MN 55133, USA

MEP: Microelectronics Education Programme
See Chapter 7. Cheviot House, Coach Lane Campus, Newcastle, NE7 7AX

MICE: Microcomputers in Computer Education
A group of teachers building up a library of programs, basically concerned with teaching computer appreciation and computer studies. Dr M. Edwards, Polytechnic of the South Bank, Borough Road, London, SE1

MICROSIFT: Microcomputer Software and Information for Teachers
A clearing house for software reviews. 500 Lindsay Building, 300 SW 6th Avenue, Portland, OR 97204, USA

MUSE: Microcomputer Users in Secondary Education
121A Chanterlands Avenue, Hull, HU5 3TG

NCC: National Computing Centre
Oxford Road, Manchester M1 7ED

NDPCAL (or NDP, for short): *National Development Programme in Computer-Assisted Learning*
A UK government-sponsored programme which ran from 1973 to 1977.

PLATO: Programmed Logic for Automatic Teaching Operation
See Chapter 3.

SALT: Society for Applied Learning Technology
For instructional technologists. 50 Culpepper Street, Warrenton, VA 22186, USA

SIGART: Special Interest Group on Artificial Intelligence
A group within the ACM (see above).

SIGCUE: Special Interest Group on Computer Uses in Education
A group within the ACM (see above).

SMDP: Scottish Microelectronics Development Programme
A government-funded agency supporting the use of microcomputers in education in Scotland. Dowanhill, 74 Victoria Crescent Road, Glasgow, G12 9JN

TICCIT: Time-shared Interactive Computer Controlled Information Television
See Chapter 3.

BIBLIOGRAPHY

Abelson, H. (1982) *Logo for the Apple II*, Peterborough, NH: Byte/McGraw-Hill.

Abelson, H. and di Sessa, A. (1976) 'Student science training program in mathematics, physics and computer science', *LOGO Memo No. 29*, MIT, Cambridge, Mass.

Abelson, H. and di Sessa, A. (1981) *Turtle Geometry: the Computer as a Medium for Exploring Mathematics*, Cambridge, Mass.: MIT Press.

Abelson, H. and Goldenberg, P. (1977) 'Teacher's guide for computational models of animal behaviour', *LOGO Memo No. 46*, MIT, Cambridge, Mass.

Aiken, R.M. and Braun, L. (1980) 'Into the eighties with microcomputer based learning', *Computing*, 13, 7, 11-16.

Alderman, D.L. (1979) 'Evaluation of the TICCIT computer-assisted instructional system in the community college', *SIGCUE Bull.*, 13, 3, 5-17.

Alderman, D.L. and Mahler, W.A. (1977) 'Faculty acceptance of instructional technology: attitudes towards educational practices and CAI at community college', *Prog. Learning and Ed. Tech.*, 14, 77-87.

Alpert, D. (1975) 'The PLATO IV system in use: a progress report', in O. Lecarme and R. Lewis (eds), *Computers in Education*, Amsterdam: North-Holland.

Alty, J.L. (1982) 'The impact of microtechnology – a case for reassessing the role of computers in learning', *Computers and Education*, 6, 1-5.

Anderson, J.R. and Bower, G.H. (1973) *Human Associative Memory*, Washington: Winston.

Anderson, R.C., Kulhavy, R.W. and André, T. (1972) 'Conditions under which feedback facilitates learning from programmed lessons', *J. Educ. Psych.*, 63, 186-8.

Aston, M.H. (1981) 'Viewdata – implications for education', *Computer Education*, 37, 43-5.

Atkinson, R.C. (1972) 'Ingredients for a theory of instruction', *Am. Psychologist,* 27, 921-31.

Atkinson, R.C. (1976) 'Adaptive instructional systems: some attempts to optimize the learning process', in D. Klahr (ed.), *Cognition and Instruction*, Hillsdale, NJ: Erlbaum.

Atkinson, R.C. and Wilson, H.A. (eds) (1969) *Computer-assisted Instruction: a Book of Readings*, New York: Academic Press.

Ausubel, D.P. (1968) *Educational Psychology: a Cognitive View,* New York: Holt, Rinehart & Winston.

Ayscough, P.B. (1977) 'CALCHEMistry', *Brit J. of Ed. Tech.*, 8, 201-3.

Bamberger, J. (1974) 'The luxury of necessity', *LOGO Memo No. 12*, MIT, Cambridge, Mass.

Bamberger, J. (1979) 'Logo music projects: experiments in musical perception and design', *LOGO Memo No. 52*, MIT, Cambridge, Mass.

Banet, B. (1979) 'Computers and early training', *Calculators/Computers*, 3, 17.

Barr, A., Beard, M. and Atkinson, R.C. (1976) 'The computer as a tutorial laboratory: the Stanford BIP project', *Int. J. Man-Machine Stud.*, 8, 567-96.

Beard, M.H., Lorton, P.V., Searle, B.W. and Atkinson, R.C. (1973) 'Comparison of student performance and attitude under three lesson-selection strategies in computer-assisted instruction', *Tech. Rep. No. 222*, Inst. for Math. Stud. in Soc. Sci., Stanford.

Beech, G. (1979) *Computer-assisted Learning in Science Education*, Oxford: Pergamon.

Bell, D. (1974) *The Coming of Post-industrial Society*, London: Heinemann.

Bitzer, D.L. (1976) 'The wide world of computer-based education', in M. Rubinoff and M. Yovits (eds), *Advances in Computers 15*, New York: Academic Press.

Bitzer, D.L. (1977) 'The million terminal system of 1985', in R.J. Seidel and M.L. Rubin (eds), *Computers and Communications: Implications for Education*, New York: Academic Press.

Boast, C.W. (1975) 'Soil water simulation computer program for teaching purposes', *J. Agronomic Educ.*, 4, 98-105.

Bobrow, D.G. and Winograd, T. (1977) 'An overview of KRL, a knowledge representation language', *Cogn. Sci.*, 1, 3-46.

Boden, M.A. (1977) *Artificial Intelligence and Natural Man*, Hassocks, Sussex: Harvester.

Boden, M.A. (1979) *Piaget*, Hassocks, Sussex: Harvester.

Boehm, B.W. (1979) 'Software engineering: R&D trends and defense needs', in P. Wegner (ed.), *Research Directions in Software Technology*, Cambridge, Mass.: MIT Press.

Bork, A.M. (1979) 'Interactive learning', *Am. J. Physics*, 47, 5-10.

Bork. A.M. (1980) 'Physics in the Irvine Educational Technology Center', *Computers and Education*, 4, 37-57.

Bork, A.M. and Robson, J. (1972) 'A computer simulation of the study of waves', *Am. J. Physics*, 40, 1288-94.

Borning, A. (1979) 'Thinglab: a constraint-oriented simulation laboratory', *Rep. No. SSL 79-3*, Xerox Palo Alto Research Center, California.

Borning, A. (1981) 'The programming language aspects of Thinglab, a constraint-oriented simulation laboratory', *ACM Trans. on Prog. Lang. & Systems*, 3, 353-87.

Bowman, W. and Flegal, B. (1981) 'ToolBox: a Smalltalk illustration system', *Byte*, 8, 6, 369-77.

Brahan, J.W. and Godfrey, D. (1982) 'A marriage of convenience: videotex and computer assisted learning', *Computers and Education*, 6, 33-8.

Bramer, M. (1980) 'Using computers in distance education: the first ten years of the British Open University', *Computers and Education*, 4, 293-301.

Braun, L. (1977) 'A speculation on the impact of LSI technology on computing', in R.J. Seidel and M.L. Rubin (eds), *Computers and Communications: Implications for Education*, New York: Academic Press.

Brebner, A. and Hallworth, H.J. (1980) 'A multi-media CAI terminal based upon a microprocessor with applications for the handicapped', Paper presented at 18th Ann. Conv. of Assoc. for Educ. Data Systems.

Brown, J.S. (1979) 'Fundamental research in technology in science education', in D.H. Deringer and A.R. Molnar (eds), *Technology in Science Education: the Next Ten Years, Perspectives and Recommendations*, Nat. Sci. Found. Report.

Brown, J.S. and Burton, R.R. (1978) 'Diagnostic models for procedural bugs in basic mathematical skills', *Cogn. Sci.*, 2, 155-92.

Brown, J.S., Burton, R.R. and Bell, A.G. (1974) 'SOPHIE: a sophisticated instructional environment for teaching electronic troubleshooting', *BBN Rep. No. 2790*, Bolt Beranek and Newman, Cambridge, Mass.

Brown, J.S. , Burton, R.R. and Bell, A.G. (1975) 'SOPHIE: a step toward creating a reactive learning environment', *Int. J. Man-Mach. Stud.*, 7, 675-96.

Brown, J.S., Burton, R.R. and de Kleer, J. (1982) 'Pedagogical, natural language and knowledge engineering techniques in SOPHIE I, II and III', in D.H. Sleeman and J.S. Brown (eds), *Intelligent Teaching Systems,* London: Academic Press.

Brown, J.S. and Van Lehn, K. (1980) 'Repair theory: a generative theory of bugs in procedural skills', *Report CIS-4*, Xerox Palo Alto Research Center, California.

Bruner, J.S. (1966) *Toward a Theory of Instruction*, Cambridge, Mass.: Belknap Press.

Bunderson, C.V. (1974) 'The design and production of learner-controlled courseware for the TICCIT system: a progress report', *Int. J. Man-Mach. Stud.*, 6, 479-92.

Burton, R.R. and Brown, J.S. (1979) 'An investigation of computer coaching for informal learning activities', *Int. J. Man-Mach. Stud.*, 11, 5-24.

Carbonell, J.R. (1970) 'AI in CAI: an artificial intelligence approach to computer-assisted instruction', *IEEE Trans. on Man-Machine Systems*, 11, 190-202.

Carnegie Commission on Higher Education (1972) *The Fourth Revolution: Instructional Technology in Higher Education*, New York: McGraw-Hill.

Carr, B. and Goldstein, I.P. (1977) 'Overlays: a theory of modelling for computer-assisted instruction', *AI Memo No. 406*, MIT, Cambridge, Mass.

Case, R. (1978) 'Piaget and beyond: toward a developmentally-based theory and technology of instruction', in R. Glaser (ed.), *Advances in Instructional Psychology*, Vol. 1, Hillsdale, NJ: Lawrence Erlbaum.

CERL (1977) 'Demonstration of the PLATO IV computer-based education system' (final report), Computer-based Education Research Laboratory, University of Illinois, Urbana.

CET (1977) *Computer-Assisted Learning in Higher Education – the next ten years*, London: Council for Educational Technology.

Chambers, J.A. and Bork, A. (1980) *Computer-Assisted Learning in U.S. Secondary/Elementary Schools*, New York: ACM.

Chambers, J.A. and Sprecher, J.W. (1980) 'Computer-assisted instruction: current trends and critical issues', *Commun. ACM*, 23, 332-42.

Chant, V.G. and Luenberger, D.G. (1974) 'A mathematical theory of instruction: instructor/learner interaction and instruction pacing', *J. Math. Psych.*, 11, 132-58.

Charp, S. and Woolson, J. (1969) 'Using a computer to teach', *AEDS Monitor*, 7, 6-7.

Clancey, W.J. (1979a) 'Tutoring rules for guiding a case method dialogue', *Int. J. Man-Mach. Stud.*, 11, 25-49.

Clancey, W.J. (1979b). 'Transfer of rule-based expertise through a tutorial dialogue', unpublished PhD thesis, Stanford Univ.

Clarke, J. (1981) *Resource-based Learning for Higher and Continuing Education*, London: Croom Helm.

Clocksin, W. and Mellish, C. (1981) *Programming in PROLOG*, New York: Springer-Verlag.

Collins, A.M. (1976) 'Processes in acquiring knowledge', in R.C. Anderson, R.J. Spiro and W.E. Montague (eds), *Schooling and the Acquisition of Knowledge*, Hillsdale, NJ: Erlbaum.

Collins, A.M. and Quillian, M.R. (1969) 'Retrieval time from semantic memory', *J. Verb. Learn. and Verb. Behav.*, 8, 240-7.

Collins, A.M., Warnock, E.H. and Passafiume, J.J. (1975)

'Analysis and synthesis of tutorial dialogues', in G.H. Bower (ed.), *The Psychology of Learning and Motivation 9*, New York: Academic Press.

Commission on Instructional Technology (1970) *To Improve Learning: a Report to the President and the Congress of the United States*, Washington: US Govt Printing Office.

Coulson, J. (ed.) (1962) *Programmed Learning and Computer-based Instruction*, New York: Wiley.

Crowder, N.A. (1959) 'Automatic tutoring by means of intrinsic programming', in E. Galanter (ed.), *Automatic Teaching: the State of the Art*, New York: Wiley.

Curtin, C., Dawson, C., Provenzano, N. and Cooper, P. (1976) 'The PLATO system: using the computer to teach Russian', *Slavic and East European J.*, 20, 280-92.

Dahl, O.J., Dijkstra, E.W. and Hoare, C.A.R. (1972) *Structured Programming*, London: Academic Press.

Dahl, O.J. and Nygaard, K. (1966). 'Simula – an Algol-based simulation language', *Commun. ACM*, 9, 671-7.

Davis, R. and Lenat, D.B. (1982) *Knowledge-based Systems in Artificial Intelligence*, New York: McGraw-Hill.

Deci, E.L. (1975) *Intrinsic Motivation*, New York: Plenum.

Denenberg, S.A. (1978) 'A personal evaluation of the PLATO system', *SIGCUE Bull.*, 12, 2, 3-10.

DES (1980) *Microelectronics in Education: a Development Programme for Schools and Colleges*, London: DES

DoI (1981) *Information Technology: the Age of Electronic Information*, London, DoI.

Dixon, N.R. (1977) 'Automatic recognition of continuous speech: status and possibilities for an operational system', in R.J. Seidel and M.L. Rubin (eds), *Computers and Communications: Implications for Education*, New York: Academic Press.

Dodge, M., Brogan, R., Brodgen, N. and Lewis, R. (1974) 'How teachers perceive media', *Ed. Tech.*, 14, 1, 21-4.

Donaldson, M. (1978) *Children's Minds*, Glasgow: Fontana.

Du Boulay, J.B.H. (1978) 'Learning primary mathematics through computer programming', unpublished PhD thesis, Dept of Art. Intell., Univ. of Edinburgh.

Du Boulay, J.B.H. (1981) 'Re-learning mathematics through Logo: helping student teachers who don't understand mathematics', in J.A.M. Howe and P.M. Ross (eds), *Microcomputers in Secondary Education*, London: Kogan Page.

Du Boulay, J.B.H. and O'Shea, T. (1976) 'How to work the Logo machine', *DAI Occ. Paper 4*, Dept of Art. Intell., Univ. of Edinburgh.

Du Boulay, J.B.H., O'Shea, T. and Monk, J. (1981) 'The black box inside the glass box: presenting computing concepts to novices', *Int. J. Man-Machine Stud.*,14, 237-49.

Duckworth, E. (1964) 'Piaget rediscovered', in R.E. Ripple and V.N. Rockcastle (eds), *Piaget Rediscovered*, Ithaca, NY: Cornell Univ. School of Education.

Dugdale, S. and Vogel, P. (1978) 'Computer-based instruction for hearing impaired children in the classroom', *American Annals of the Deaf*, 123, 730-43.

Dwyer, T.A. (1971) 'Some principles for the human use of computers in education', *Int. J. Man-Machine Stud.*, 3, 219-39.

Ennals, J.R. (1982) *Beginning Micro-PROLOG*,Chichester: Ellis Horwood.

Evans, C. (1979) *The Mighty Micro*, London: Gollancz.

Feigenbaum, E.A. (1980) 'Themes and case studies of knowledge engineering', in D. Michie (ed.), *Expert Systems in the Microelectronic Age*, Edinburgh: Edinburgh Univ. Press.

Feurzeig, W., Papert, S., Bloom, M., Grant, R. and Solomon, C. (1969) 'Programming languages as a conceptual framework for teaching mathematics', *Rep. No. 1899*, Bolt Beranek & Newman Inc., Cambridge, Mass.

Fielden, J. (1978) 'The cost of innovation and change in education', *Prog. Learning and Ed. Tech.*, 15, 16-25.

Fielden, J. and Pearson, P. (1978) *The Cost of Learning with Computers*, London: Council for Ed. Tech.

Fischer, G. (1981) 'Computational models of skill acquisition processes', in R. Lewis and E.D. Tagg (eds), *Computers in Education*, Amsterdam: North-Holland.

Flavell, J.H. (1973) *The Developmental Psychology of Jean Piaget*,

New York: Van Nostrand.

Fletcher, J.D. and Suppes, P. (1976) 'The Stanford project on computer-assisted instruction for hearing-impaired students', *J. Computer-based Inst.*, 3, 1-12.

Foltz, R. and Gross, D. (1980) 'Integration of CAI into a music program', *J. Computer-based Inst.*, 6, 72-6.

Forester, T. (ed.) (1980) *The Microprocessor Revolution*, Oxford: Blackwell.

Francis, L.D. (1973) 'Computer-simulated qualitative inorganic chemistry', *J. Chem. Educ.*, 50, 556-8.

Fraser, R. (1981) 'Design and evaluation of educational software for group presentation', in J.A.M. Howe and P.M. Ross (eds), *Microcomputers in Secondary Education*, London: Kogan Page.

Frenzel, L. (1980) 'The personal computer – last chance for CAI?', *Byte*, 5, 7, 86-96.

Frijda, N.H. (1972) 'Simulation of human long-term memory', *Psych. Bull.*, 77, 1-31.

Gagné, R.M. (1977) *The Conditions of Learning*, New York: Holt, Rinehart & Winston.

Galanter, E. (ed.) (1959) *Automatic Teaching: the State of the Art*, New York: Wiley.

Gallagher, P. (1980) 'Application of microcomputers to the education of the gifted: meeting an instructional challenge with computer literacy', *T.H.E. Journal*, 7, 4, 40.

Gerard, R.W. (ed.) (1967) *Computers and Education*, New York: McGraw-Hill.

Gilbert, L.A. (1980) 'New technologies and alternative forms of education', *Euromicro Journal*, 6, 221-5.

Gilkey, T.J. and Koffman, E.B. (1974) 'Generative computer-assisted instruction in high school algebra', in A. Gunther (ed.),*International Computing Symposium 1973*, Amsterdam: North-Holland.

Gilman, D.A. (1969) 'Comparison of several feedback methods for correcting errors by computer-assisted instruction', *J. Educ. Psych.*, 60, 503-8.

Glaser, E.L. and Heath, F.G. (1978) 'Design of digital systems in the age of LSI', *IUCC Newsletter*, 6, 1, 16-23.

Goldberg, A. (1974) 'Design of a computer tutor for elementary mathematical logic', *Proc. IFIP Congress 4*, Amsterdam: North-Holland.

Goldberg, A. (1977) 'Smalltalk in the classroom', *Rep. No. SSL 77-2*, Xerox Palo Alto Research Center, California.

Goldberg, A. (1979) 'Educational uses of a Dynabook', *Computers and Education*, 3, 247-66.

Goldberg, A. and Kay, A. (1977) 'Methods for teaching the programming language Smalltalk', *Rep. No. SSL 77-2*, Xerox Palo Alto Research Center, California.

Goldberg, A., Robson, D. and Ingalls, D.H.H. (1982) 'Smalltalk-80: the Interactive Programming Environment', forthcoming.

Goldberg, A. and Ross, J. (1981) 'Is the Smalltalk-80 system for children?', *Byte*, 8, 6, 347-68.

Goldstein, I.P. (1979) 'The genetic graph: a representation for the evolution of procedural knowledge', *Int. J. Man-Mach. Stud.*, 11, 51-77.

Gould, L. and Finzer, W. (1981) 'A study of TRIP: a computer system for animating time-rate-distance problems', in R. Lewis and E.D. Tagg (eds), *Computers in Education*, Amsterdam: North-Holland.

Grignetti, C.M., Hausmann, C. and Gould, L. (1975) 'An "intelligent" on-line assistant and tutor: NLS-SCHOLAR', *Proc. ACM Nat. Comp. Conf.*, 775-81.

Grubb, R.E. (1968) 'Learner controlled statistics', *Prog. Learning and Ed. Tech.*, 5, 38-42.

Gruber, H.E. and Voneche, J.J. (eds) (1977) *The Essential Piaget: an Interpretive Reference and Guide*, New York: Basic Books.

Guthrie, J.T. (1971) 'Feedback and sentence learning', *J. Verb. Learn. and Verb. Behav.*, 10, 23-8.

Hansen, J.B. (1974) 'Effects of feedback, learner control, and cognitive abilities on state anxiety and performance in a computer-assisted instruction task', *J. Educ. Psych.*, 66, 247-54.

Hartley, J.R. (1978) 'An appraisal of computer-assisted learning in the United Kingdom', *Prog. Learning and Ed. Tech.*, 15. 136-51.

Hartley, J.R. and Bostrom, K. (1982) 'An evaluation of micro-

CAL in schools', *Int. J. Man-Machine Stud.*, forthcoming.

Hayes, R.M. (1967) 'Library – handling books and their contents', in R.W. Gerard (ed.), *Computers and Education*, New York: McGraw-Hill.

Hebenstreit, J. (1980) '10,000 microcomputers for the French secondary schools', *Computer*, 13, 17-22.

Hewitt, C. (1976) 'Viewing control structures as patterns of passing messages', *Memo No. 410*, MIT AI Lab., Cambridge, Mass.

Hilgard, E.R. and Bower, G.H. (1975) *Theories of Learning*, Englewood Cliffs, NJ: Prentice-Hall.

Hofstetter, F.T. (1979) 'Controlled evaluation of a competency-based approach to teaching aural interval identification', *Proc. ADCIS Conf.*, 3, 935-8.

Hooper, R. (1977) *The National Development Programme in Computer Assisted Learning: Final Report of the Director*, London: Council for Ed. Tech.

House, E.R. (1974) *The Politics of Educational Innovation*, California: McCrutchan.

Howe, J.A.M. (1980) 'Learning through model building', in D. Michie (ed.), *Expert Systems in the Microelectronic Age*, Edinburgh: Edinburgh Univ. Press.

Howe, J.A.M. and O'Shea, T. (1978) 'Computational metaphors for children', in F. Klix (ed.), *Human and Artificial Intelligence*, Berlin: Deutscher Verlag.

Howe, J.A.M., O'Shea, T. and Plane, F. (1980) 'Teaching mathematics through Logo programming: an evaluation study', in R. Lewis and E.D. Tagg (eds), *Computer Assisted Learning: Scope, Progress and Limits*, Amsterdam: North-Holland.

Jamison, D., Suppes, P. and Wells, S. (1974) 'The effectiveness of alternative instructional media: a survey', *Rev. Educ. Res.*, 44, 1-68.

Jenkin, J.M. (1982) 'Some principles of screen design and software for their support', *Computers and Education*, 6, 25-31.

Johnson, D.C., Anderson, R.E., Hansen, T.P. and Klassen, D.L. (1981) 'Computer literacy and awareness', in J.A.M. Howe and P.M. Ross (eds), *Microcomputers in Secondary Education*, London: Kogan Page.

Bibliography

Jones, M.C. (1978) 'Concerning the evaluation of TICCIT computer-based English composition and mathematics instruction', Paper presented at AEDS Annual Convention, Washington: Assoc. for Ed. Data Systems.

Jones, R. (1980) *Microcomputers: their Uses in Primary Schools*, London: CET.

Judd, W.A., Bunderson, C.V. and Bessant, E.W. (1970) 'An investigation of the effects of learner control in computer assisted instruction prerequisite mathematics', *Maths. Tech. Rep. No. 5*, CAI Lab., Univ. of Texas at Austin.

Kahn, R.A. (1977) 'Public access to personal computing: a new role for science museums', *Computer*, 10, 56-66.

Kane, D. and Sherwood, B. (1980) 'A computer-based course in classical mechanics', *Computers and Education*, 4, 15-36.

Kay, A. (1977) 'Microelectronics and the personal computer', *Scientific American*, 226, 230-44.

Kay, A. and Goldberg, A. (1977) 'Personal dynamic media', *Computer*, 10, 31-41.

Kaye, A. and Rumble, G. (1981) *Distance Teaching for Higher and Adult Education*, London: Croom Helm.

Kearsley, G.P. and Hunka, S. (1979) 'Documentation in computer-based instruction', *SIGCUE Bull.*, 13, 1, 3-13.

Kimball, R.B. (1973) 'Self-optimizing computer-assisted tutoring: theory and practice', *Tech. Rep. No. 206*, Inst. for Math. Stud. in the Soc. Sci., Standford.

Kimball, R.B. (1982) 'A self-improving tutor for symbolic integration', in D.H. Sleeman and J.S. Brown (eds), *Intelligent Teaching Systems*, London: Academic Press.

Klahr, D. and Wallace, J.G. (1976) *Cognitive Development: an Information Processing View*, Hillsdale, NJ: Erlbaum.

Koffman, E.B. (1972) 'A generative computer-assisted instruction tutor for computer science concepts', *Proc. Spring. Jt. Comp. Conf.* Montvale, NJ: AFIPS Press.

Koffman, E.B. and Blount, S.E. (1975) 'Artificial intelligence and automatic programming in CAI', *Art. Intell.*, 6, 215-34.

Kolstad, R. and Lidtke, D. (1981) 'Gifted and talented', in *Topics: Computer Education for Elementary and Secondary Schools*,

New York: ACM.

Kopstein, F.F. and Seidel, R.J. (1969) 'Computer-administered instruction versus traditionally-administered instruction: economics', in R.C. Atkinson and H.A. Wilson (eds), *Computer-assisted Instruction: a Book of Readings*, New York: Academic Press.

Krasner, G. (1981) 'The Smalltalk-80 virtual machine', *Byte*, 6, 8, 300-21.

Kulhavy, R.W. (1977) 'Feedback in written instruction', *Rev. Educ. Research*, 47, 211-32.

Kulik, J.A., Kulik, C-L.C. and Cohen, P.A. (1980) 'Effectiveness of computer-based college teaching: a meta-analysis of findings', *Rev. Educ. Research*, 50, 524-44.

Kuhn, W. and Lorton, P. (1981) 'Computer assisted instruction in music: ten years of evolution', in R. Lewis and E.D. Tagg (eds), *Computers in Education*, Amsterdam: North-Holland.

Last, R.W. (1979) 'The role of computer-assisted learning in modern language teaching', *Assoc. for Literary and Linguistic Computing Bull.*, 7, 165-71.

Laubsch, J.H. (1970) 'Optimal item allocation in computer-assisted instruction', *IAG Journal*, 3, 295-311.

Laubsch, J.H. (1975) 'Some thoughts about representing knowledge in instructional systems', *Proc. 4th Int. Jt. Conf. on Art. Intell.*, Tbilisi, USSR.

Laubsch, J.H. and Chiang, A. (1974) 'Application of mathematical models of learning in the decision structure of adaptive computer-assisted instruction systems', in A. Gunther (ed.), *International Computing Symposium 1973*, Amsterdam: North-Holland.

Laver, M. (1976) *An Introduction to the Uses of Computers*, Cambridge: Cambridge Univ. Press.

Lawler, R.W. (1981) 'The progressive construction of mind', *Cogn. Sci.*, 5, 1-30.

Learning Research Group (1976) 'Personal dynamic media', *Rep. No. SSL 76-1*, Xerox Palo Alto Research Center, California.

Levien, R.E. (1972) *The Emerging Technology: Instructional Uses of the Computer in Higher Education*, New York: McGraw-Hill.

Levine, M. (1975) *A Cognitive Theory of Learning: Research on Hypothesis Theory*, Hillsdale, NJ: Erlbaum.

Lewis, B.N. and Pask, G. (1964) 'The theory and practice of adaptive teaching machines', in R. Glaser (ed.), *Teaching Machines and Programmed Learning II*, Washington: Nat. Educ. Assoc.

Lewis, J.W. and Tagg, W. (1981) 'Data storage and retrieval and its application', in R. Lewis and D. Tagg (eds), *Computers in Education*, Amsterdam: North-Holland.

Licklider, J.C.R. (1979) 'Impact of information technology on education in science and technology', in D.H. Deringer and A.R. Molnar (eds), *Technology in Science Education: the Next Ten Years, Perspectives and Recommendations*, Nat. Sci. Found. Report.

Luehrmann, A. (1972) 'Should the computer teach the student, or vice versa?' *Proc. AFIPS Conf.*, 40, 407-10.

Luehrmann, A. (1977) 'Intelligent videodisc systems – implications for education', in R.J. Seidel and M.L. Rubin (eds), *Computers and Communications: Implications for Education*, New York: Academic Press.

Lumsdaine, A.A. and Glaser, R. (eds) (1960) *Teaching Machines and Programmed Learning: a source book*, Washington: Nat. Educ. Assoc.

Maggs, P.B. and Morgan, T.D. (1975) 'Computer-based legal education at the University of Illinois: a report of two years' experience', *J. of Legal Educ.*, 27, 138-56.

Malone, T.W. (1980) 'What makes things fun to learn?: a study of intrinsically motivating computer games', unpublished PhD thesis, Dept of Psychology, Stanford Univ.

Malone, T.W. (1981) 'Toward a theory of intrinsically motivating instruction', *Cogn. Sci.*, 4, 333-69.

Martin, J. and Butler, D. (1982) *Viewdata and Information Society*, Hemel Hempstead: Prentice-Hall.

Mayer, R.E. (1981) 'The psychology of how novices learn computer programming', *Computing Surveys*, 13, 121-41.

McCall, K. and Tesler, L. (1980) 'TinyTalk, a subset of Smalltalk-76 for 64kb microcomputers', *ACM Sigsmall Newsletter*, 6, 197-8.

McDonald, B. (1977) 'The educational evaluation of NDPCAL', *Brit. J. Ed. Tech.*, 8, 176-89.
McKeachie, W.J. (1974) 'Instructional psychology', in M.R. Rosenzweig and L.W. Porter (eds), *Annual Review of Psychology*, 24, Palo Alto: Annual Reviews Inc.
McKenzie, J. (1977) 'Computers in the teaching of undergraduate science', *Brit. J. Ed. Tech.*, 8, 214-24.
McKenzie, J. (ed.) (1978) *Interactive Computer Graphics in Science Teaching*, Chichester: Ellis Horwood.
McNally, D.W. (1977) *Piaget, Education and Teaching*, Hassocks, Sussex: Harvester.
Merrill, M.D. (1974) 'Premises, propositions and research underlying the design of a learner controlled computer assisted instruction system: a summary for the TICCIT system', *Working Paper No. 44*, Div. Inst. Services, Brigham Young Univ.
Merrill, M.D. (1980) 'Learner control in computer based learning', *Computers and Education*, 4, 77-95.
Michie, D. (ed.) (1980) *Expert Systems in the Microelectronic Age*, Edinburgh: Edinburgh Univ. Press.
Millward, R.B. and Wickens, T.D. (1974) 'Concept-identification models', in D.H. Krantz (ed.), *Contemporary Developments in Mathematical Psychology 1*, San Francisco: Freeman.
Minsky, M.L. (1975) 'A framework for representing knowledge', in P.H. Winston (ed.), *The Psychology of Computer Vision*, New York: McGraw-Hill.
Minsky, M.L. and Papert, S. (1972) 'Artificial intelligence progress report', *AI Memo No. 252*, MIT, Cambridge, Mass.
Mitre Corporation (1974) 'An overview of the TICCIT program', *Report M74-1*, Washington: Mitre Corporation.
Mitre Corporation (1976) 'An overview of the TICCIT program', *Report M76-44*, Washington: Mitre Corporation.
Montanelli, R.G. (1979) 'Evaluating PLATO in the teaching of computer science', *J. Computer-Based Inst.*, 5, 72-6.
Moore, G.E. (1965) 'Cramming more components onto integrated circuits', *Electronics*, 38, 114-16.
Morgan, R.P. (1977) 'Potential impacts of educational telecommunications systems', in R.J. Seidel and M.L. Rubin (eds), *Computers and Communications: Implications for Education*,

New York: Academic Press.

Morrison, F. (1975) 'Planning a large-scale computer-assisted instruction installation – the TICCIT experience', in O. Lecarme and R. Lewis (eds), *Computers in Education*, Amsterdam: North-Holland.

Murphy, R.T. and Appel, L.R. (1977) 'Evaluation of the PLATO IV computer-based education system in the community college', *Nat. Sci. Found. Contract No. NSF-C731*, Princeton, NJ: Educational Testing Service.

NCET (1969) *Computer Based Learning Systems: a Programme for Research and Development*, London: Council for Educational Technology.

Naur, P. (1963) 'Goto statements and good Algol style', *BIT*, 3, 204-5.

Newell, A. and Simon, H.A. (1972) *Human Problem Solving*, Englewood Cliffs, NJ: Prentice-Hall.

Nilles, J.M. (1980) 'Personal computers in the future: an overview', *IEEE Trans. Systems, Man and Cybernetics*, 10, 474-6.

Obertino, P. (1974) 'The PLATO reading project: an overview', *Educational Technology*, 14, 8-13.

Oettinger, A.G. (1971) *Run, Computer, Run: the Mythology of Educational Innovation*, Harvard: Harvard Univ. Press.

Ojemann, R.H. and Wilkinson, F.R. (1939) 'The effect on pupil growth of an increase in teacher's understanding of pupil behaviour', *J. Exper. Educ.*, 8, 143-7.

O'Shea, T. (1979) *Self-improving Teaching Systems*, Basel: Birkhauser Verlag.

Palmer, B.G. and Oldehoeft, A.E. (1975) 'The design of an instructional system based on problem-generators', *Int. J. Man-Mach. Stud.*, 7, 249-71.

Papert, S. (1973) 'Uses of technology to enhance education', *AI Memo No. 298*, MIT, Cambridge, Mass.

Papert, S. (1980) *Mindstorms: Children, Computers and Powerful Ideas*, New York: Basic Books.

Papert, S., Watt, D., di Sessa, A. and Weir, S. (1979) 'Final report of the Brookline LOGO Project', *LOGO Memo No. 53*, MIT, Cambridge, Mass.

Pask, G. (1975) *Conversation, Cognition and Learning*, New York: Elsevier.

Pask, G. and Scott, B.C.E. (1972) 'Learning strategies and individual competence', *Int. J. Man-Mach. Stud.*, 4, 217-53.

Peplinski, C. (1970) 'A generative computer-assisted instruction program that teaches algebra', *Tech. Rep. No. 90*, Dept of Comp. Sci., Univ. of Wisconsin.

Perlman, R. (1976) 'Using computer technology to provide a creative learning environment for preschool children', unpublished MSc thesis, MIT, Cambridge, Mass.

Piaget, J. (1954) 'Language and thought from the genetic point of view', *Acta Psychologica*, 10, 51-60.

Piaget, J. (1964) 'Development and learning', in R.E. Ripple and V.N. Rockcastle (eds), *Piaget Rediscovered*, Ithaca, NY: Cornell Univ. School of Education.

Piaget, J. (1966) *The Origin of Intelligence in the Child*, London: Routledge & Kegan Paul.

Piaget, J. (1970) *The Science of Education and the Psychology of the Child*, New York: Orion Press.

Placek, R.W. (1980) 'A model for integrating computer-assisted instruction into the music curriculum', *J. Computer-Based Inst.*, 6, 99-105.

Quillian, M.R. (1969) 'The teachable language comprehender', *Commun. ACM*, 12, 459-76.

Resnick, C.A. (1975) 'Computational models of learners for computer assisted learning', unpublished PhD thesis, Univ. of Illinois at Urbana-Champaign.

Resnick, L.R. and Ford, W.W. (1981) *The Psychology of Mathematics for Instruction*. Hillsdale, NJ: Erlbaum.

Richardson, J.E. (1980) 'Computer-based education for the hearing impaired: a look toward the future', College Educational Resources paper, Kendall College, Washington, DC.

Rigney, J.W. (1962) 'Potential uses of computers as teaching machines', in J.E. Coulson (ed.), *Programmed Learning and*

Computer-Based Instruction, New York: Wiley.

Rockart, J.F. and Morton, M.S.S. (1975) *Computers and the Learning Process in Higher Education*, New York: McGraw-Hill.

Rowntree, D. (1979) *Educational Technology in Curriculum Development*, London: Harper & Row.

Rubin, A. (1980) 'Making stories, making sense', *BBN Report*, Cambridge, Mass.

Ruth, G.R. (1976) 'Intelligent program analysis', *Art. Intell.*, 7, 65-85.

Saettler, P. (1968) *A History of Instructional Technology*, New York: McGraw-Hill.

Samuel, A.L. (1959) 'Some studies in machine learning using the game of checkers', *IBM J. Res. Develop.*, 3, 210-29.

Sandals, L.H. *et al.* (1980) 'An overview of a 6-year computer-assisted learning project for special needs children and adolescents', *Computer Applications Unit Report*, Univ. of Calgary.

Schank, R.C. (1982) *Reading and Understanding: Teaching from the Perspective of Artificial Intelligence*, London: Lawrence Erlbaum.

Schneider, E.W. (1977) 'Applications of videodisc technology to individualised instruction', in R.J. Seidel and M.L. Rubin (eds), *Computers and Communications: Implications for Education*, New York: Academic Press.

Self, J.A. (1974) 'Student models in computer-aided instruction', *Int. J. Man-Mach. Stud.*, 6, 261-76.

Sharples, M. (1981) 'A computer-based teaching scheme for creative writing', in R. Lewis and E.D. Tagg (eds), *Computers in Education*, Amsterdam: North-Holland.

Sherwood, B.A. (1976) *The TUTOR Language*, Eagan, Minnesota: Control Data Education Company.

Sherwood, B.A. (1978) 'Fast text-to-speech algorithms for Esperanto, Spanish, Italian, Russian and English', *Int. J. Man-Mach. Stud.*, 10, 669-92.

Shortliffe, E.H. (1976) *Computer-based Medical Consultations: MYCIN*, New York: American Elsevier.

Siklossy, L. (1970) 'Computer tutors that know what they teach',

Proc. Fall Jt. Comp. Conf., 36, Montvale, NJ: AFIPS Press.

Skinner, B.F. (1938) *The Behaviour of Organisms: an Experimental Analysis*, New York: Appleton-Century-Crofts.

Skinner, B.F. (1954) 'The science of learning and the art of teaching', *Harvard Educ. Rev.*, 24, 86-97.

Skinner, B.F. (1958) 'Teaching machines', *Science*, 128, 969-77.

Skinner, B.F. (1965) 'The technology of teaching', *Proc. Royal Soc.*, B, 162, 427-43.

Skinner, B.F. (1968) *The Technology of Teaching*, New York: Appleton-Century-Crofts.

Sleeman, D.H. (1975) 'A problem-solving monitor for a deductive reasoning task', *Int. J. Man-Mach. Stud.*, 7, 183-211.

Smallwood, R.D. (1962) *A Decision Structure for Teaching Machines*, Cambridge: MIT Press.

Smallwood, R.D. (1970) 'Optimal policy regions for computer-directed teaching systems', in W.H. Holtzmann (ed.), *Computer-assisted Instruction, Testing and Guidance*, New York: Harper & Row.

Smallwood, R.D. (1971) 'The analysis of economic teaching strategies for a simple learning model', *J. Math. Psych.*, 8, 285-301.

Smith, R.L. and Blaine, L.H. (1976) 'A generalized system for university mathematics instruction', *SIGCUE Topics*, 2, 280-8.

Smith, S.G. and Sherwood, B.A. (1976) 'Educational uses of the PLATO computer system', *Science*, 192, 344-52.

Sorlie, W.E. and Essex, D.L. (1979) 'The University of Illinois basic medical sciences PLATO IV project – an evaluation', *J. Computer-Based Inst.*, 5, 50-6.

Steele, G.L. and Sussman, G.J. (1978) 'Constraints', *Memo No. 502*, AI Lab., MIT, Cambridge, Mass.

Steinberg, E. (1977) 'Review of student control in computer-assisted instruction', *J. Computer-Based Inst.*, 3, 84-90.

Stevens, A., Collins, A. and Goldin, S.E. (1979) 'Misconceptions in student's understanding', *Int. J. Man-Machine Stud.*, 11, 145-56.

Stolurow, L. (1969) 'Computer-assisted instruction', in H.J. James (ed.), *The Schools and the Challenge of Innovation*, New York: McGraw-Hill.

Sturges, P.T. (1978) 'Delay of informative feedback in computer-assisted testing', *J. Educ. Psych.*, 70, 378-87.

Sugarman, R. (1978) 'A second chance for computer-aided instruction', *IEEE Spectrum*, 15, 29-37.

Suppes, P. (1966) 'The uses of computers in education', *Sci. Am.*, 215, 2, 206-20.

Suppes, P. (1979) 'Current trends in computer-assisted instruction', in M.C. Yovits (ed.), *Advances in Computers 18*, New York: Academic Press.

Suppes, P., Jerman, M. and Brian, D. (1968) *Computer-assisted Instruction: the 1965-66 Stanford Arithmetic Program*, New York: Academic Press.

Suppes, P. and Morningstar, M. (1972) *Computer-assisted Instruction at Stanford, 1966-68; Data, Models and Evaluation of the Arithmetic Programs*, New York: Academic Press.

Tait, K., Hartley, J.R. and Anderson, R.C. (1973) 'Feedback procedures in computer-assisted arithmetic instruction', *Brit. J. Educ. Psych.*, 43, 161-71.

Tawney, D.A. (1979) *Learning through Computers*, London: MacMillan.

Taylor, E.F. (1969) 'Automated tutoring and its discontents', *Am. J. Physics*, 36, 496-504.

Tesler, L. (1981) 'The Smalltalk environment', *Byte*, 6, 8, 90-147.

Thompson, G.G. and Hunnicutt, C.W. (1944) 'The effect of praise or blame on the work achievement of "introverts" and "extroverts" ', *J. Educ. Psych.*, 35, 257-66.

Thorndike, E.L. (1898) 'Animal intelligence: an experimental study of the associative processes in animals', *Psychol. Rev. Monogr. Suppl.*, 2, No. 8.

Thorndike, E.L. (1906) *Principles of Teaching*, New York: A.G. Seiler.

Turing, A.M. (1950) 'Computing machinery and intelligence', *Mind*, 59, 433-60.

Uhr, L. (1969) 'Teaching machine programs that generate problems as a function of interaction with students', *Proc. 24th Nat. ACM Conf.*, 125-34.

Uttal, W.R. (1962) 'On conversational interaction', in J.E.

Coulson (ed.), *Programmed Learning and Computer-Based Instruction*, New York: Wiley.

Uttal, W.R., Pasich, T., Rogers, M. and Hieronymus, R. (1969) 'Generative computer assisted instruction', *Comm. No. 243*, Mental Health Res. Inst., Univ. of Michigan.

Van der Veer, G. (1970) 'Mathematical learning models as tools for computer-assisted instruction', in B. Scheepmacher (ed.), *Proc. IFIP World Conf. on Comp. Education*.

Virgo, P. (1981) *Learning for Change*, London: Bow Publications.

Wasserman, A.I. and Gutz, S. (1982) 'The future of programming', *Commun. ACM*, 25, 196-206.

Waterman, D. (1975) 'Adaptive production systems', *Proc. 4th Int. Jt. Conf. on Art. Intell.*, Tbilisi, USSR.

Watson, P.G. (1978) 'Utilization of the computer with deaf learners', *Educational Technology*, 18, 47-9.

Wegner, P. (ed.) (1979) *Research Directions in Software Technology*, Cambridge, Mass.: MIT Press.

Weir, S. (1981) 'Logo as an information prosthetic for the handicapped', *DSRE Working Paper 9*, MIT, Cambridge, Mass.

Weir, S. and Emanuel, R. (1976) 'Using Logo to catalyse communication in an autistic child', *DAI Research Report No. 15*, Dept of Art. Intell., Univ. of Edinburgh.

Weizenbaum, J. (1976) *Computer Power and Human Reason*, San Francisco: Freeman.

Westrom, M.L. (1974) 'National author language, NATAL-74, author guide', *Report No. NRC-14243*, National Research Council, Canada.

Wexler, J.D. (1970) 'A teaching program that generates simple arithmetic problems', *Int. J. Man-Mach. Stud.*, 2, 1-27.

Weyer, S. and Kay, A. (1977) 'Information manipulation on a personal computer', *Int. Report*, Learning Research Group, Xerox Palo Alto Research Center, California.

Wilcox, T.R., Davis, A.M. and Tindall, M.H. (1976) 'The design and implementation of a table driven, interactive diagnostic programming system', *Commun. ACM*, 19, 609-16.

Winograd, T. (1975) 'Frame representations and the declarative/

procedural controversy', in D. Bobrow and A. Collins (eds), *Representation and Understanding*, New York: Academic Press.

Winston, P.H. (1975) 'Learning structural descriptions from examples', in P.H. Winston (ed.), *The Psychology of Computer Vision*, New York: McGraw-Hill.

Winston, P.H. (1977) *Artificial Intelligence*, New York: Addison-Wesley.

Wirth, N. (1973) *Systematic Programming*, New York: Prentice-Hall.

Woods, P. and Hartley, J.R. (1971) 'Some learning models for arithmetic tasks and their use in computer-based learning', *Brit. J. Educ. Psych.*, 41, 35-48.

Young, R.M. (1976) *Seriation by Children: an Artificial Intelligence Analysis of a Piagetian Task*, Basel: Birkhauser Verlag.

Young, R.M. (1980) 'Production systems for modelling human cognition', in D. Michie (ed.), *Expert Systems in the Microelectronic Age*, Edinburgh: Edinburgh Univ. Press.

Young, R.M. and O'Shea, T. (1982) 'Errors in children's subtraction', *Cogn. Sci.*, 5, 153-77.

Zinn, K.L. (1970) 'An evaluative review of uses of computers in instruction', *Final Report, Project No. 8-0509*, US Dept Health, Education and Welfare.

ACKNOWLEDGEMENTS

We would like to thank the following publishers for permission to
reprint excerpts from the titles listed below:

Academic Press: *Int. J. Man-Machine Stud.*, Vol.7, pp. 204-5,
264-5, 583-4, 680-7; Vol. 11, pp. 35-40.

Academic Press: *Advances in Computers*, Vol 15, pp. 261-7.

American Assoc. for the Advancement of Science: *Science*, Vol.
192, pp. 344-52.

Council for Educational Technology: *The National Development
Programme in Computer Assisted Learning*, by R. Hooper, p.
83.

W.H. Freeman & Co.: *Scientific American*, Vol. 215, p. 207.

Inst. of Electrical and Electronics Engineers, Inc.: *IEEE Trans. on
Man-Machine Systems*, Vol. 11, pp. 142-4.

McGraw-Hill Book Co.: *The Psychology of Computer Vision*, by
P. Winston, p5.55-5.58.

INDEX

302